Cool ways to work with application windows

✔ To shrink a window so that it shows up as only a little button on the Taskbar, click the leftmost button with the little line in it in the window's upper-right corner.

✔ To customize the size and shape of a window instead of having it cover the entire screen, click the middle button in the upper-right corner of the window. (The button should have two boxes in it before you do this.) Then you can drag the lower-right corner of the window border to make the window smaller or larger or move the window by dragging its title bar.

✔ To make a window fill the entire screen, click the middle button in the upper-right corner of the window. (The button should have only one box in it before you do this.)

✔ To arrange the windows on your screen, right-click a blank area of the Taskbar and choose one of the Tile commands.

Seven shortcuts to save you scads of time

1. To move quickly to list box entries that begin with a specific letter, press the letter.

2. To select a list box entry and choose a dialog box's suggested command button, double-click the entry.

3. To move the insertion point to the beginning of a list or line, press Home.

4. To move the insertion point to the end of a list or line, press End.

5. To close a window or dialog box, click the box in the upper-right corner with an x in it.

6. To move to the next field in a dialog box, press Tab.

7. To move to the previous field in a dialog box, press Shift+Tab.

Quick editing tricks

Action	Shortcut
Cut the selected information	Press Ctrl+X.
Copy the selected information	Press Ctrl+C.
Paste whatever you've just copied or cut	Press Ctrl+V.
Undo the last action	Press Ctrl+Z.

...For Dummies: #1 Computer Book Series for Beginners

COMPUTER BOOK SERIES FROM IDG

Small Business Windows® 95 For Dummies®

Cheat Sheet

Windows Explorer and My Computer tricks

Task	Trick
Start Windows Explorer in a flash	Right-click the Start button and choose Explore.
Copy a file to a disk	Select the file and drag it to the disk.
Copy a file to a different folder	Select the file, hold down Ctrl, and drag the file to the other folder.
Move a file to a disk	Select the file, hold down Shift, and drag the file to the disk.
Move a file to a different folder	Select the file and drag it to the other folder.
Select several files individually	Select the first file and hold down Ctrl as you select any subsequent files.
Select a group of files	Select the first file you want to include in the group, hold down Shift, and select the last file you want to add to the group. Doing so selects all the files in between as well.
Rename a file or folder	Select the file or folder and press F2.
Find a file or folder	Press F3.
Delete a file or folder permanently without moving it to the Recycle Bin	Press Shift+Del.

Speedy shortcuts for working with files

Action	Shortcut
Create a file	Press Alt+F and then N.
Open a file	Press Alt+F and then O.
Save a file	Press Alt+F and then S.
Save a file under a different name	Press Alt+F and then A.
Print a file	Press Alt+F and then P.

The two top tips

- ✔ Whenever possible, turn off your computer in the right way. As long as your computer hasn't frozen up, shut it down before turning off the power. To do so, click the Start button and choose Shut Down. In the Shut Down Windows dialog box, choose Shut Down and click OK. Don't turn off your computer until Windows tells you that doing so is okay.

- ✔ To yelp for help from just about anywhere, press F1.

...For Dummies: #1 Computer Book Series for Beginners

SMALL BUSINESS

WINDOWS® 95

FOR

DUMMIES®

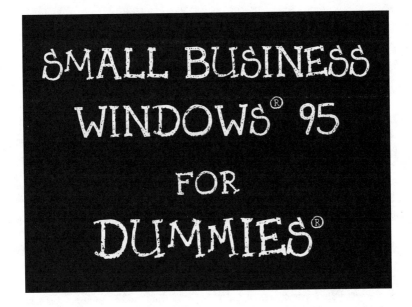

SMALL BUSINESS WINDOWS® 95 FOR DUMMIES®

by Stephen L. Nelson

IDG BOOKS WORLDWIDE™

IDG Books Worldwide, Inc.
An International Data Group Company

Foster City, CA ♦ Chicago, IL ♦ Indianapolis, IN ♦ Southlake, TX

Small Business Windows® 95 For Dummies®

Published by

IDG Books Worldwide, Inc.
An International Data Group Company
919 E. Hillsdale Blvd.
Suite 400
Foster City, CA 94404
www.idgbooks.com (IDG Books Worldwide Web site)
www.dummies.com (Dummies Press Web site)

Library of Congress Catalog Card No.: 98-70131

ISBN: 0-7645-0352-9

Printed in the United States of America

10 9 8 7 6 5 4 3 2 1

1E/RT/QS/ZY/IN

Distributed in the United States by IDG Books Worldwide, Inc.

Distributed by Macmillan Canada for Canada; by Transworld Publishers Limited in the United Kingdom; by IDG Norge Books for Norway; by IDG Sweden Books for Sweden; by Woodslane Pty. Ltd. for Australia; by Woodslane Enterprises Ltd. for New Zealand; by Longman Singapore Publishers Ltd. for Singapore, Malaysia, Thailand, and Indonesia; by Simron Pty. Ltd. for South Africa; by Toppan Company Ltd. for Japan; by Distribuidora Cuspide for Argentina; by Livraria Cultura for Brazil; by Ediciencia S.A. for Ecuador; by Addison-Wesley Publishing Company for Korea; by Ediciones ZETA S.C.R. Ltda. for Peru; by WS Computer Publishing Corporation, Inc., for the Philippines; by Unalis Corporation for Taiwan; by Contemporanea de Ediciones for Venezuela; by Computer Book & Magazine Store for Puerto Rico; by Express Computer Distributors for the Caribbean and West Indies. Authorized Sales Agent: Anthony Rudkin Associates for the Middle East and North Africa.

For general information on IDG Books Worldwide's books in the U.S., please call our Consumer Customer Service department at 800-762-2974. For reseller information, including discounts and premium sales, please call our Reseller Customer Service department at 800-434-3422.

For information on where to purchase IDG Books Worldwide's books outside the U.S., please contact our International Sales department at 650-655-3200 or fax 650-655-3295.

For information on foreign language translations, please contact our Foreign & Subsidiary Rights department at 650-655-3021 or fax 650-655-3281.

For sales inquiries and special prices for bulk quantities, please contact our Sales department at 650-655-3200 or write to the address above.

For information on using IDG Books Worldwide's books in the classroom or for ordering examination copies, please contact our Educational Sales department at 800-434-2086 or fax 817-251-8174.

For press review copies, author interviews, or other publicity information, please contact our Public Relations department at 650-655-3000 or fax 650-655-3299.

For authorization to photocopy items for corporate, personal, or educational use, please contact Copyright Clearance Center, 222 Rosewood Drive, Danvers, MA 01923, or fax 978-750-4470.

is a trademark under exclusive license to IDG Books Worldwide, Inc., from International Data Group, Inc.

About the Author

Stephen L. Nelson, a CPA with a master's degree in finance and accounting, writes about using computers for personal financial and business management. The author of dozens of books and over a hundred magazine articles, Nelson is one of the world's best-selling technology writers. His books have sold more than 2,000,000 books in English and have been translated into 11 other languages.

Nelson is also the author of IDG's best-selling *Quicken 98 For Dummies* and *QuickBooks 5 For Dummies*.

ABOUT IDG BOOKS WORLDWIDE

Welcome to the world of IDG Books Worldwide.

IDG Books Worldwide, Inc., is a subsidiary of International Data Group, the world's largest publisher of computer-related information and the leading global provider of information services on information technology. IDG was founded more than 25 years ago and now employs more than 8,500 people worldwide. IDG publishes more than 275 computer publications in over 75 countries (see listing below). More than 60 million people read one or more IDG publications each month.

Launched in 1990, IDG Books Worldwide is today the #1 publisher of best-selling computer books in the United States. We are proud to have received eight awards from the Computer Press Association in recognition of editorial excellence and three from *Computer Currents*' First Annual Readers' Choice Awards. Our best-selling *...For Dummies*® series has more than 30 million copies in print with translations in 30 languages. IDG Books Worldwide, through a joint venture with IDG's Hi-Tech Beijing, became the first U.S. publisher to publish a computer book in the People's Republic of China. In record time, IDG Books Worldwide has become the first choice for millions of readers around the world who want to learn how to better manage their businesses.

Our mission is simple: Every one of our books is designed to bring extra value and skill-building instructions to the reader. Our books are written by experts who understand and care about our readers. The knowledge base of our editorial staff comes from years of experience in publishing, education, and journalism — experience we use to produce books for the '90s. In short, we care about books, so we attract the best people. We devote special attention to details such as audience, interior design, use of icons, and illustrations. And because we use an efficient process of authoring, editing, and desktop publishing our books electronically, we can spend more time ensuring superior content and spend less time on the technicalities of making books.

You can count on our commitment to deliver high-quality books at competitive prices on topics you want to read about. At IDG Books Worldwide, we continue in the IDG tradition of delivering quality for more than 25 years. You'll find no better book on a subject than one from IDG Books Worldwide.

John Kilcullen
CEO
IDG Books Worldwide, Inc.

Steven Berkowitz
President and Publisher
IDG Books Worldwide, Inc.

IDG Books Worldwide, Inc., is a subsidiary of International Data Group, the world's largest publisher of computer-related information and the leading global provider of information services on information technology. International Data Group publishes over 275 computer publications in over 75 countries. Sixty million people read one or more International Data Group publications each month. International Data Group's publications include: **ARGENTINA:** Buyer's Guide, Computerworld Argentina, PC World Argentina; **AUSTRALIA:** Australian Macworld, Australian PC World, Australian Reseller News, Computerworld, IT Casebook, Network World, Publish, Webmaster; **AUSTRIA:** Computerwelt Osterreich, Networks Austria, PC Tip Austria; **BANGLADESH:** PC World Bangladesh; **BELARUS:** PC World Belarus; **BELGIUM:** Data News; **BRAZIL:** Annuário de Informática, Computerworld, Connections, Macworld, PC Player, PC World, Publish, Reseller News, Supergamepower; **BULGARIA:** Computerworld Bulgaria, Network World Bulgaria, PC & MacWorld Bulgaria; **CANADA:** CIO Canada, Client/Server World, ComputerWorld Canada, InfoWorld Canada, NetworkWorld Canada, WebWorld; **CHILE:** Computerworld Chile, PC World Chile; **COLOMBIA:** Computerworld Colombia, PC World Colombia; **COSTA RICA:** PC World Centro America; **THE CZECH AND SLOVAK REPUBLICS:** Computerworld Czechoslovakia, Macworld Czech Republic, PC World Czechoslovakia; **DENMARK:** Communications World Danmark, Computerworld Danmark, Macworld Danmark, PC World Danmark, Techworld Denmark; **DOMINICAN REPUBLIC:** PC World Republica Dominicana; **ECUADOR:** PC World Ecuador; **EGYPT:** Computerworld Middle East, PC World Middle East; **EL SALVADOR:** PC World Centro America; **FINLAND:** MikroPC, Tietoverkko, Tietoviikko; **FRANCE:** Distributique, Hebdo, Info PC, Le Monde Informatique, Macworld, Reseaux & Telecoms, WebMaster France; **GERMANY:** Computer Partner, Computerwoche, Computerwoche Extra, Computerwoche FOCUS, Global Online, Macwelt, PC Welt; **GREECE:** Amiga Computing, GamePro Greece, Multimedia World; **GUATEMALA:** PC World Centro America; **HONDURAS:** PC World Centro America; **HONG KONG:** Computerworld Hong Kong, PC World Hong Kong, Publish in Asia; **HUNGARY:** ABCD CD-ROM, Computerworld Szamitastechnika, Internetto online Magazine, PC World Hungary, PC-X Magazin Hungary; **ICELAND:** Tolvuheimur PC World Island; **INDIA:** Information Communications World, Information Systems Computerworld, PC World India, Publish in Asia; **INDONESIA:** InfoKomputer PC World, Komputek Computerworld, Publish in Asia; **IRELAND:** ComputerScope, PC Live!; **ISRAEL:** Macworld Israel, People & Computers/Computerworld; **ITALY:** Computerworld Italia, Macworld Italia, Networking Italia, PC World Italia; **JAPAN:** DTP World, Macworld Japan, Nikkei Personal Computing, OS/2 World Japan, SunWorld Japan, Windows NT World, Windows World Japan; **KENYA:** PC World East African; **KOREA:** Hi-Tech Information, Macworld Korea, PC World Korea; **MACEDONIA:** PC World Macedonia; **MALAYSIA:** Computerworld Malaysia, PC World Malaysia, Publish in Asia; **MALTA:** PC World Malta; **MEXICO:** Computerworld Mexico, PC World Mexico; **MYANMAR:** PC World Myanmar; **NETHERLANDS:** Computer! Totaal, LAN Internetworking Magazine, LAN World Buyers Guide, Macworld Netherlands, Net, WebWereld; **NEW ZEALAND:** Absolute Beginners Guide and Plain & Simple Series, Computer Buyer, Computer Industry Directory, Computerworld New Zealand, MTB, Network World, PC World New Zealand; **NICARAGUA:** PC World Centro America; **NORWAY:** Computerworld Norge, CW Rapport, Datamagasinet, Financial Rapport, Kursguide Norge, Macworld Norge, Multimediaworld Norge, PC World Ekspress Norge, PC World Nettverk, PC World Norge, PC World ProduktGuide Norge; **PAKISTAN:** Computerworld Pakistan; **PANAMA:** PC World Panama; **PEOPLE'S REPUBLIC OF CHINA:** China Computer Users, China Computerworld, China InfoWorld, China Telecom World Weekly, Computer & Communication, Electronic Design China, Electronics Today, Electronics Weekly, Game Software, PC World China, Popular Computer Week, Software Weekly, Software World, Telecom World; **PERU:** Computerworld Peru, PC World Profesional Peru, PC World SoHo Peru; **PHILIPPINES:** Click!, Computerworld Philippines, PC World Philippines, Publish in Asia; **POLAND:** Computerworld Poland, Computerworld Special Report Poland, Cyber, Macworld Poland, Networld Poland, PC World Komputer; **PORTUGAL:** Cerebro/PC World, Computerworld/Correio Informático, Dealer World Portugal, Mac*In/PC*In Portugal, Multimedia World; **PUERTO RICO:** PC World Puerto Rico; **ROMANIA:** Computerworld Romania, PC World Romania, Telecom Romania; **RUSSIA:** Computerworld Russia, Mir PK, Publish, Seti; **SINGAPORE:** Computerworld Singapore, PC World Singapore, Publish in Asia; **SLOVENIA:** Monitor; **SOUTH AFRICA:** Computing SA, Network World SA, Software World SA; **SPAIN:** Communicaciones World España, Computerworld España, Dealer World España, Macworld España, PC World España; **SRI LANKA:** Infolink PC World; **SWEDEN:** CAP&Design, Computer Sweden, Corporate Computing Sweden, Internetworld Sweden, it.branschen, Macworld Sweden, MaxiData Sweden, MikroDatorn, Nätverk & Kommunikation, PC World Sweden, PCaktiv, Windows World Sweden; **SWITZERLAND:** Computerworld Schweiz, Macworld Schweiz, PCtip; **TAIWAN:** Computerworld Taiwan, Macworld Taiwan, NEW ViSiON/Publish, PC World Taiwan, Windows World Taiwan; **THAILAND:** Publish in Asia, Thai Computerworld; **TURKEY:** Computerworld Turkiye, Macworld Turkiye, Network World Turkiye, PC World Turkiye; **UKRAINE:** Computerworld Kiev, Multimedia World Ukraine, PC World Ukraine; **UNITED KINGDOM:** Acorn User UK, Amiga Action UK, Amiga Computing UK, Apple Talk UK, Computing, Macworld, Parents and Computers UK, PC Advisor, PC Home, PSX Pro, The WEB; **UNITED STATES:** Cable in the Classroom, CIO Magazine, Computerworld, DOS World, Federal Computer Week, GamePro Magazine, InfoWorld, I-Way, Macworld, Network World, PC Games, PC World, Publish, Video Event, THE WEB Magazine, and WebMaster; online webzines: JavaWorld, NetscapeWorld, and SunWorld Online; **URUGUAY:** InfoWorld Uruguay; **VENEZUELA:** Computerworld Venezuela, PC World Venezuela; and **VIETNAM:** PC World Vietnam.
3/24/97

Author's Acknowledgments

A book like this one represents the efforts of many people. For example, truth be told, IDG's Mary Bednarek turned my vague, half-baked idea into a real book concept and table of contents. And IDG's Ellen Camm negotiated the contract (leaving me, along the way, with my shirt, my pride, and a fair deal). Jeff Adell, a freelance programmer, turned my rough Visual Basic programs (the ones described in Appendixes B and C) into real, working, dependable tools. Coworker Kaarin Dolliver helped write several key chapters, reviewed all of the chapters I wrote, and worked closely with the IDG editorial team as they turned a raw manuscript into this book.

Which of course brings up the huge and essential contribution of IDG's editorial and production team. Rev Mengle, the book's project editor, made sure that we not only got the book done but also got it done right. Tammy Castleman, our copy editor, not only fixed my grammar errors but also added clarity. Allen Wyatt, our technical editor, not only checked the statements of facts but also (appropriately) challenged my statements of opinion. The IDG Production Department, headed up by Regina Snyder, created the interior pages of the book.

Publisher's Acknowledgments

We're proud of this book; please send us your comments about it by using the IDG Books Worldwide Registration Card at the back of the book or by e-mailing us at feedback/dummies@idgbooks.com. Some of the people who helped bring this book to market include the following:

Acquisitions, Development, and Editorial

Project Editor: Rev Mengle

Product Development Director: Mary Bednarek

Media Development Manager: Joyce Pepple

Permissions Editor: Heather Heath Dismore

Senior Copy Editor: Tamara Castleman

Technical Editor: Allen L. Wyatt

Editorial Manager: Leah P. Cameron

Editorial Assistant: Donna Love

Production

Project Coordinator: Regina Snyder

Layout and Graphics: Lou Boudreau, Angela F. Hunckler, Brent Savage, Janet Seib, Michael A. Sullivan

Proofreaders: Michelle Croninger, Kathleen Prata, Nancy Price, Rebecca Senninger, Carrie Voorhis, Janet M. Withers

Indexer: Sherry Massey

Special Help: Joell Smith, Associate Technical Editor; Access Technology, Inc., CD interface design; Stephanie Koutek, Proof Editor

---

General and Administrative

IDG Books Worldwide, Inc.: John Kilcullen, CEO; Steven Berkowitz, President and Publisher

IDG Books Technology Publishing: Brenda McLaughlin, Senior Vice President and Group Publisher

Dummies Technology Press and Dummies Editorial: Diane Graves Steele, Vice President and Associate Publisher; Mary Bednarek, Acquisitions and Product Development Director; Kristin A. Cocks, Editorial Director

Dummies Trade Press: Kathleen A. Welton, Vice President and Publisher; Kevin Thornton, Acquisitions Manager

IDG Books Production for Dummies Press: Beth Jenkins Roberts, Production Director; Cindy L. Phipps, Manager of Project Coordination, Production Proofreading, and Indexing; Kathie S. Schutte, Supervisor of Page Layout; Shelley Lea, Supervisor of Graphics and Design; Debbie J. Gates, Production Systems Specialist; Robert Springer, Supervisor of Proofreading; Debbie Stailey, Special Projects Coordinator; Tony Augsburger, Supervisor of Reprints and Bluelines; Leslie Popplewell, Media Archive Coordinator

Dummies Packaging and Book Design: Patti Crane, Packaging Specialist; Kavish + Kavish, Cover Design

◆

The publisher would like to give special thanks to Patrick J. McGovern, without whom this book would not have been possible.

◆

Contents at a Glance

Cartoons at a Glance

By Rich Tennant

page 7

page 247

page 159

page 95

page 287

page 201

Fax: 978-546-7747 • E-mail: the5wave@tiac.net

Table of Contents

· ·

Introduction

● ●

Do you remember that television show *Twin Peaks*? If you do, you know that strange things happen in this hotel called the Great Northern. This may seem irrelevant to this book and Windows except that one summer afternoon I was actually at the hotel (which in real life is the Salish Lodge at Snoqualimie Falls, Washington) with Mary B., the IDG Books acquisitions director, and her husband, Gene. We're having a nice lunch. And we're talking about the fact that people always write books for computer users as if everybody has, essentially, the same information needs. If you're talking about Windows, for example, you assume that everybody wants the same coverage of the same topics using the same example cases. At a point in our lunch somewhere between the spinach salad and the chocolate mousse, I said to Mary, "And you know what else? Small business people should have their own Windows book, because they have unique interests and problems and, as a result, special information needs."

I didn't really expect something to come of this comment any more than of my suggestion that we order a second bottle of wine. But, as you know if you watched *Twin Peaks,* strange things happen at the Great Northern hotel. So it shouldn't have surprised me when Mary said, "Hey, you know what? We've been thinking the same thing. You are a small business guy, so why don't you write the book for us?"

A few weeks later, the book was written: A *Windows For Dummies* book specifically for small business people.

About This Book

You can probably guess what this book's slant is from its title and the preceding discussion. But just so there's no misunderstanding, let me be very explicit and say that this is a Windows reference book written especially for small business and home office users. As you would expect from any Windows reference, the book explains all the basic stuff that everybody needs to know about Windows. But after this work is done, the book focuses on the needs and interests of small business users. For example, the book talks about Windows features that are particularly useful to small business users — like setting up a network — and yet are often ignored in the other, one-size-fits-all books. This book considers and discusses computing opportunities (like the Internet and Web publishing) from the perspective of the small business person. And, this book uses business examples in all its illustrations.

How to Use This Book

You can use this book in one of two ways. One way is to start reading Chapter 1 and then continue all the way to the end (which means through Chapter 17 and the three appendixes). I actually don't believe that this start-to-finish approach is bad, because you'll discover a bunch of stuff.

But you can also use this book like an encyclopedia. If you want to know how to perform some Windows task or learn about some Windows topic, you can look the task or topic up in the table of contents or the index. Then you can flip to the correct chapter or page and read as much as you need or enjoy.

Either way works. You pick.

How This Book Is Organized

This book is organized into six parts.

Part I: Getting Started

The first part, which includes four chapters, covers the basics of using and working with Windows 95. Chapter 1 describes what Windows is, including how you start and stop programs, choose commands, and work with windows and dialog boxes. Chapter 2 talks about how you use Windows to organize and manage the information you create and store on a computer. Chapter 3 explains how you get help when your computer has you tired, angry, or confused. And Chapter 4 describes how you print business documents by using Windows and Windows programs (such as your word processor).

By the way, any Windows user can actually glean the basics of Windows 95 from Part I; you don't need to be a small business person.

Part II: Profiting from the Internet

Part II talks about the Internet and how you can profit from it. Chapter 5, for example, explains what the Internet and World Wide Web are and how you can use them for business. Chapter 6 explains how you, too, can become a Web publisher. And then Chapter 7 explains how you can use another of the Internet's nifty features — electronic mail — for things like business correspondence and research.

Perhaps I should mention, too, that Part II includes coverage (and, in fact, emphasizes) Microsoft's new Internet Explorer 4.0 Web browser, which you'll find on the CD that comes with this book.

Part III: Teamwork

Many small businesses want and need to share the business information they create and store on their computers. For this reason, Part III talks about how you accomplish this feat. Chapter 8 explains how you share information if you're working on a stand-alone computer. (It's in Chapter 8, for example, that you can read about exporting documents, moving stuff from a Windows PC to your accountant's Apple Macintosh, and using Windows' information sharing tools like the Clipboard.) Chapter 9 provides easy-to-follow instructions for setting up a peer-to-peer network. Chapter 10 explains how you and your office mates work on a network.

Part IV: Business Accessories and Tools

In Part IV, I talk about a bunch of tools that Windows provides to make your life and computing easier or safer. Chapter 11 talks about those Windows accessory programs that are most useful to small business users. (Accessory programs are little, freebie programs that you get from Microsoft when you buy Windows.) Chapter 12 tells you how to customize Windows so it looks and works the way you want. Chapter 13 describes how you use the system management tools that come with Windows to perform do-it-yourself repair and maintenance.

Part V: The Part of Tens

By tradition, a ...*For Dummies* book includes a bunch of laundry-list-like chapters that cover stuff that doesn't fit well into a real chapter. This book continues the tradition. Chapter 14 provides some quick-and-dirty crash courses on ten, popular small business software programs. (You can also use Chapter 14 to glean information about some of the most useful small business accounting programs available to you.) Chapter 15 talks about some general, management issues related to buying and using computers in a small business. Chapter 15 shares ten ideas that potential Web publishers may find useful. And Chapter 17 provides ten tips for home-based businesses.

Part VI: Appendixes

The first appendix in this book gives an overview of all of the neat stuff packed on the companion CD for this book. It also tells you how you can install the programs on the CD. The next two appendixes describe how you use two new, available-only-to-readers-of-this-book Windows accessories. Okay, this is just one man's opinion — mine — but I've always thought that Windows should include a couple of additional accessories for business users: A business calculator that does loan and investment calculations and then a profit-volume-cost analyzer that does business forecasting and break-even calculations. I stewed about this a bit and then figured, "What the heck, I used to be a programmer, I'll just do this myself!" So Appendixes B and C describe how you use these two programs, called BizCalculator and PVCAnalyzer.

Windows 98 Preview

You may have noticed that one chunk of this book is printed on canary yellow paper. That's because that section provides a short primer and preview of the next version of Windows, Windows 98. You can argue, I guess, that the next version of Windows shouldn't really be considered a business accessory or tool. But this information — which you'll actually find useful — would have been lost if I'd stuck it at the very back of the book in an appendix. *Note:* The information in this section is based on the prerelease version of Windows 98, which may differ slightly from the final version.

Special Icons Used Here

You're ready to begin using this book, but let me quickly tell you one last thing. Like many computer books, this one uses icons, or little pictures, to flag things that don't quite fit into the flow of things. The *...For Dummies* books use a standard set of icons that flag these little digressions, such as the following:

This icon points out nerdy technical material that you may want to skip.

This icon points out a tip or provides a bit of useful information.

This icon identifies money and timesaving advice.

This icon marks instructions, tips, and information about programs on the companion CD.

This icon is just a friendly reminder to do something.

This icon is a friendly reminder *not* to do something.

Conventions Used in This Book

To make the best use of your time and energy, you should know about the following conventions used in this book.

When I want you to type something, such as **Hydraulics screamed as the pilot lowered his landing gear**, I put it in bold letters.

You can choose menu commands and select dialog box elements with the mouse or the keyboard. To select them with the mouse, you just click them. To select them with the keyboard, you press Alt and the underlined letter in the menu, command, or dialog box. I identify the keyboard selection keys by underlining them in the text. For example, the letter F in File and the letter O in Open are underlined so that you can choose the File➪Open command by pressing Alt+F, O. If you see a command that begins with the word Start, such as Start➪Programs➪Windows Explorer, it means you first click the Start button on the left side of the Windows Taskbar at the bottom of your screen and then choose the appropriate commands from the Start menu.

Part I
Getting Started

The 5th Wave — By Rich Tennant

"Hold on there, boy! You think you're gonna install Windows 95 on old '286' yourself? Well you'd better hope to high heaven she's in a good mood today."

In this part . . .

You discover what Windows is and how you do stuff like start, stop, work with programs, manage business documents, and print.

Chapter 1

With Windows, You're the Boss

● ●

In This Chapter

▶ Starting and stopping programs

▶ Choosing commands

▶ Working with dialog boxes

▶ Working with windows

● ●

*I*f you are new to Windows 95 — perhaps you're new to computers or have migrated from the old 3.*x* version of Windows or the Apple Macintosh — this chapter provides basic information about working with the Windows 95 interface.

If you don't know how to do the things listed in the introductory bullets at the top of this page, or if you aren't sure that you know how to do these things, please read through this chapter (at least briefly). Even if you only become a casual user of Windows 95, you need to know how to do everything this chapter describes.

Starting and Stopping Programs

Before you can use a Windows program, you need to start the program. Fortunately, starting programs isn't difficult, but different methods are available. Different methods work best in different situations. You can, for example, save yourself substantial amounts of time by becoming document-centric in your work (something discussed in greater detail in the section entitled "Opening a document") and by using shortcut icons.

To start Windows 95, you simply turn on your computer.

You can start Windows programs in three ways: by telling Windows that you want to start the actual program, by telling Windows that you want to open a document, and by using a shortcut icon that points either to the program you want to start or the document you want to open. These three choices may sound confusing, but let me quickly explain how they work — and make some suggestions about when you'll want to use each.

Starting the program directly

The most obvious way to start a program, like Microsoft Word, for example, is to tell Windows that you want to start the program. To do so, take the following steps:

1. **Click the Start button to display the Start menu.**

2. **Click the Programs item.**

   The Programs menu appears.

3. **Click the program item — for example, Microsoft Word — that appears on the Programs menu (see Figure 1-1).**

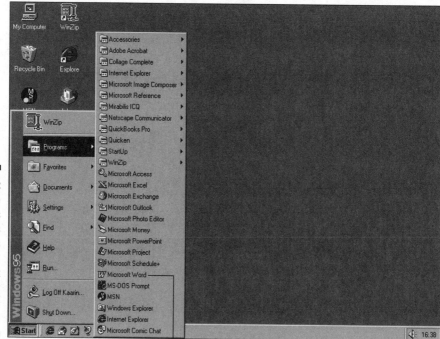

Figure 1-1: The Programs menu lists programs that you can start simply by clicking the menu item.

The Microsoft Word program item

To click an item on your screen, roll your mouse across the top of your desk or tabletop so the mouse pointer (which appears on the screen) points to the item you want to click. Then quickly depress the mouse's left button. To double-click an item, simply click the item twice quickly.

Note that you start other programs in the same manner. You click Start, then Programs, and then the menu item representing the program you want.

When you install software programs, Windows 95 adds the individual programs to your Programs menu.

Some of the items shown on the Programs menu aren't programs but rather lists, or *submenus,* of still more programs. For example, the Accessories item, which appears on the Programs menu, isn't a program. If you click the Accessories item, Windows displays the Accessories submenu. It lists additional programs and even a few more submenus. (Chapter 11, by the way, talks about the Windows Accessories.)

Opening a document

Clicking some program listed on the Programs menu is not actually the most logical way to start programs. You see, Windows 95 is document-centric, which means that you don't need to start a program before opening a document file in that program. You just need to tell Windows that you want to work with the document file. When you do so, Windows starts the program that you're most likely to use for working on the kind of document you chose, and then tells this program to open the document file you said you wanted to work with. Makes sense, right? Rather than starting a program in order to work with a document file, you just say, basically, "I want to work with that Word document or with that Excel workbook."

Documents, files, and programs

The terms document, file, and program are easy to confuse and misuse, so let me quickly describe and define all three terms. A *file* is what the operating system stores on your disk drives (or any other storage device you happen to have). For example, a sales proposal that you create with a word-processing program like Microsoft Word is a file that gets stored someplace — presumably on your hard drive. What's more, the Word software program itself is a file that gets stored on the hard drive, too. To differentiate these various types of files, people generally categorize them in two ways: program files (like the Word software program) and document files (like the sales proposal you created with Word).

You actually have two tools, roughly speaking, to identify to Windows which document you want to work with: the Documents menu and a shell program like Windows Explorer. Both tools are easy to use.

Opening a document with the Documents menu

Windows lists the last 15 document files you've worked with on the Documents menu. Because you probably work with the documents you create more than once and over a short period of time, you can often start a program and, at the same time, open the document you want simply by choosing a document file from the Documents menu.

You can open any of the Documents menu's document files by following these steps:

1. Click the Start button.

2. Click the Documents item.

The Documents menu appears.

3. Click the document file you want to open (see Figure 1-2).

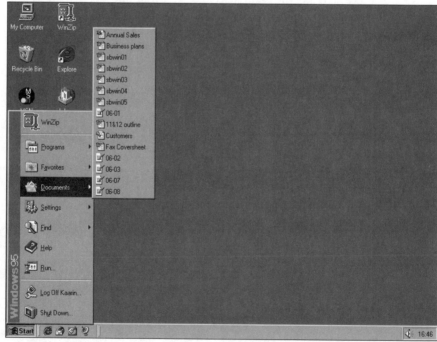

Figure 1-2:
The Documents menu lists the last 15 document files you've worked with.

Windows uses the program icons to identify the program it thinks you used to create a document file. For example, the first document file listed on the Documents menu in Figure 1-2 shows an "X" and then a smaller page behind the "X" to identify it as an Excel workbook. The second Document file listed on the Documents menu in Figure 1-2 shows a "W" and then a smaller page behind the "W" to identify it as a Word document.

Opening a document with Windows Explorer

If a document isn't one that you've recently opened, it won't appear on the Documents menu. You can still start the program and open the document at the same time, however, if you know how to use Windows Explorer to display the folder with the document file. Doing so isn't really very difficult — you can start the program and open the document file simply by double-clicking the document file. To do so, follow these steps:

1. **Click the Start button.**

2. **Click the Programs item.**

3. **Click Windows Explorer.**

   The Windows Explorer program starts (see Figure 1-3).

4. **Use the folder pane to select the folder that stores the document file.**

   (You can select a folder by clicking it with the mouse.)

5. **Double-click the document file when you see it listed in the Contents pane.**

Notice that Windows Explorer, like the Documents menu, uses icons to identify the program that Windows thinks you used to create a document file. For more information about Windows Explorer, refer to Chapter 2.

Using shortcut icons

Shortcut icons represent a third method of starting programs. Sort of. Let me explain. Shortcut icons are simply clickable buttons that point to a program you want to start or document file you want to open. If you take a look at Figure 1-4 (which shows the Windows desktop), you'll notice a bunch of icons that appear along the left edge of the screen: My Computer, Recycle Bin, MSN, Network Neighborhood, and so on. These icons are shortcut icons. And if you double-click a shortcut icon, Windows starts the program file (if that's what the shortcut icon represents) or opens the document (if that's what the shortcut icon represents). For example, if you double-click the My Computer shortcut icon, Windows starts the My Computer program. (My Computer is, essentially, a "lite" version of Windows Explorer.) And if you double-click Explore, Windows starts the Internet Explorer program.

The contents pane

The folder pane of Explorer

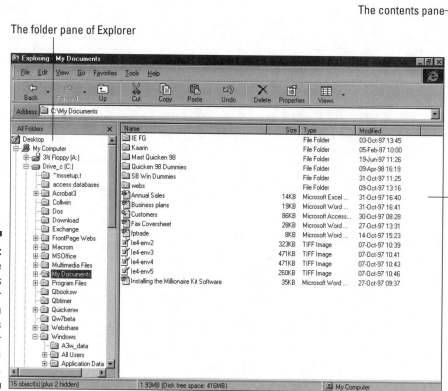

The neat thing about shortcut icons is that although you need to create them yourself — Windows only comes with a handful of shortcut icons on its desktop — they actually save you a great deal of time. Think about it for a minute: Rather than clicking the Start button and then choosing some item from the Programs menu or the Documents menu, you simply double-click a shortcut icon. Rather than using Windows Explorer to find some document you want to open, you simply double-click the shortcut icon.

Shortcut icons aren't difficult to create. For more information about shortcut icons and for step-by-step instructions on how to create them, refer to Chapter 2.

Figure 1-4:
You can place clickable shortcut icons on your Windows desktop.

Stopping Programs

You need to stop programs when you finish working with them. This makes sense, right? When you work with any tool, you should put it away when you're done with it. Otherwise the tool — in this case, a software program — unnecessarily uses up space on your desktop.

Fortunately, stopping a program is very easy. You stop programs in one of three ways: by using the Close box, by choosing File⇨Exit, or, in a pinch, by having Windows end the program. You'll want to know about all three ways.

Using the Close box

The easiest way to close a program is to click its window's Close box. If you take a look at Figure 1-5 — which shows Microsoft Word's program window — you'll notice two square buttons labeled with an "X" in the upper-right corner. These are the Close boxes. If you click the Close box in the very corner of the Word program window (or in the very corner of any other program window), Windows stops the program.

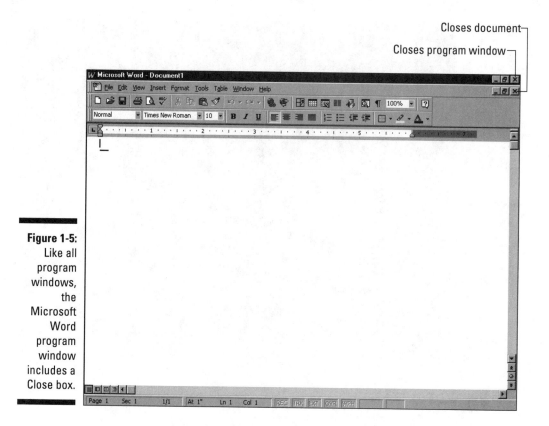

Closes document

Closes program window

Figure 1-5:
Like all
program
windows,
the
Microsoft
Word
program
window
includes a
Close box.

If you look closely at Figure 1-5, you'll notice a second Close box, as well. That's the document window's Close box. If you click it, Windows closes the document you've opened or created. *Document windows* are the windows that appear inside program windows. Just as you may guess, programs use document windows to display any documents you've opened or created. (The last section of this chapter talks more about document windows.)

Using File⇨Exit

A slightly more difficult way to stop a program is to choose File⇨Exit. While the upcoming "Choosing Commands" section talks more about how this works, know that if you click the word File (to display the File menu) and then click the word Exit (to choose the Exit command), Windows stops the program. (See Figure 1-6.) Almost every other program you'll ever encounter provides a File menu with an Exit command.

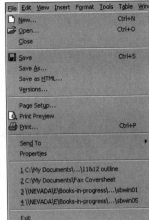

Figure 1-6:
The
Microsoft
Word File
menu.

Using the Windows 95 emergency stop procedure

Unfortunately, you can have a problem stopping a program. When you can't tell the program to stop, you need to tell Windows to stop the program.

To tell Windows 95 to stop a program, press the Ctrl, Alt, and Del keys simultaneously so that Windows displays the Close Program dialog box. (If you haven't been able to close the program in one of the usual ways — such as by clicking the Close box or by choosing File➪Exit — Windows will probably identify the program as not responding.) Click the program you want to close — it should show as highlighted after you click it — and then click the End Task command. If Windows 95 displays a dialog box asking you to confirm that you want to end the task, click the dialog box's End Task button.

If you close a program by telling Windows 95 to stop the program, you will probably lose any changes you made to open document files since last saving them.

Multi-tasking Programs

You'll sometimes want to use more than one program at a time — or perform what's called *multi-tasking*. For example, suppose that you want to run both Word and Excel to create a business report. In this situation, you may use Word to collect and prepare the actual business report. But you may also want to use Excel to analyze some information you're using in the report. (Perhaps the report makes a financial forecast, for example.) Fortunately, multi-tasking programs is easy with Windows.

Starting multiple programs

To multi-task, all you do is start more than one program. If you want to multi-task both Word and Excel, for example, you start Word. And then you start Excel. You start programs in any of the ways I describe earlier in the chapter. You can start the program directly. You can start a program indirectly by telling Windows you want to open a document file it thinks you created with the program. Or you can double-click a shortcut icon that points either to the program you want to start or the document file you want to open. If you have questions about how any of these techniques work, refer to the earlier chapter section entitled, "Starting and Stopping Programs."

Switching between programs

Windows puts a button on the task bar to represent each of the programs you start (see Figure 1-7). If you start Word, for example, it displays the Word program and then places a button labeled Microsoft Word on the task bar. If you next start Excel, it displays the Excel program (on top of the Word program) and then places a button labeled Microsoft Excel on the Taskbar. To use a program, you simply click its Taskbar button.

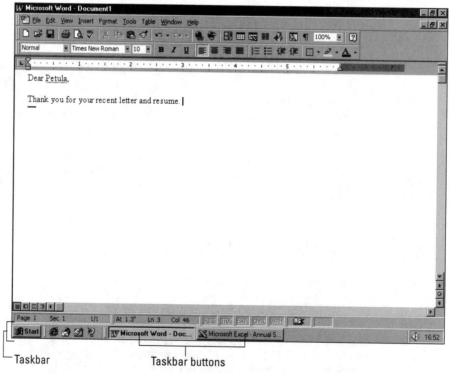

Figure 1-7: You can only see the Word program window in this figure, but as you can tell by looking at the Taskbar, both the Word and Excel programs are running.

Taskbar   Taskbar buttons

To indicate to Windows that you want to work with a particular program in another way, simultaneously press the Alt and the Tab keys.

You don't need to click a program's task bar button or press Alt+Tab to activate a program if the program already shows on your screen. Just click the mouse somewhere in the program window and then begin typing. The later chapter section, "Working with Windows," talks more about program windows.

Choosing Commands

You tell Windows and Windows programs what you want them to do by issuing commands. In fact, if you've been reading this chapter from the beginning and following along in front of your computer, you've actually already issued several commands to Windows. When you tell Windows to start some program, for example, you issue a command. And when you tell a program like a Windows program to stop, you again issue a command.

Understanding how to choose commands is important, however. So the following paragraphs describe more fully how you use the mouse, the keyboard, toolbar buttons, and shortcuts menus to issue commands.

Using the mouse

Often the easiest way to issue some command is with the mouse. For example, suppose that you start Windows Explorer but then decide that you don't want to work with Windows Explorer. In this situation, you may want to tell Windows that it should close the Windows Explorer program. (This scenario is somewhat artificial, but it lets these paragraphs more effectively explain how choosing commands with a mouse works. And don't worry about what you're doing — just pay attention to command mechanics.)

To issue the "close Windows Explorer" command, choose File⇨Close by following these steps:

1. **Click on the word File (see Figure 1-8).**

2. **When Windows opens the File menu, click on the word Close.**

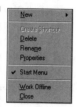

Figure 1-8:
The
Windows
Explorer
File menu.

While the Close command appears on the File menu, some commands don't appear on menus. They instead appear on submenus. And in this case, you go to slightly more work to choose the command because you have to open the menu, then open the submenu, and then choose the command. To rearrange the information shown in the Windows Explorer window, for example, you choose View⇨Arrange Icons and then choose one of the commands that appears on the submenu. To arrange document and program files alphabetically by name, follow these steps:

1. **Click the word View.**

2. **When Windows Explorer opens the View menu, click the words Arrange Icons.**

3. **When Windows Explorer opens the Arrange Icons submenu, click by Name (see Figure 1-9).**

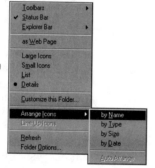

Figure 1-9:
The
Windows
Explorer
View menu.

You now know how to choose menu commands with the mouse. But before I move on to discussing other ways of choosing commands, let me make a couple of quick observations. First of all, if you inadvertently open a menu but don't want to choose one of its commands, you can close the menu by clicking someplace — it doesn't matter where — other than on the menu. (If you click another menu name, of course, Windows opens that menu.)

A second, minor point is this: You can always tell which menu commands display submenus because those programs display an arrow head following the command. Take another look at Figure 1-9, for example. See the arrow head that follows the Arrange Icons command? It tells you that when you choose the Arrange Icons command, you actually tell Windows to display the Arrange Icons submenu.

Using the keyboard

If the mouse usually represents the easiest way to choose command, the keyboard often represents the fastest way (at least it does if you're a touch-typist). Let me explain. You can open any menu by pressing the Alt key and the letter that's underlined in the menu name. And, after you open a menu, you can choose any of its commands by pressing the letter that's underlined in the command name. For example, suppose you wanted to choose the File menu's Close command in Windows Explorer. (Refer to Figure 1-8 to see what this menu looks like.)

In this case, you could follow these steps:

1. **Press the Alt key.**

   Doing so tells Windows Explorer that you want to open a menu.

2. **Press the F key.**

   Doing so tells Windows Explorer that you want to open the File menu.

3. **Press the C key.**

   Doing so tells Windows that you want to choose the Close command.

Some commands also provide keyboard shortcuts. If you look at the Edit menu shown in Figure 1-10, for example, you see that following the Cut command is the keyboard combination, Ctrl+X. This indicates that you can also choose the Edit menu's Cut command simply by simultaneously pressing the Ctrl key and then the "X" letter key. If you use a particular command regularly, check to see if a keyboard shortcut combination is provided. If one is, you may want to memorize the shortcut and then begin using it in place of one of the other command choice methods.

Figure 1-10:
The Word
Edit menu.

Using the toolbar buttons

The toolbar's buttons and boxes represent another, albeit slightly less precise way, to choose menu commands. In a nutshell, toolbars supply clickable buttons that you use in place of choosing commands. For example, if you want to see the information in the Windows Explorer window presented in a different way, you can use the commands shown on the Arrange Icons submenu, as mentioned earlier. But you can also click the Views toolbar button appearing on the Windows Explorer window (see Figure 1-11).

If you don't have Internet Explorer 4.0 installed, the last four buttons on the toolbar let you rearrange the information shown in the Explorer Window.

The one problem with toolbar buttons — at least for people new to Windows or a particular Windows program — is that figuring out what a particular button does can be tough. Fortunately, Windows and Windows programs provide three aids to help you learn or remember what a toolbar button does. The programmers who create these software programs put pictures on the buttons to help you identify what a particular button does. Okay, I admit these pictures aren't perfect. But if you pay attention to them, you should often be able to figure out (or more easily remember) what a particular button does.

Go ahead and experiment with the Back, Up, Properties, and Views toolbar buttons to verify that you know how these simple-to-use tools work. But don't use any of Windows Explorer's other toolbar buttons — in particular the Cut and Delete buttons — until you review Chapter 2.

Toolbar buttons are not the only aid that Windows and Windows programs provide in order to help you learn or remember what a particular toolbar button does. Sometimes (especially when a button doesn't have a text label) when you move the mouse pointer so that it rests on a particular button, the

Click to select a different way of viewing information in Windows Explorer

Toolbar

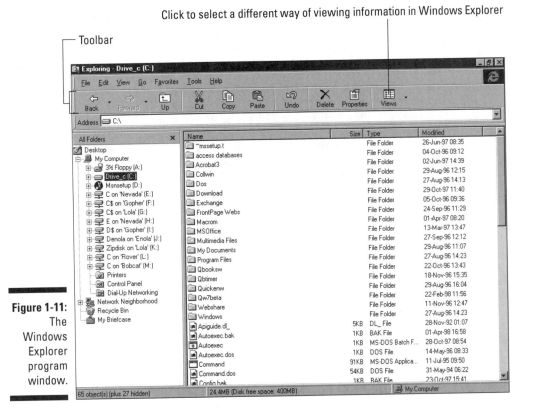

program you're working with displays the toolbar button name in a small box called a *tool tip.* You can often use tool tips to jog your memory about what a particular toolbar button does and even sometimes to learn enough about a toolbar button to begin experimenting with the button.

Some Windows programs provide a third aid that you can use to learn and remember what various toolbar buttons do. They include a picture of the equivalent toolbar button next to the menu commands. For example, the little picture that's next to the Cut command on an Edit menu may look like the pair of scissors on the Cut toolbar button.

Toolbar buttons possess one other characteristic worth mentioning here. Sometimes, a program requires additional information from you before it executes a command you issue. The program gets this information when you fill out a dialog box, something described later in the "Working with Dialog Boxes" section. If you choose a menu command, you get to fill out the dialog box and in doing so get to describe exactly how you want the command carried out. If you click a toolbar button, however, the program typically doesn't display the dialog box and instead just guesses as to how you want the command carried out.

You can usually tell which commands display dialog boxes by looking at the menu. If choosing a command causes Windows to display a dialog box, the command name is followed by an ellipsis (...).

This "sometimes-you-get-a-dialog-box-sometimes-you-don't" business sounds a little complicated (even though it's not), so let me give you a quick example. Many Windows programs (although not Windows Explorer) provide a Print command on their File menus as well as a Print toolbar button. You can use either the menu command or the toolbar button to tell a program you want to print some document file. If you choose the File⇨Print command, the program displays a dialog box that asks you several questions about the document you want to print: which printer to use (if you have more than one), whether to print the entire document or just a few pages, how many copies you want to print, and so forth. If you click the Print toolbar button, the program just prints the document without, in effect, asking any of these questions. The program makes best-guess assumptions about how it should carry out the command. (For more information about printing, refer to Chapter 4.)

Using shortcut menus

Let me be blunt. One of the problems with menus and menu commands is that there are just too many of them. If you've spent even a few minutes working with Windows or just about any Windows programs, you've already seen that you have several menus and together these menus provide dozens and dozens of commands. And that means that finding a command you need is often really difficult — particularly when you're still learning Windows or a Windows program.

To deal with the "too-many-commands" problem, Windows and most Windows programs also supply shortcut menus. A *shortcut menu* is simply a menu of commands that are available to work with a particular item. To indicate that you want to see the shortcut menu of commands for working with an item, you right-click the item. In other words, you point to the item with the mouse and, instead of clicking the mouse's left button (which is the usual way of clicking some item), you click the mouse's right button.

This shortcut menu business may sound complicated, but a quick example will help you see exactly what how it works. Say, for the sake of illustration, that you've started Windows Explorer (see Figure 1-12). If you want to do something with one of the files shown in the window, you can choose a menu command in one of the ways I've already described. Or, you can simply right-click the file. If you do right-click the file, Windows displays the shortcut menu.

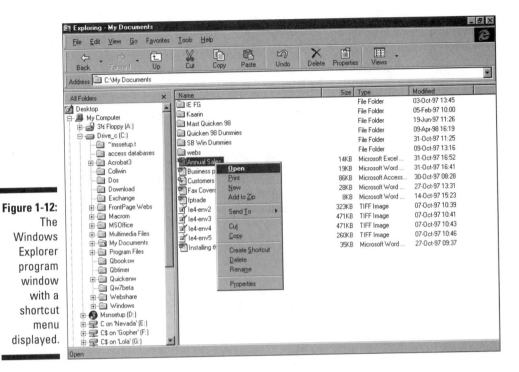

Figure 1-12:
The
Windows
Explorer
program
window
with a
shortcut
menu
displayed.

After Windows Explorer displays the shortcut menu, you choose its commands in the usual way. For example, you can click a command with the mouse. Or you can press the letter key that corresponds to the underlined letter in the command name. So if you want to choose the Open command you can click it or you can press the "O" key.

Working with Dialog Boxes

Sometimes when you choose a command, the program you're issuing the command to needs more information to carry out the command. Suppose, for example, that you're working with the WordPad accessory that comes with Windows. If you tell WordPad to change the font of some word or text selection, it needs more information than that. WordPad not only needs to know that you want to make the change, but it also needs to know how you want to make a change. In the case where you're changing the format of the word or text selection, for example, WordPad needs to know what typeface you want to use, how big or small the characters should be, what color you want to use, and so on.

When a program needs more information to carry out a particular command, the program displays a dialog box. The dialog box provides a bunch of buttons and boxes that you use to provide more specific instructions about how the program is supposed to carry out the command you've given. To see how this feature works, do the following:

1. Close the Windows Explorer program by clicking its Close box.

2. Start WordPad by clicking Start⇨Programs⇨Accessories⇨WordPad.

3. Once WordPad starts, choose File⇨Print.

Figure 1-13 shows the Print dialog box that WordPad displays when you choose File⇨Print. This dialog box illustrates many of the buttons and boxes that dialog boxes use.

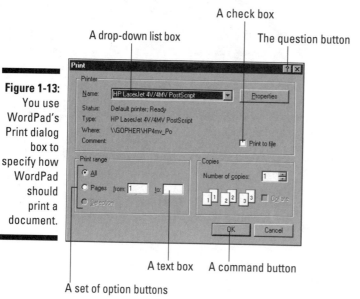

A check box

A drop-down list box

The question button

Figure 1-13: You use WordPad's Print dialog box to specify how WordPad should print a document.

A text box   A command button

A set of option buttons

The question button

The most important button on a dialog box is the question button (see Figure 1-13). If you have a question about what some dialog box button or box does or how it works, you click the question button and then the button or box you want to know more about. When you do so, the program displays a pop-up box that provides (hopefully) helpful information about whatever you just clicked. For example, if you are working with the Print dialog box and want to know what the Name drop-down list box does (this drop-down list box is labeled in Figure 1-13), you click the Question button and then the Name drop-down list box. When you do, WordPad (with Windows' help) displays a pop-up box.

List boxes

Programs use list boxes to present you with a limited set of choices. As just mentioned, for example, WordPad uses a list box to let you specify what printer you want to use to print a document. Typically, list boxes don't show the list of choices until you say you want to see the list. But if you click the downward-pointing arrowhead at the right end of the list box or, alternatively, press the Alt key and then the underlined letter in the list box's name, the program drops down the list. For example, if you click the downward-pointing arrow head that's at the right end of the Name box or press Alt+N, WordPad drops down a list of printers that Windows can use to print your WordPad document, as shown in Figure 1-14.

Figure 1-14:
The Printer
Name
drop-down
list box.

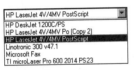

To select a choice from a list box, click it with the mouse or type the first character of the list box choice. With the list box just shown, for example, typing the letter "H" selects the first list box choice and typing the letter "L" selects the fourth list box choice. After you select a list box choice, the program highlights the entry.

Windows programs like WordPad don't actually print their document files. When you issue the print command, the program hands off a copy of the document to Windows. Windows then goes to the actual work of printing the document file.

Check boxes

Check boxes work like on-off switches. By checking a box, you turn it on. If you uncheck the box, you turn it off. If you look back at Figure 1-13, for example, you'll notice that a callout points to the Print To File box. This is a check box. If you check it, Windows doesn't send the document file to the printer but instead saves a printable copy of the document file to your hard disk. (You'll probably never need to do this, by the way, so don't worry about ever using this check box.) To check and uncheck a box, click it with the mouse. Or, alternatively, press the Alt key and then the underlined letter in the check box's name. For example, to check and uncheck the Print To File box, you can press Alt+L.

Option buttons

Options buttons represent mutually exclusive choices. For example, if you want to print some WordPad document, you can print the entire document or some portion of the current document. But you can't simultaneously print the entire document and only a portion of the entire document. (This makes sense, right? It's just another variant of the logical reality that you can't both have your cake and eat it, too.) To make these sorts of choices, programs provide option button sets. You select which option you want to pick by clicking the appropriate button. If you take another peek at Figure 1-13, you'll notice that I've labeled the Print range option buttons. If you want to print the entire WordPad document, you click the All button. If you have, say a 100-page business plan and want to print only a specified range of pages — say pages 23 through 29, you click the Pages button; then you enter the page range into the box just right of the Pages option button. (The box you use to specify the page range is called a text box. I describe how text boxes work next.)

If you don't have a mouse or don't like using one for some reason, note that you can also select an option button by pressing the Alt key and the underlined letter in the option button name. For example, to select the All option button, press Alt+A. To select the Pages option button, press Alt+G.

If you look closely at the Print range option button set, you'll also notice another button named Selection. (You'll need to look closely; the Selection button is "grayed-out" and only shows faintly.) Windows and Windows programs, like WordPad, disable commands and dialog box options when they don't make sense in a given situation. In Figure 1-13, the Selection option button is grayed-out and disabled for just this reason.

Text boxes

A *text box* is just a box you fill with information by typing something with your keyboard keys — or, in special circumstances by copying or moving text from some other text box. I'm going to spend a bit more time than you may expect describing how text boxes work, but I have a good reason for doing so. Once you know how to enter text into a text box, you also know how to enter text into other documents such as WordPad. In other words, once you know how to type stuff into a text box, you know almost everything you need to know to provide information to Windows and Windows programs. You'll want, therefore, to have a thorough understanding of how text boxes work.

One-line text boxes

The simplest text boxes are the short, one-line text boxes. For example, in Figure 1-13, you may choose to print out only specified range of pages. To do so, you can click the Pages option button (as described in the "Option buttons" section) and then you enter the page range into the Pages from and to text boxes, which follow the Pages option button. To enter the page range into these text boxes, click the text box and then type the text.

You have several editing techniques that you can use to change the stuff you type into a text box. You can insert characters into your existing entry by clicking the mouse at the exact location where you want to insert the new characters — doing so positions the insertion point — and then typing the next characters you want to insert. If you want to erase the character preceding the insertion point, press the Backspace key. If you want to erase the character following the insertion point, press the Delete key.

The *insertion point* is the vertical bar that shows where any text you type will be inserted. You can move the insertion point by clicking the mouse or, after you click the text box once (to place an insertion point inside the text box), by pressing the left and right arrow keys.

If you make a mistake, you can replace your entire entry or some portion of the entry by selecting whatever you want to replace and then typing the replacement text or numbers. You can select the text box's entire contents by triple-clicking inside the text box. You select a single word or chunk of text by double-clicking the word or text chunk. You can also select some portion of the text box's contents by clicking on the first character you want to select and then dragging the mouse to the last character you want to select. (When you select a text box's contents, the Windows program identifies your selection by highlighting it.)

Text boxes that have buttons

Let me mention one final thing about the Print dialog box shown in Figure 1-13. If a text box accepts only numeric values — 1, 2, 3, and 4 or 10%, 20%, 30%, and 40% — some programs add a set of buttons to the right end of the text box. You can then use these buttons to incrementally adjust the value already shown in the text box. (These buttons, then, save you from having to click the text box and type a new value.) The Number of Copies text box, for example, includes just such a set of buttons. If you click the upward-pointing arrow, the program adds 1 to the value already shown in the Number of Copies text box. If you click the downward-pointing arrow, the program subtracts one from the value already shown in the Number of Copies text box.

Scrolling text boxes

Once you understand how one-line text boxes work — and they really aren't difficult to use — working with scrolling text boxes is a snap. The Print dialog box doesn't include a scrolling text box, but many program windows and some dialog boxes do. (If you're following along at your computer, close the Print dialog box by clicking its Close box.) For example, if you're working with WordPad, the WordPad window itself, shown in Figure 1-15, consists primarily of a large scrolling text box. The area into which you type text is actually a scrolling text box.

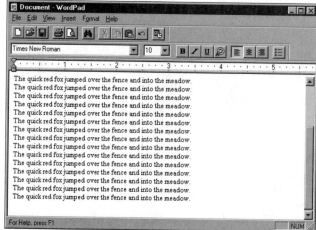

Figure 1-15: How the WordPad looks after you type a bit of text.

Basically, scrolling text boxes are just text boxes that accept more than one line of text. In Figure 1-15, for example, you can type as much information into the scrolling text box as you want. If you get to the end of a line, the program automatically moves the insertion point to the start of the next line. If you want to end a line of text, you can also press the Enter key to end the current line and move to the next line. (In effect, when you press Enter, you end one paragraph and start another.)

If you're following along in front of your computer, go ahead and type several lines of text. You can type anything you like. If you're stuck, use a text fragment from your high school typing class such as "The quick red fox jumped over the lazy dog's back."

As soon as you type more text into the scrolling text box than it can show at one time (see Figure 1-15), the program adds a scroll bar to the right edge of the text box, making the box a scrolling text box. You can scroll a scrolling text box's text by clicking the arrow heads that appear at either end of the scroll bar. You can also drag the *scroll bar marker* (the rectangular button that appears on the scroll bar between the scroll bar's arrow heads). And you can click the scroll bar when there's room: Click above the scroll bar marker to scroll up and click below the scroll bar marker to scroll down.

Tabs

Let me quickly describe how dialog box tabs work. If you choose View⇨Options, WordPad displays the Options dialog box shown in Figure 1-16. In Figure 1-16, you see several tabs across the top of the Options dialog box: Options, Text, Rich Text, Word 6, Write, and Embedded.

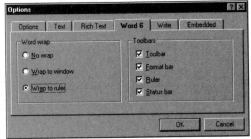

Figure 1-16:
The Options
dialog box.

Tabs amount to different dialog box pages. When a program can't fit all of the buttons and boxes onto a single dialog box — even though they should all go there — the program segregates the buttons and boxes into homogenous groups and then uses a separate page, or tab, for each group. To move to a page, you click its page tab. For example, to move to the Options page, you click the Options page tab. To move to the Text page, you click the Text page tab.

Combo boxes

You already know what list boxes and text boxes are, so I should mention that Windows programs sometimes use a hybrid of the two boxes. In other words, you'll occasionally see a box that is part list box (because the program provides a list of choices you can select) and part text box (because you can also enter a some bit of information — a word or number, for example — into the box). The Font Size tool (see Figure 1-17), which appears on the WordPad toolbar, is really a combo box, for example. You can type a value directly into the box. (To do so, click the box and then type a number.) You can also activate the list box's drop-down list and select a point size. (To do so, click the box's downward-pointing arrow head to display the list box and then click a point size.)

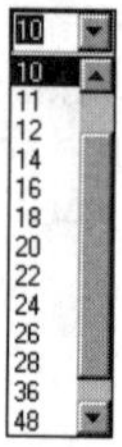

Figure 1-17:
The Font
Size combo
box.

Command buttons

All dialog boxes provide command buttons. Figure 1-18 shows the Print
dialog box again. (I'm repeating it so that you don't have to flip back to
Figure 1-13, which is where I first show it to you.) See those rectangular
buttons along the bottom of the dialog box labeled: OK and Cancel? Those
are command buttons. Another command button, labeled Properties,
appears to the right of the Name drop-down list box.

Figure 1-18:
The Print
dialog box,
like all
dialog
boxes,
provides
command
buttons you
use to tell a
program
what you
want to do
when you
finish with a
dialog box.

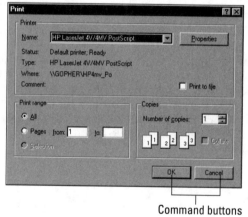

Command buttons

You use command buttons to tell Windows and Windows programs what you
want to do after you finish with a dialog box. For example, after you use the
Print dialog box to describe in precise detail how you want to print some
WordPad document, you click OK. In other words, clicking OK is the final
step you take to issue the Print command. After you click the Print dialog
box's OK command button, WordPad sends a printable copy of the WordPad
document to Windows so Windows can print the document file. And
WordPad closes the Print dialog box. If you display the Print dialog box
accidentally or decide that you don't want to issue the Print command, you
click Cancel. WordPad closes the Print dialog box, but nothing else happens.

Clicking a dialog box's Close button is equivalent to clicking its Cancel command button. In other words, if you click the Close button, the program closes the dialog box and doesn't execute the command.

The Print dialog box, like many dialog boxes, also provides other command buttons. On the Print dialog box, for example, you can click the Properties command button to display and change information about the printer you've selected to use. (Chapter 4 describes how you make changes to the way a printer works.)

The easiest way to choose a command button is to click it. You can also typically choose a command button in two other ways. If a command button's label shows an underlined letter, you can press the Alt key and the underlined letter key to choose the command button. For example, in the case of the Print dialog box shown in Figure 1-18, you can press Alt+P to choose the Properties command button. (You can go ahead and try this if you're following along at your computer. Remember that to close the new dialog box you display, you just click its Cancel button or its Close button.)

You can also choose a command button by selecting the button and then pressing Enter. To select the button, you press the Tab key or the Alt+Tab key combination until Windows highlights the command button. You may need to press Tab or Alt+Tab several times because as you press Tab or Alt+Tab, Windows selects the next button or box on the dialog box. So the first time you press Tab with the WordPad Print dialog box showing, Windows selects the Properties command button. And then the next time you press Tab, Windows selects the Print to file check box. And then the next time you press Tab — well, you get the picture right? Pressing Tab just selects the next box or button. (Pressing Alt+Tab, by the way, selects the previous box or button.) Anyway, you keep pressing Tab or Alt+Tab until Windows selects the command button you want to choose. (You can tell when a command button is selected because Windows draws a dark border around the command button.) Then, after the command button is selected, you press Enter.

You can choose a command button in another way, too. Sort of. Windows typically selects one of a dialog box's command buttons as the default command button. (You can tell which command button is selected because Windows draws a dark border around the button.) You can choose the selected command button by pressing Enter. For example, you can choose File⇨Print, make a change or two to the dialog box's buttons and boxes, and then press Enter to issue the command because the OK command button is the one that's initially selected.

Working with Windows

Thus far in this chapter, the discussion has avoided the subject of windows (lowercase "w") — which is rather paradoxical because this is, after all, a chapter about working with the Windows (uppercase "w") interface. Before I wrap up this discussion of the Windows interface, therefore, I need to spend just a few minutes explaining what windows are, how you resize them, and how you move them.

Application windows vs. document windows

Windows (the operating system) gets its name from the fact that it uses rectangular boxes called windows. When you start a program like Windows or WordPad, for example, Windows displays the program's menus, commands, toolbars, and document files in a window called a *program window* or an *application window.*

Both terms — "program window" and "application window" — are used, although the term "application window" is more common. Nevertheless, this book calls them program windows.

Many programs like those that make up the Microsoft Office suite of programs also display windows inside their own program windows. Specifically, they typically display what's called a *document window* for each document file you open. For example, if you start Microsoft Word and then open a couple of Word documents (say a letter to a customer and a memo to a coworker), you see the Word program; inside the Word program window, you see two document windows. See Figure 1-19 for an example.

Many other Windows programs supply program windows and document windows that work the same way. For example, if you start Excel and then open up a couple of Excel workbooks, you see the Excel program window, and then inside the program window you see document windows for each of the Excel workbooks you opened. If you start Outlook and then open up a couple of Outlook items, you see the Outlook program window and then inside the program window you see document windows for each of the Outlook items.

Resizing windows

You can resize both program windows and document windows. The easiest way to do so is by clicking the Minimize, Restore, and Maximize buttons that appear in the upper-right corner of windows next to the Close button.

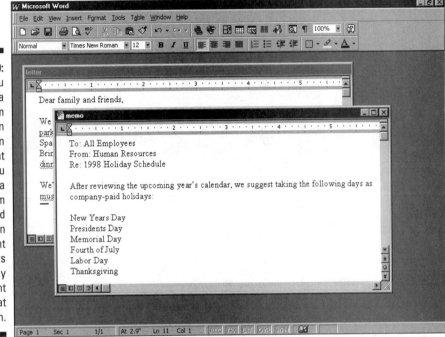

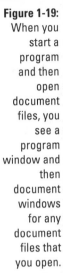

 ✔ Click the Minimize button to shrink a window into a button. If you minimize a program window, it shrinks to a button that appears only on the task bar. If you minimize a document window, it shrinks to a button that appears at the bottom of the program window.

✔ Click the Maximize button to expand a program window so it fills the screen or to expand a document window so it fills the program window.

If you point to a document-window window button, the program displays a pop-up box with the window button name.

After you click a window's Minimize or Maximize button, Windows replaces the Minimize or Maximize button with a Restore button, which you can use to undo the effect of your previous click. In other words, if you click a Minimize button, Windows replaces the Minimize button with a Restore button, and you can click this Restore button to un-minimize the window. And if you click a Maximize button, Windows replaces the Maximize button with a Restore button, and you can click this Restore button to un-maximize the window.

Window buttons are the easiest way to resize windows — you just need to click them. However, you can resize windows in another way. Windows also supplies a *resize box* for each program window and document window. The resize box appears in the lower-right corner of any program window or document window that isn't already maximized, as shown in Figure 1-20.

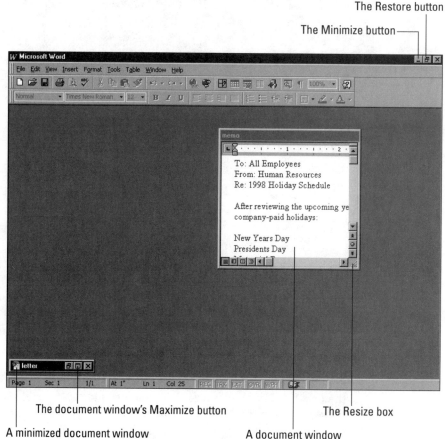

The Restore button

The Minimize button

Figure 1-20:
Resizing
and
minimizing
document
windows.

The document window's Maximize button

A minimized document window

A document window

The Resize box

You can drag the resize box to change the window size. Any additional instructions provided here about the resize box will only make it sound more complicated than it really is. Therefore, if you're curious about how this works — or are confused — start a program like WordPad, click the Restore button if necessary (to un-minimize the program window), and then drag the resize box.

Moving windows

If your screen shows more than one program window or a program window shows more than one document window, things can get a little, well, cluttered. Fortunately, it's easy to rearrange program windows and document windows so the one you want to work with is visible.

If you only have a single program or document window open, you can always move the window by dragging its title bar. The *title bar* is the colored bar along the top edge of the window that names the program or document file and provides the window buttons and the Close box. ***Note:*** You can't move a maximized program or document window because you have no place to move the window. You've run out of room.

If your screen shows more than one program window or more than one document window, moving windows is only slightly more involved. If you can see a window, you can still move the window by dragging its title bar. If you can't see a window, you may need to move the window to the top of the stack. To move a program window to the top of the stack of program windows, just click its task bar button. Note that clicking a program's task bar button makes that program window "active." The active program window appears on top of any other program windows, and Windows assumes that any commands you issue are commands to the active program. Suppose, for example, that you start both Word and Excel and then use the keyboard to choose File⇨Print command. When you choose this command, Windows assumes that you're issuing the command to the active program.

If you minimize a program window, clicking its task bar button both un-minimizes the program window and makes the program window active.

To move a document window to the top of a stack of document windows, open the program's Windows menu (see Figure 1-21) and then choose the document file. For example, suppose that you're working with Word and you open a Word document named "Letter" and another Word document named "Memo." If the Letter document shows on top but you want to reshuffle the document windows so that the "Memo" document shows on top, choose the Window menu's "Memo" command.

Figure 1-21:
The
Window
menu.

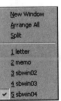

Typically, when you open a document file with a Windows program, the program adds a new, numbered command to the Windows menu for the document. To make a document the active document, choose its Windows menu command. ***Note:*** Some programs (including WordPad) can only work with one document at a time. When you open a new document with these programs, you also close the old document.

Chapter 2

Your Business Is Information

*N*ot that long ago, Walter Wriston, the former chairman of Citicorp Bank, said that businesses are all about information. Now Wriston's point wasn't that a delivery company's trucks and customers are unimportant. Quite the contrary. His observation, gleaned from decades of experience, was that the knowledge about things like what a truck can do and a true understanding of customer needs is what ultimately made for business success. In other words, information — Wriston used the term *intellectual capital* — is the essence of the business.

This notion may seem irrelevant in a book about Windows 95. However, Windows' primary role is the management of the information you store on your personal computer. For this reason, once you understand how Windows works — Chapter 1 describes that — the very next thing you need to know is how you work with the business documents you store electronically on your computer. And that's what this chapter does.

Organizing Your Business's Information

I'm going to start from the very beginning. Your computer uses a variety of devices for storing your information. You may be able to grab data and even place data on a compact disc, or CD. Your computer probably has a floppy drive into which you can insert floppy disks. Your computer also provides a hard disk, which you typically use as your principal warehouse of information. Although you can also use other pieces of equipment to store your information, for the most part, you're just storing information on disks: compact disks, floppy disks, hard disks, and so on. And this is the first thing you need to understand. (I'm sure that you understand this point, by the way. What I'm saying here is akin to, "Hey, you know those music CDs your teenager buys? The music is *stored* on the CD. Oooh . . .")

So now that you have this first critical piece of data in your mind — which you probably knew before you started reading — I need to tell you something else. Because the storage devices that your computer uses store tons of information, you use folders to break up the disk into little compartments. You can even break a folder compartment into smaller compartments called *subfolders.*

Believe it or not, you now understand pretty much everything you need to understand about how your computer organizes its information. Your computer uses disks to store files. Just to make sure that the disk doesn't become a complete mess, people typically break a disk's storage space into compartments called folders and subfolders. And that's really it.

Files, files, and more files

In Chapter 1, I made some gross generalizations about program files and document files. But in the interest of fair and full disclosure, you may just want to know three more things about the files stored on your computer:

✔ A program like your word processor is made up of dozens and dozens of program files — maybe even more. And the Windows operating system — which is itself a program — is made up of hundreds of program files. I mention this because if you start snooping around your disk and looking in mysteriously named folders and subfolders, you'll see all sorts of weird stuff you can't identify. You don't need to worry about this weird stuff. Just say to yourself, "Oh, that's probably just part of some program."

✔ Not all of the document files that get stored on your computer hold your information.

The Windows operating system and the programs you run often essentially create their own document files to store information. Your disks — particularly your hard disk — will quite possibly be storing hundreds and hundreds of these things.

✔ Sometimes, programs store collections of items together in a single document file. For example, while a single invoice may be a document file (say in the case where you create the invoice with a word processor), an accounting program typically groups all your invoices together along with your other financial records into one really big document file. Because the label "document" doesn't truly work for these big files that store a bunch of different items, people often call these big files *databases* and the individual items in the database file *records.*

Viewing Disks and Folders

You can view your disks, folders, and files in two basic ways: by using the Windows Explorer program (which is part of Windows 95) or by using the Internet Explorer 4.0 Web browser. In this chapter, I'm going to emphasize how you view disks and folders the Windows Explorer way. But I'll also briefly describe how and why you may want to view your disks and folders with Internet Explorer.

To start Windows Explorer, click Start➪Programs➪Windows Explorer.

Understanding the Windows Explorer window

Windows Explorer shows a visual representation of your computer from the perspective of your desktop. To be really honest, this visual map doesn't make much sense. And that's probably the first (and most important) thing you need to understand. In the left pane of the program window, for example, you see My Computer, Network Neighborhood, Recycle Bin, and My Briefcase. These four items roughly correspond to the four general locations you can store programs and documents:

- **My Computer:** Your own computer's disks, folders, and subfolders. (I talk about My Computer later in this chapter.)

- **Network Neighborhood:** The disks, folders, and subfolders of the computers that your computer can access by way of a network. (I discuss networking in Chapters 9 and 10.)

- **Recycle Bin:** The garbage dump where folders and program and document files go when you delete them. (I talk more about this just a bit later in the chapter.)

- **My Briefcase:** A weird container you can use to move documents between computers. (I talk more about this in Chapter 11.)

On the left pane of the Windows Explorer window, you see more information about whatever item you click on the left half of the window. If you click My Computer, for example, you see the contents of My Computer listed in the right pane of the window. These contents include system folders for Dial-Up Networking, Printers, and the Control Panel (which you don't have to know anything about to work your disks, so I'm going to postpone talking about these folders) and then the disks connected to your computer. Your Windows Explorer window almost certainly looks different than mine (which is shown in Figure 2-1) because your computer is different.

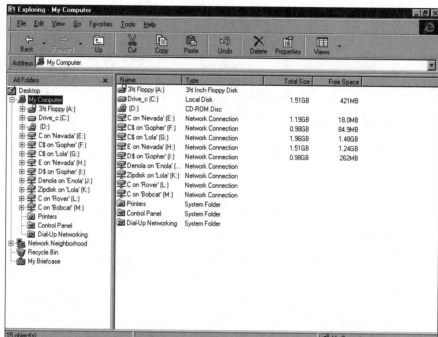

Figure 2-1:
The
Windows
Explorer
window.

Viewing a disk's contents

To view the contents of a disk, click its icon in the right half of the Windows
Explorer window. (The icons are just those labeled pictures that represent
disks.) For example, to see what's stored on the disk named "C," double-
click the "C" icon. When you do, Windows Explorer uses the pane to show
the folders, programs, and documents on your "C" disk. If you look closely
at the stuff shown in the right pane in Figure 2-2, you'll notice that different
items use different icons. Some of the items show an icon that looks sort of
like a manila file folder. These items are folders. Other items show little
pictures that look, well, different. These other items are programs (also
called applications) and documents (also called files).

To view folder and file details in Windows Explorer, choose View⇨ Details.

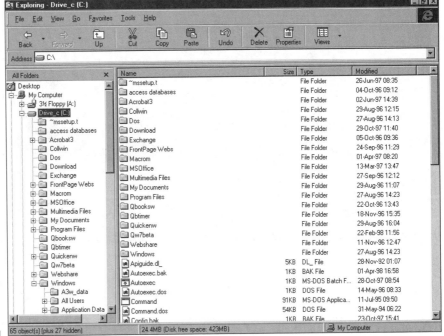

Figure 2-2:
The
Windows
Explorer
window
showing the
contents of
the "C"
disk.

Viewing a folder's contents

To view the contents of a folder, click its icon in the right half of the Windows Explorer window. When you do, Windows Explorer displays its subfolders and files. To see a subfolder's contents, click its icon. To move back up to the parent folder, click the Up One Level button (which appears on the toolbar), or activate the Go to different level drop-down list box and select the folder or disk you want to view.

You can learn the names of toolbar buttons and boxes by pointing to them with the mouse. When you point to a button, Windows displays the button name in a pop-up box.

If a folder stores subfolders that aren't displayed, Windows Explorer shows a plus symbol in front of the folder icon. To show the folder's subfolders — some people call this "expanding the folder tree" — click the plus symbol. After you expand a branch of the folder tree, Windows Explorer changes the plus symbol to a minus symbol. To collapse a folder tree that you previously expanded, click this minus symbol.

About file extensions

Windows doesn't typically show you this, but it turns out that Windows and Windows programs append a suffix — called a *file extension* — to the end of the file name you give a document. Windows uses this file extension to identify the file type of a document. A document you create with Microsoft Word, for example, uses the file extension DOC. A worksheet you create with Microsoft Excel uses the file extension WKB. Web pages you view with a browser like Internet Explorer use the file extension HTM. And JPEG graphic images (like those you often see in Web pages) use the file extension JPG. If you're interested in seeing the file extensions that different document types use, start Windows Explorer and choose View⇨Folder Options. Then, when the Folder Options dialog box appears, click the View tab and unmark the Hide file extensions for known file types box.

You can control how much information Windows Explorer displays about the folders and files it shows by using the last four buttons on the toolbar: Large icons, Small icons, List, and Details. If you click either the Large icons or Small icons button, Windows Explorer shows icons for folders and files — although the icons are of different size. If you click the List button, Windows Explorer lists the files and folders. If you click the Details button, Windows Explorer lists the files and folders but also provides additional information about items, including their type, size, and the date the file was last changed.

Saving and Opening Business Documents

Once you know how Windows 95 organizes your documents by using disks, folders, and subfolders, and that it stores program files and your document files using these disks, folders, and subfolders, you're ready to discover how to save and open these documents.

Saving a document for the first time

To save a document the first time — I'm assuming that you've already been working hard on creating the document — you take the following steps:

1. Choose File⇨Save As.

Windows displays the Save As dialog box as shown in Figure 2-3.

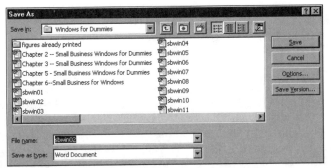

Figure 2-3:
The Save
As dialog
box.

2. **Activate the Save in drop-down list box and select the disk and folder you want to use for storing the document.**

   If the folder you want to use for storing the document is actually a subfolder, you may need to select this subfolder from the list box that appears beneath the Save In box.

   Note: You may even need to repeat this step a second time if the folder is really a sub-subfolder.

3. **In the File name box, provide a descriptive name for the document by using letters, numbers, and spaces.**

   You can use most symbols, too, but for safety's sake, stick with letters, numbers, and spaces.

4. **Click Save, and the program saves the document using the name you provided and in the specified location.**

   Pretty straightforward, right?

Saving a document a subsequent time

To save a document a subsequent time using the same name (which you usually want to do) and in the same location (which you also usually want to do), choose File⇨Save, or click the Save button on the toolbar (if you have one).

To save a document a subsequent time using a different name or in a different location, use File⇨Save As. In other words, go ahead and use the same command as you used to originally save the document the first time. By providing a new name or specifying a new location, you actually create a second copy of the document.

Opening a document the new and usually right way

The right way to open a document you've already saved is to just tell Windows that you want to open the document. If the document appears on the Documents menu, for example, you can just choose the document from that menu (as I discuss in Chapter 1). You can also start Windows Explorer, root around your disks and folders until you find the document, and then double-click it to open it. (If you use this last approach, of course, it helps if you know the document name and have some faint idea about where it's located.)

You can preview the contents of many document files — without actually opening a document — by using the QuickView command. To use QuickView, right-click a document to display the shortcut menu. If Windows can preview a document file's contents, you'll see a QuickView command on the shortcut menu. To preview the document, choose the QuickView command.

When you open a document the new and usually right way, note that you don't first start the program you'll use to work with the document. No way. Weird, right? Well, here's what happens. Windows knows which program you used to create a document. So when you tell Windows that you want to open up a document that you created with Microsoft Word, for example, it's smart enough to know that the right way to do so is to start Microsoft Word and then have it open the document.

If you ask Windows to open some document that Windows can't identify, it asks you what program to use. To provide this information, Windows displays the Open with dialog box. To use this dialog box, you click its Browse button so that the Browse window appears. The Browse window basically works like a miniature Windows Explorer program. You use it to find the program that Windows should use to open the document. (By the way, you should know what program this is, because presumably you created the document.)

Opening a document the old way

You can also open a document by using a program's File➪Open command. For example, if you're working with Microsoft Word, you use the Word program's File➪Open command. To do so, take the following steps:

1. Select File➪Open.

Windows displays the Open dialog box as shown in Figure 2-4.

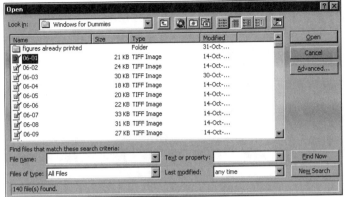

Figure 2-4:
The Open
dialog box.

2. **Activate the Look in drop-down list box and select the disk and folder you used for storing the document.**

3. **If the folder you used for storing the document is actually a subfolder, you may need to select this subfolder from the list box that appears beneath the Look In box.**

   Note: You may even need to repeat this step a second time if the folder is really a sub-subfolder.

4. **When you see the document listed in the list box beneath the Look in box, double-click it.**

   Note: If you have too many documents listed to fit completely inside the box, Windows adds scrollbars to the box and you use these to scroll through the list.

By default, Windows only lists documents that are native to the program from which you're opening the document. If you're working with Word, for example, you typically only see Word documents. In fact, Windows is even more picky than that. If you're working with Word version 8, you may only see documents that were created by Word version 8. To override the way that Windows lists the documents shown in the Open dialog box, activate the Files of Type drop-down list box and select the entry that describes the category of files you want to open.

Closing Documents

You can close an open document by clicking the document window's Close box, or by choosing File⇨Close. If you close, or stop, the program, the program automatically closes all of its open document files as a part of stopping.

As you may guess, Windows doesn't close a document that includes changes you haven't saved without first suggesting that you save your changes (by re-saving the document). For example, if while working with some financial report, you make a bunch of changes and then ask Windows to close the document, Windows won't immediately close the document. Windows will first ask you if you want to save your changes. If you answer this question, "Yes," Windows saves the revised version of the document.

A Quick Word about Shortcut Icons

In Chapter 1, I mention that Windows lets you use shortcut icons — clickable buttons — to start programs and open documents. You may also be interested in knowing that you can easily create shortcut icons yourself, too. To do so, follow these steps:

1. **Right-click the program file or document for which you want to create a shortcut icon.**

2. **Choose the shortcut menu's Create Shortcut command.**

   Windows places the shortcut in the same folder with the original program or document file.

You can copy or move the shortcut icon (for instance to the desktop) in the same manner as you copy and move other files. (See the next section for information on how to do this.)

Copying and Moving Business Documents

You have a bunch of different ways to copy and move business documents. And that puts you and me in a bit of a pickle. I can tell you about every way (and bore you half to death), or I can pick one good way and explain how it works. Because I'm a small business person, too, and seem to have more work than time, I'm going to just give you one really good, fast way to do this stuff.

Copying business documents

Okay here's how you copy a business document. First, you start Windows Explorer by clicking Start➪Programs➪Windows Explorer. Then, you take the following steps:

1. **Make sure that the folder pane of the Windows Explorer window shows the folder to which you want to copy a document (see Figure 2-5).**

   If it doesn't, you can expand the folder tree — the map of folders and subfolders — by clicking the plus symbols that appear in front of disks and in front of folders with subfolders.

2. **View the folder or subfolder with the document you want to copy.**

   To do so, click the disk, then the folder, and then, if necessary, the subfolder.

3. **Click the document you want to copy.**

   This step selects the document.

4. **Hold down the Ctrl key and drag the document to the icon in the folder pane that represents the folder to which you want to copy the document.**

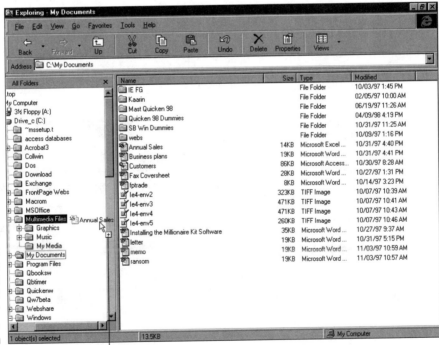

Figure 2-5: Copying a business document to another folder.

The plus icon verifies that you're creating a copy of the document in another location.

You can copy a document to the folder that's holding the original document, but the two documents can't have the same name if they're both stored in the same folder. For this reason, if you do copy a document to the same folder with the original, Windows changes the name of the document copy by tacking on the phrase "Copy of" to the document's name.

If you want to copy a document to a different drive on your computer or to a different computer on your network, you don't need to hold down the Ctrl key.

Moving business documents

Moving a document works almost the exact same way as copying a document. First, you start Windows Explorer, and then you take the following steps:

1. **Make sure that the folder pane of the Windows Explorer window shows the folder to which you want to move a document (see Figure 2-6).**

   If it doesn't, you can expand the folder tree by clicking the plus symbols that appear in front of disks and in front of folders with subfolders.

2. **View the folder or subfolder with the document you want to move.**

   You do so as described earlier in the chapter: Click the disk, then the folder, and then, if necessary, the subfolder.

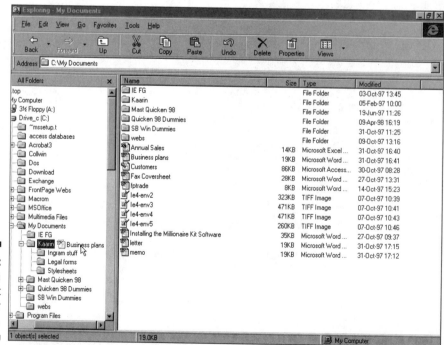

Figure 2-6: Moving a document to another folder.

3. **Click the document you want to move.**

   This step selects the document.

4. **Drag the document to the icon in the folder pane that represents the folder to which you want to move the document.**

You don't want to move a document that somebody else or some program created. This makes sense, right? I mean, it's okay to move a bunch of word-processing documents you created (with your word processor's help) to a new folder you've set up. But you don't want to start fiddling around with program files or other, weird files that you're not sure about, such as files the guy in the next office created. If you do, only bad things can happen. Windows won't know where to find the program file for some program you want to start. Or the guy in the next cubicle won't know where to find the legal correspondence documents he's been saving for the last four years.

Other Cool Stuff You Can Do with Your Documents

You can do a bunch of other stuff with the documents you see on a disk or in a folder. Most of this is so easy that you almost don't need my help. But let me just quickly tell you about seven handy things you'll want to know how to do with Windows Explorer:

- ✔ **Deleting documents:** If you want to delete a document, click it, and then click the Delete button.

- ✔ **Renaming documents:** If you want to rename a document, click it once. Then click the document name once again. (You need to do these two clicks slowly so that Windows doesn't think that you're double-clicking.) Windows opens an editable text box over the document name, and you can use it to type a new name.

- ✔ **Hiding documents:** If you want to hide a document so people can't see it, right-click the document so that the shortcuts menu shows, choose the Properties command, and then check the Hidden box.

- ✔ **Unhiding previous hidden documents:** To unhide a document, first choose View➪Folder Options, click the View tab, and then mark the Show All Files button, which appears in the Hidden Files list of settings. (When you click OK, Windows Explorer updates the folder and file information shown in its windows so hidden folders and files appear.) Next, right-click the hidden document you want to unhide (the document is now visible), choose the Properties command, and then uncheck the Hidden box.

✔ **Undeleting a document:** You can usually undelete a document you previously deleted, because when you delete a document, Windows typically doesn't delete it. It moves the document to a special folder, called the Recycle Bin. (This is the same Recycle Bin that appears in the left-hand pane of the Windows Explorer window.) To move a document from the Recycle Bin to its old location, double-click the Recycle Bin icon to display its contents, find and then right-click the document you want to undelete, and then choose the Restore command.

✔ **Really deleting a document:** To really delete a document, first delete the document from its regular folder location (so that the document gets moved to the Recycle Bin). Then, double-click the Recycle Bin icon to display its contents, find the document you want to delete, and then press Delete.

✔ **Emptying the Recycle Bin:** To empty the recycle bin of all its documents, right-click the Recycle Bin icon and then choose the Empty Recycle Bin command from the shortcuts menu.

Typically, you'll want to fiddle with files by using the Windows Explorer. But you can also do some of this stuff by displaying the Save As and Open dialog boxes (see Figures 2-3 and 2-4). Specifically, if you display the Save As or Open dialog box (as described earlier in this chapter) and then right-click a document that appears in the list box, Windows displays a shortcut menu that includes commands for doing stuff like opening, renaming, and deleting files.

Formatting Floppy Disks

Before you can copy or move files to a floppy disk, you or someone else needs to format the disk. If you buy floppy disks that aren't preformatted, you first need to format them yourself. To format a disk, follow these steps:

1. **Insert the floppy disk in your floppy disk drive.**

2. **Start Windows Explorer by clicking Start⇨Programs⇨Windows Explorer.**

3. **Right-click the floppy disk icon in the folder pane so that Windows Explorer displays the shortcut menu.**

4. **Choose the Format command.**

   Windows Explorer displays the Format dialog box (see Figure 2-7).

Figure 2-7:
The Format
dialog box
in Windows
Explorer.

5. **Verify that the Capacity drop-down list box correctly shows the floppy disk's capacity.**

   If it doesn't, activate the list box and select the correct capacity. If you don't know the capacity, look at the box the floppy disks came in, or look on the disk itself. (If you see the letters HD or the words High Density, select the 1.44MB setting. If you see the letters DD or the words Double Density, select the 720K setting.) If you can't find the disk's capacity, you can also just ignore this step and let Windows try to format the disk at the selected capacity. If the capacity is incorrect, Windows will tell you so and you can try the other capacity.

6. **Select the Format type button that describes how you want to format the disk:**

   • **Quick:** Select Quick if the floppy disk has already been formatted before. Use this option to recycle old disks by erasing all of the files off of them.

   • **Full:** Select Full to truly format the disk (say because it's unformatted or because you want to recycle a Macintosh-formatted disk).

   • **Copy system files:** Select Copy system files only to make a disk that you can use to boot your computer using the old MS-DOS operating system.

7. **Check the Display summary when finished box.**

   This way, you can see if the disk is damaged. If the summary shows that the disk has any bad sectors, throw the disk away and start with a new one.

8. **Click Start.**

   Windows formats the disk according to your instructions.

The Lost Files

Windows comes with a really useful tool called Find File. What this tool does is look for files — typically documents — that you've lost on a disk. For example, if you're trying to find a copy of a letter you wrote to some customer sometime last year, but you can't find the darn thing, you can use Find File.

Using Find for a simple search

Although Find File is a powerful tool, you can use it to perform simple, no-brain searches. Here's how:

1. **Click Start⇨Find.**

2. **When Windows displays the Find submenu of commands, choose the Files or Folders command.**

   Windows starts the Find File tool as shown in Figure 2-8.

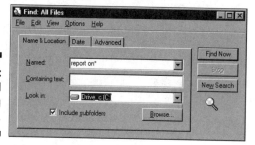

Figure 2-8: The Find: All Files dialog box.

3. **If necessary, click the Name & Location tab so that the Name & Location tab shows.**

4. **Enter the document's name in the Named box.**

   If you know part of the name but not all of the name, you can use the ? wildcard character to represent any single character. For example, if you want to find a document that's named either letter-a, letter-b, or letter-c, you could enter the name as **letter-?**. You can use the * wildcard character to represent any set of characters. So, if you want to find documents that start with the word "report" such as " report on competitors," "report on customers," and "report on vendors," you can enter the name as **report on***.

5. **Use the Look in box to specify which disk you want to search.**

6. **Check the Include subfolders box so that Find looks in all of the folders (including any subfolders) of the selected disk.**

7. **Click Find Now.**

Find searches the specified disk for a document with a name like what is entered in the Named box, and then displays a list of the documents matching your search criteria. It shows the disk, folder, and subfolder for a document. (This collection of information is called a path, but who cares, right?) Some other information is shown as well, such as the document size, its file type, and the date and time you last saved it.

8. **To open document you see listed, double-click it.**

Searching for documents that include specific text

If you're the observant type, you may have noticed that the Name & Location tab also shows a Containing text box (see Figure 2-8). This box lets you provide some snippet of text, which Find then uses to search for the document you want. You can do this to search for a document when you don't know the document name but do know something about the information a document stores, for example. Suppose, for sake of illustration, that you can't remember what you named a letter you wrote to your attorney asking about common real estate lease terms. In this case, you could search for documents containing the phrase "real estate lease."

But I should warn you that text-based searches typically take a long time. Although Windows can search through a list of the files stored on your hard disk in a few seconds, or perhaps in a few minutes, searching through actual documents can take quite a few minutes. If you do decide to execute a text-based search, therefore, don't sit and wait. Remember, too, that you can multitask Windows programs (as I describe in Chapter 1) and that means you can do other work with your computer while Windows is searching your hard disk.

Searching for documents by date

The Find: All Files dialog box also provides a Date and Advanced tab. These tabs provide extra search options that can be really useful — especially in office settings where you're producing or collecting lots and lots of documents on your computer. To use the Date tab, you start the Find tool in the usual way, and use the Name & Location tab to describe where you want to search (and to provide additional information about the document name or its contents). Then, you take the following steps:

1. **Mark the Find all files button to indicate that you want to search for documents based on their last modification dates (see Figure 2-9).**

Figure 2-9:
The Date
tab.

2. Describe how you want to use document last modification dates:

- To search for documents with dates that fall within a range, mark the between button and then use the between boxes to provide a range of dates. Enter the starting and ending dates in the form MM/DD/YY where MM represents the month number, DD represents the day number, and YY represents the year number.

- To search for documents with dates that fall during the previous month or months, mark the during previous months button and then indicate how far back — how many months — you want to go.

- To search for documents with dates that fall during the previous day or days, mark the during previous days button and then indicate how far back — how many days — you want to go.

3. To begin searching by using your dates criteria, click Find Now.

The Find tool combines the search criteria you enter on each of the Find: All Files dialog box tabs. Does that make sense? What I mean is that if you enter search criteria on the Name & Location tab to say you want to search disk "C" for documents that begin with the word "report" and then you use the Date tab to say you want to look for documents created in the previous month, Find looks for documents that match all of these criteria: documents stored on disk "C" that have their names starting with the word "report" and that were created in the last month. If you use any of the Advanced tab's buttons or boxes to create additional search criteria, well, then these also apply.

Using Advanced Search Options

If you click the Advanced tab on the Find: All Files dialog box, you can provide additional search criteria to Find (see Figure 2-10). You can use the Of type drop-down list to specify that you're looking for specific types of files. (This drop-down list displays a lengthy list of rather specific files, so to see what choices you have, activate the list box and then take the time to scroll through its entries.) You can also use the Size is boxes to specify that you're looking for a file that is either at least the size you specify or at most the size you specify.

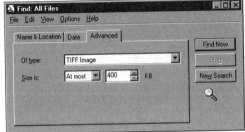

Figure 2-10:
The Find: All
Files
Advanced
tab.

A Final Few Words About Information Strategy

Now the usual tack in a book like this — after you understand what disks, folders, and files are and how you noodle around with them — is to just stop the chapter. But you know what? I'm not going to do that here. Remembering what Walter Wriston said, I'm going to reflect for just a moment or two on strategies and tactics you can and should use to make sure that your business's information — the very essence of your business — gets organized in way that supports your activities and helps you succeed.

You gotta get organized

Okay, the first thing I want to say is that, well, you really do want to keep your computer's information organized. That sounds so darned obvious, I know, but with the dozens of folders and thousands of files you'll find even on a brand-new, right-out-of-the-box computer, you need to keep your information organized from the very start. And if you've already gone along in a haphazard way, storing your business documents here and there, you want to take the time to get organized before you go any further. You really do. So here's what you want to do:

✔ Store all of the documents that you create in one folder. You can use the folder that Windows provides exactly for this purpose, My Documents. Or you can create a new folder — perhaps one with a slightly shorter name like Data. Either way works. The choice is yours. Move existing documents to this folder (as described earlier in this chapter), and from now on, save your documents here, too.

- ✔ If you work with a bunch of documents, go ahead and create meaningful subfolders within this folder. (I use separate folders for collecting documents for the individual books I write, for legal documents, letters to customers, and so forth.)

- ✔ Name your documents with meaningful filenames but don't duplicate information that's already provided automatically by Windows such as the document file type or date.

Play it safe, will you?

I suggest that you need to think about the safety of your information. You don't want to lose valuable information, and you don't want to divulge secret information. Fortunately, as long as you're not trying to mimic the Central Intelligence Agency's secrecy standards, you can rather easily increase your information safety:

- ✔ Make backup copies of really important documents and files, and then store these copies on another disk — preferably either a disk on another computer (just in case the computer with the data is stolen) or better yet on a removable disk you can store in some offsite location (just in case something bad like a fire happens).

- ✔ Hide or at least camouflage documents you don't want people to easily view or tamper with. You can create a folder and hide it, for example, just by following the steps I described earlier; doing so keeps most people out of your files. You can also hide the individual documents. *Note:* After you hide a folder or document, the Find tool doesn't find them.

- ✔ Secure documents you absolutely don't want people to look at or copy by using program-level security. Most programs let you assign passwords to documents so that only people who know (or can guess) the password can view the document. How you do this is beyond the scope of this book because program password security varies between programs. But do be aware that this functionality is almost always available, and consider using it if security concerns warrant.

Spring cleaning is essential

With the large hard disks now available, you can rather easily fall into the habit of never cleaning your disks and folders. However, I really think you need to do this. So, on a regular basis, look through the folder or subfolders in which you have your documents stored, and then delete the old documents you know you won't use anymore. (I describe how you delete documents earlier in the chapter.) Be sure to regularly empty your Recycle Bin, too, to free up storage space on your computer.

Backing up important documents

To create a backup copy of an important document, all you need to do is copy the document to another storage device. While you can use a floppy disk or handful of floppy disks to do this, you'll probably want to use some other storage device. A floppy disk, for example, stores at most about a megabyte of information. (You can store about 500 pages of Microsoft Word documents or around twenty average-sized JPEG photographic images in a megabyte, for example.) But you can get Iomega Zip drives — which are sorta like monster floppy disks — that store 100 megabytes or more. If you get a CD disk that lets you write to blank CDs, you can store as much as 600 megabytes on the disk. And you can also get tape drives that let you store hundreds of megabytes of information or more on a tape. (These tapes look like cassette tapes.) In my office, by the way, I use Iomega Zip disks for backups because they're pretty cheap, reusable, and don't go bad as easily as, say, floppy disks. (Check any PC supplies catalog for up-to-date information.)

Another thing you can do is use Find to build a list of the temporary documents that Windows programs create — these files all use the extension TMP — and delete these files, too. (These files are typically stored in the Temporary subfolder in the Windows directory.)

Chapter 3

Getting Help

● ●

● ●

*I*n a large organization an information systems or computer department supports users and helps them solve problems. What's more, in a large organization, you can always find a few people around with strong technology skills — people to whom you can turn for help. Alas, this isn't the case for the small business Windows user.

Therefore, as remedial as it sounds, once you know what Windows is and how you work with it, you need to know how to get help when you have a question or encounter a problem. You can't afford to waste time finding help on how to get help — you have a business to run.

A Brief Description of Using Help

Windows comes with a built in Help program. In a nutshell, the Help program just lets you read and wade through a heavily-indexed document that describes how Windows works and what to do when Windows doesn't work.

Starting Help

To start the Help program, click Start⇨Help. When you start Help, Windows displays a window like the one shown in Figure 3-1.

Figure 3-1:
The Help
window.

As Figure 3-1 shows, the Help window uses three tabs to organize its information. In the paragraphs that follow, I describe how you work with each tab.

Using the Contents tab

The Contents tab works like a book's table of contents. By looking through the Help program's table of contents, you see what information the Help program provides.

The Help program's table of contents — the stuff you see on the Contents tab — doesn't show more detail than you request. This sounds tricky, but let me explain. If you take a look at Figure 3-1, you'll notice that the first item listed in the Contents tab is If you've used Windows before. See it? Good. This "If you've used Window before" thing is a help topic — basically a little article or essay that describes help information useful to people who've used Windows before.

Okay, now notice that preceding this help topic is a little icon that looks something like a miniature page with a big question mark on it. See that? That icon identifies the "If you've used Windows before" thing as a help topic. If you double-click a help topic, the Help program opens a Window that displays (hopefully) helpful information. Figure 3-2 shows the "If you've used Windows before" help topic.

Figure 3-2:
The Help window showing information that is (hopefully) useful to people who've used Windows before — perhaps the prior version of Windows, for example.

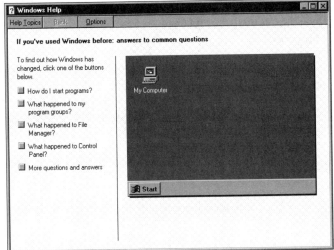

As Figure 3-2 shows, the Help window's information provides both text and pictures. You'll also see that the bulleted list of text chunks includes little gray buttons. (These gray buttons don't show up all that well on the page, but if you follow along with your computer you'll see exactly what I mean.) If you click a gray button, the Help program displays different information in the Help window. For example, if you click the little gray button that's just left of the bullet text that says How do I start programs?, the Help program displays information about how you start programs. This makes sense, right?

But now go back to the Contents tab, and I'll describe a few more useful tidbits about how it works. To go back, by the way, just click the Help Topics button. (This button appears in the top left corner of the Help information window.)

Take a look at the second item on the Contents tab list. See the one that says, Introducing Windows? Do you see how the little icon that precedes this help thing is a little book? Okay, good. The little book icon shows you that "Introducing Windows" isn't really a help topic in the way that "If you've used Windows before" is. The "Introducing Windows" help thing is really a set of help topics.

You can see which help topics make up a set of help topics by clicking the little closed-book icon. When you do, Help shows all the help topics and subsets of help topics within the set. If you double-click the little closed-book icon for the Introducing Windows set, for example, Help shows the subsets of help topics shown in Figure 3-3.

Rather than double-clicking a help topic to display the Help information window and rather than double-clicking a help topics set or subset to display its contents, you can select the help topic, set, or subset and then click the Display button. However, I suggest that you double-click these items because doing so is both faster and easier.

Figure 3-3: The Contents tab after it shows what's in the "Introducing Windows" set of help topics.

If you click one of these subsets, Help then shows the help topics within the subset, as shown in Figure 3-4. Notice that when Help shows the subset's help topics, it replaces the little closed-book icon with a little open-book icon. You can see this both in Figure 3-3 (where the "Introducing Windows" set of help topics is shown) and in Figure 3-4 (where the "Welcome" subset of help topics is shown). If you click one of the help topics shown in the "Welcome" subset, Help displays the Help information window shown in Figure 3-2.

You actually now know what you need to know to work with Help. In most situations, you can use the Contents tab to find a help topic that provides the information you need or want. Oh sure, you always have to do a bit of searching — that's to be expected. But what you'll find is that the more you look through the sets and subsets of help topics and then the actual topics shown on the Contents tab, the more familiar you'll became both with the information provided in Help and how Help organizes its data.

Double-click the little open-book icon
to collapse a help topics set or subset.

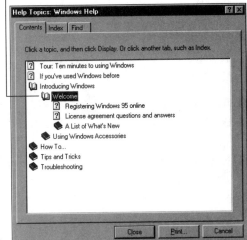

Figure 3-4:
The
Contents
tab after it
shows
what's
in the
"Welcome"
subset of
help topics.

TIP

When you choose a Help menu command within a software program like
Word or WordPerfect, Excel or Quicken, you start the same Help program
described earlier in this chapter. The Help program displays information
from a different help document (one for the software program — Microsoft
Word, perhaps — that you used to start Help). So once you know how the Help
program works, you can use it to get help with Windows or with any other
software program, too.

Using the Index tab

If you're new to Windows and want online help, first try using the Contents tab.
If that doesn't work, use the Index tab. (You may also want to use the Index tab
after you've worked with Windows long enough to know the lingo — in other
words, to know which terms Windows uses to refer to whatever item you have a
question about.) As you may expect, the Index tab works like a book's index.

To use the Index tab, start the Help program and then click the Index tab.
When you do, Help displays the Index tab as shown in Figure 3-5. To use the
index, type in the word or phrase that best describes the help topic you
have question about. If you want to know how to turn on Windows' screen
saver, for example, type the phrase **screen saver** into the text box that
appears at the top of the Index tab. As you type, Help scrolls through its
index of help topics. If it finds one that matches, it selects that topic.
Figure 3-5 shows the "screen savers" topic selected. To display help information about the selected help topic, double-click the help topic. (You can
scroll through the help topic index by pressing the Page Up and Page Down
keys and by using the help topic index list box's scroll bar.)

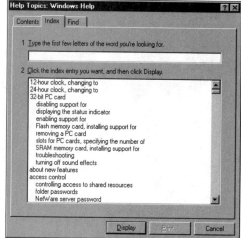

Figure 3-5:
The Index
tab lets you
search and
view the
Help
program's
index of
help topics.

You can print the selected help topic shown in the Contents tab or the Index tab. To do so, select the help topic (click it) and then click the Print command button.

Using the Find tab

If neither the Contents tab nor the Index tab works, you can also try using the Find tab. From the start, you should know that the Find tab is a long shot. In essence, the Find tab works like a concordance to the help file — it searches through the text of all of the help topics, looking for the word or phrase you supply. You can search for the word, "printer," for example. Or the phrase, "control panel."

Recognize, however, that Find typically doesn't provide you with much value, which makes sense if you think about. What you find by using Find is information that doesn't appear on the Contents tab and doesn't appear on the Index tab. Consider the significance of this point for just a moment. If you are looking for a help topic that uses the word, "printer," the only new information you can find with Find are help topics that use the word "printer" but that weren't germane enough to appear as printer-related topics on either the Contents tab or the Index. See my point?

To use the Find tab, click it. The first time you display the Find tab, Help starts the Find Setup wizard. The Find Setup wizard in effect builds a second index of terms and phrases according to your instructions. To build this index, the Find Setup wizard asks one or more questions. The first question is whether you want to minimize the size of the index — what the Find Setup wizard calls a database. The Find Setup wizard may also ask you (depending on your answer to the first question) about which specific help topics you want to include in this new index you're building. Your best bet for either question is just to accept the default, or suggested answer. If you want to do something else, however, just read the on-screen instructions. When you finish answering a question, click the Next button. (When you answer the last question, click the Finish button instead of the Next button.)

You can rerun the Find Setup wizard by clicking the Rebuild command button, which appears on the Find tab. In other words, while the Find Setup wizard appears only the first time you click the Find tab, if you click the Find tab's Rebuild button, you tell Help to run the Find Setup wizard over again. Doing so lets you rebuild the Find tab's index in different way.

After you finish answering the Find Setup wizard's questions, Help creates the new index, database, or help topics and displays the Find tab (see Figure 3-6). To search through this index, type in the word or phrase that best describes the help topic you have questions about. (This works the same way as for the regular Index tab.) If you want to know how to view a video, for example, type the word **video** into the text box that appears at the top of the Find tab. As you type, Help scrolls through this new index of terms and phrases. If it finds one that matches, Help selects the topic. Figure 3-6 shows two "video" topics selected, Video and video. Beneath this list of matching index entries, the Find tab displays a list of help topics that use the index entry or entries, "Video" or "video." To display the selected help topic, check its box. (You can display more than one help topic by checking more than one box.) Then click the Display button. Or, to print a copy of the help topic, check its box and then click the Print button. (As you may expect, you can also print more than one help topic by checking more than one box.)

Figure 3-6:
The Find tab lets you create and then use a custom index of words and phrases used in the Help information files.

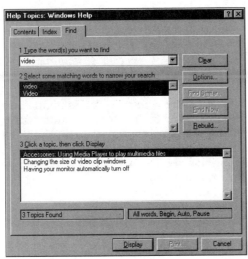

One worthwhile feature of the Find tab is that you can use it to find help topics that reference more than one word or phrase. For example, if you enter the word "graphic," you can track down help topics having to do with graphic images. And if you enter the word "printing," you can track down help topics having to do with printing. But — and this is the neat part — with the Find tab you can enter the words "graphic" and "printing" and then track down help topics that to do with printing graphic images.

You can click the Find tab's Find Similar button to display a list of help topics that the Help program thinks are similar to the topic about which you want more information.

Before I wrap up this discussion of the Find tab, let me mention one more thing. You can click the Find tab's Options command button to display a dialog box that lets you more closely control how Help finds (or attempts to find) what you're looking for. Figure 3-7 shows this dialog box.

Figure 3-7:
The Find
Options
dialog box
lets you
specify how
Help is
supposed to
find what
you're
looking for.

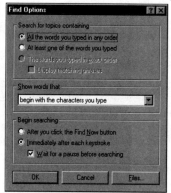

Most of the Find Options options are self-descriptive, but let me quickly describe what each does. The Find Options dialog box provides four options related to how it searches for the help topics:

> ✔ **All the words you typed in any order:** Mark this option button if the order of the words you're trying to find doesn't matter. For example, if you're trying to find information about how you go about "printing graphics," the order doesn't matter. Any topic that talks both about printing and about graphics may be useful to you. (Chapter 4 talks in detail about how you print in Windows.)

✔ **At least one of the words that you typed:** Mark this option button if you are interested in help topics that use only one of the words you entered. For example, if you enter the words "printing" and "graphics" into the Find tab's text box, you may mark this option button if in addition to information about printing graphic images, you're also interested in general information about printing and general information about graphics.

✔ **The words you typed in exact order:** If you type more than one word and the order in which you typed the words does matter (say because the words need to be in the typed order for accuracy's or meaning's sake), you mark this option. For example, if you're interested in help topics having to do with the Windows Control Panel tool and so enter the phrase "control panel" into the Find tab, you probably want to find only those help topics that use the words "control" and "panel" and in that order. You don't want to find help topics that discuss volume "control" and then how you can split windows into "panels," or frames, in some programs. (Chapter 12 talks about how you use Control Panel tools to personalize your computer.)

✔ **Display matching phrases check box:** This check box, which is enabled only if you mark the "word you typed in exact order" option button, tells Help that you're searching for the exact phrase you entered in the Find tab. For example, if you enter the phrase "graphic printing," and only want to see help topics that use this exact phrase but not other phrases such as "graphic image printing," you check this box.

The Find Options dialog box provides three options related to how it starts its search for help topics matching the words you enter on the Find tab:

✔ **After you click the Find Now button:** Mark this option button if you want Help to begin searching only after you click the Find Now command button. (The Find Now command, as shown in Figure 3-7, appears on the Find Options dialog box.)

✔ **Immediately after each keystroke:** Mark this option button if you want Help to begin searching as you start typing the words. (By default, this button is marked.)

✔ **Wait for a pause before searching:** This check box, which is enabled only if you mark the Immediately After Each Keystroke option button, essentially tells Help to give you a moment to type most or all of your entry before beginning the search. (By default, this check box is checked.)

How to Use Online Help Options

Microsoft Corporation, through its corporate Web site (www.microsoft.com) provides technical support for the Windows operating system and most of its application programs. In addition, many PC manufacturers (and hopefully whomever you bought your computer from) also provide technical support via the Internet. I'm only going to describe how Microsoft's Windows Support Online Web site works here, but do recognize that you may be able to get similar information about your computer from the manufacturer's Web site.

For purposes of this discussion, I need to assume that you have an Internet connection and that you know how to work with a Web browser such as Internet Explorer 4.0. If you don't yet possess this information, you'll need to turn to Chapter 5.

Finding the Windows support Web site

I personally find the Support Online Web site incredibly valuable. When I have a problem that I can't find an answer to, I often conduct a search of Microsoft's Online technical support resources by using Support Online.

The way you use Support Online changes over time (as Microsoft updates and polishes its technical support system). Nevertheless, let me just quickly overview how it works as I'm writing this book. If you have a general idea as to how Support Online works and what it's capable of, you'll have little problem applying the general principles described here to your future problem solving.

To get Windows product support from Microsoft's Support Online Web site, start your Web browser and go to the following Web page:

```
http://support.microsoft.com/support/
```

When you do, your Web browser displays the Support Online search page as shown in Figure 3-8. To conduct a search, follow these steps:

1. **Select the Microsoft product you have a question about in the My Question Is About drop-down list box.**

   For example, you may select Windows 95 if you have a question about Windows 95.

2. **Describe your question by entering a key word or phrase in the My Question Is text box.**

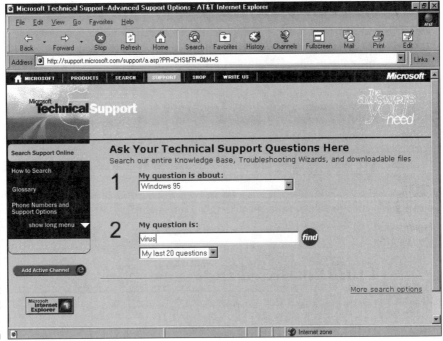

Figure 3-8:
The
Microsoft
Windows
product
support
Web site.

3. Click Find.

If Support Online finds any articles that match your search criteria, it displays a list of the first 25 matching articles. (See Figure 3-9.)

4. Click an article's headline to read the article.

Addresses change over time. Therefore, don't freak out if the *URL,* or Internet address, that I just provided for the Windows product support changes. Instead, use your Web browser to view the Microsoft Corporation home page (which is at `www.microsoft.com/`). Then look for a hyperlink labeled "Support" or "Product Support" or something along these lines. (A *hyperlink* is just a graphic or an underlined piece of text that takes you to another Web page. You can tell if an element on a Web page is a hyperlink because your mouse pointer turns into a pointing finger when you move it over the hyperlink.) If you click this hyperlink, you should see another Web page that provides hyperlinks to the appropriate Windows Web site. (You may have to select Windows 95 from a list box and click "Go.")

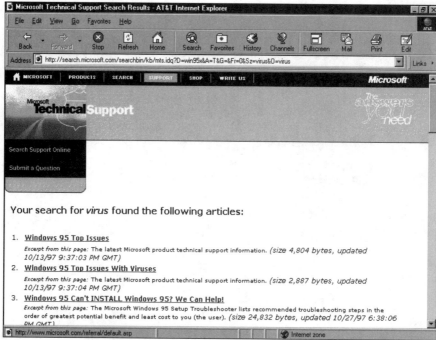

Figure 3-9:
My search
on the word
virus
returned
this list of
articles.

Getting answers to frequently asked questions

The Microsoft product support Web site lists and provides answers to frequently asked questions. I don't find the Frequently Asked Questions information as useful as, say, the Knowledge Base stuff. The Frequently Asked Questions stuff usually appears in the Help program's document. But, especially if you're a brand-new-to-Windows user, you may find the Frequently Asked Questions Web site useful.

To use the Frequently Asked Questions Web site, follow these steps:

1. **Start your Web browser and then go to the following Web page:**
   ```
   http://support.microsoft.com/support/windows/faq/
   default.asp
   ```

2. **Click the category of frequently asked questions that your question falls into.**

3. **When you see the list of frequently asked questions, click the question you want to have answered.**

   Figure 3-10 shows an answer to a frequently asked question.

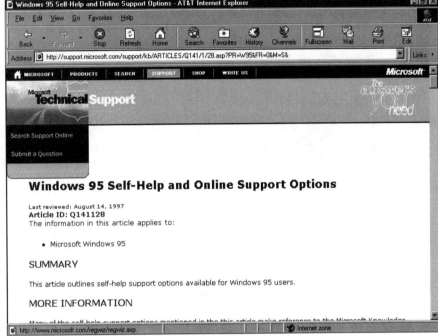

Figure 3-10:
This Web
page shows
the answer
to one
frequently
asked
question,
"Where can
I find more
information
about
Windows 95
usage and
trouble-
shooting?"

Browsing a Windows support newsgroup

As you may know (and as is discussed a bit further in Chapter 6) a
newsgroup amounts to an electronic bulletin board where people post and
read messages, or news articles. If you click the Newsgroups hyperlink
supplied by the Windows product support Web page and then identify
Windows 95 as the Microsoft product you want more help with, you ultimately get a Web page that lists Windows 95 newsgroups having to do with a
bunch of different stuff. To view a newsgroup, you click the appropriate
hyperlink.

I'm not going to discuss support newsgroups in more detail. For most small
business users, the newsgroups useful-news-to-useless-news (or signal-to-
noise) ratio is too low to justify the time you spend. But if you have time and
find yourself intrigued with the whole Internet thing, do explore this option.
(You may have to do a bit of fiddling in order to get your *newsgroups reader*
working correctly — this is a special program you use to read and post
messages to a newsgroup — but just follow the on-screen instructions, and
you'll be fine.)

Where to Turn When Help is No Help

And now, predictably, I come to big question. What do you do when you need help but the established and traditional sources of help — the Help program, the product support Web site, and even this book — are no help?

The obvious answer is simply to call Microsoft and ask to talk with a product support specialist. Microsoft changes the direct telephone numbers you're supposed to call. Just call the main Microsoft number (1-425-882-8080) and ask the receptionist what number you're supposed to call for Windows 95 product support, and he or she will give you the direct number. As I'm writing this, product support calls are free for Windows 95.

Be forewarned that product support calls aren't always free. (Microsoft Corporation does charge Windows NT users for their support calls, for example.) And you have to pay for long-distance telephone charges (a cost that may be prohibitive for people calling outside of the United States).

If you can't just call Microsoft or you've tried that it and it doesn't work, let me throw out one final idea: You may not really need help at all. Let me explain by way of example what I mean.

A few years ago, I needed to install a Windows NT server for printing the large desktop publishing documents — called postscript files — that we work with in my small business. (I talk more about Windows NT, servers, and building your own network in Chapters 9 and 10, but don't worry if you don't know what postscript files are.) So my question was, "How to do I print postscript documents by using the new NT server?" In other words, what special tricks did I need to know?

I figured that I could get answers to this question pretty easily. I tried to look up, "printing postscript documents with Windows NT" by using the Help program and could find no help. I checked the printed user's guide but got not help. So I called a few friends, but they didn't really have any answers. Next, I resorted to Microsoft's Support Online — and saw references to really esoteric problems related to printing postscript documents with Windows NT — but still didn't find an article that said, "Okay to get started, here's what you need to do." As this point, feeling totally frustrated, I called Microsoft (which got me no answer) and then called the company that made the desktop publishing software program (which also got me no answer).

In a fit of desperation, I ultimately just said to myself, "Heck, I'll try doing this and see how far I get . . ." At this point, I figured that I didn't really have anything to lose. I mean, whatever damage I did would be minimal. You can probably guess what happened. I didn't have a problem. In other words, printing postscript files with Windows NT works exactly like printing anything with Windows. And so all the time I thought I had this big technical problem, I really didn't. My problem was that I thought I had a problem.

Now I'm not telling you all this to embarrass myself. But I think my little problem, in a general way, is more common that you think. You think you have some big problem with the "electrofuzzer doohickey" because it won't "combobulate." So you're out trying to look for Help topics that relate to "electrofuzzer doohickeys" and "combobulation," but you can't find anything. And the reason that you can't solve your problem is because "electrofuzzer doohickeys" don't "combobulate" at all. Maybe that's the job of the "gizmolator," for example. Or maybe the "electrofuzzer doohickey" always "combobulates" — there's no way it can't. So the real problem is that something else isn't working right. (Maybe you forgot to plug the machine in or maybe you just need to assume that the thing is already working correctly.)

Do you see what I mean? If you can't get an answer to a problem by using the Help program or the product support Web site or telephone product support, it may be that either you don't have a problem or you don't have the problem you think you do.

Chapter 4

Printing

· ·

· ·

*U*ndoubtedly, one of the principal tasks you have for your small business's computers is printing. You may have originally purchased a computer in order to produce attractive customer proposals or sales letters; to save time printing customer invoices or checks; or even to produce some portion of your firm's product — instructions to customers or a product booklet. For these reasons, after you master the stuff covered in Chapters 1, 2, and 3, the next thing you want to figure out is how to print in Windows. Fortunately, printing is really easy.

How to Print a Business Document

You may have already guessed this, but you print documents by using Windows. In order words, a program, like your word processor, doesn't actually do the printing. It's Windows.

Printing from within a program

To print within a program — such as your word processor — you first start the program and open the document you want to print. After you get to this point, you choose between the easy way and the "you're the man" or "you're the woman" way.

To print a document in the easy way, you click the Print toolbar button, which typically appears near the top of the Window. Figure 4-1, for example, shows the Word program window, which includes a Print toolbar button. (Note that other program's Print toolbar buttons look very similar.) When you click the Print button, the program prints the document in the usual way with all the usual settings. The benefit of this technique is that you don't *have* to make decisions about how the document should print. However, this approach also suffers from a disadvantage: You also don't *get* to make decisions about how the document should print.

If you want to use the "you're the man" or "you're the woman" way, you also need to start the program and open the document. Then, at this point, you choose File⇨Print. The program (with Windows' help) displays a dialog box that looks something like the one shown in Figure 4-2.

The Print toolbar button

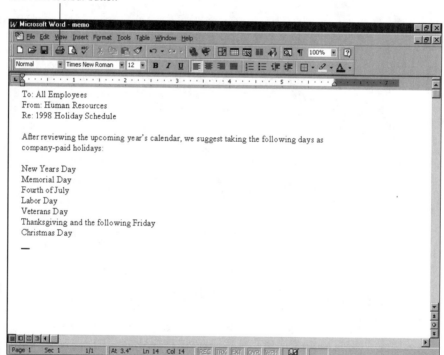

Figure 4-1:
A Word
document.

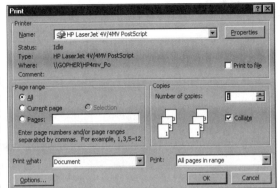

Figure 4-2:
Most Print
dialog
boxes look
very similar
to this one.

To use this Print dialog box, take the following steps:

1. **Use the Printer Name box to select a printer if you or your office mates have installed multiple printers.**

   If you don't change the printer shown in the Printer Name box, you'll print the document using the default Windows printer.

2. **Specify which pages you want to print.**

   If you're printing a multiple-page document, you typically have the option of specifying which pages to print by using buttons and boxes like those shown in the Print Range box. For example, you can specify that all the pages of a document should print, or you can specify that only some range of pages should print.

3. **Specify how many copies you want.**

   If you want to print more than one copy of a document, you typically have the option of making this specification by using a Copies box.

4. **Specify how the program should print a document and click OK.**

   The program sends a printable copy of the document to Windows and then Windows carefully passes the pages of this printable copy to the printer you choose.

Different programs display different Print dialog boxes, but most of them closely resemble the dialog box shown in Figure 4-2. If you see buttons or boxes that you don't understand, click the question button (in the upper right corner of the dialog box) and then the button or box.

Printing outside a program

You don't have to start a program in order to print a document. At least you don't have to do so directly. If you're working with Windows Explorer and you see a document that you want to print, you can right-click the document (to display a shortcuts menu) and then choose the Print command. When you do, Windows opens the document for you (by starting the appropriate program and by telling it to open the document). Then Windows instructs the program to print the document in the usual way with the usual, or default, settings. And then Windows closes the document and stops the program.

I should tell you, by the way, that not all documents can be printed in this manner. Windows needs to know which program it should use for printing a document. (Windows looks at a document file's extension to determine what type of document file it is and whether Windows can automatically print the document.) If Windows doesn't know, the shortcut menu doesn't include a Print command.

How to Add and Configure Printers

Before Windows can print with a specific printer — say a new printer that you just brought — you need to tell Windows about the printer. This process of telling Windows about the printer is called *adding a printer*. I don't know why — I suppose that term is supposed to make the whole process sound more friendly or less complicated.

Adding a local printer

A *local printer* is a printer you've connected to your computer. In other words, you used the printer cable (which should have come in the printer box) to connect your computer to the printer. (You usually have to purchase the printer cable separately. If you haven't already bought or connected the printer, ask your salesperson which cable you need.) To add a local printer, you follow these steps:

1. **Click Start⇨Settings⇨Printers to display the Printers folder (see Figure 4-3).**

Double-click the Add Printer icon to add a new printer

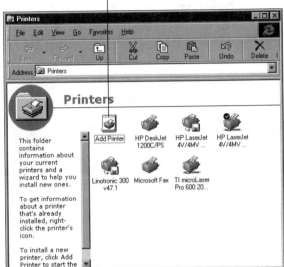

Figure 4-3:
The Printers
folder lists
the printers
you have
installed.

2. **Double-click the Add Printer icon.**

   Doing so tells Windows to start the Add Printer wizard.

3. **When the Add Printer wizard displays its first dialog box (the one that says, basically, "Hey, you use this wizard to install a printer") click Next.**

4. **When the second Add Printer Wizard dialog box asks whether you want to install a local printer or a network printer, click the local printer button and then click Next.**

   The Add Printer wizard displays the third Add Printer Wizard dialog box (see Figure 4-4).

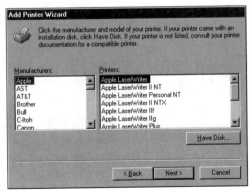

Figure 4-4:
You use the
third Add
Printer
Wizard
dialog box
to identify
the printer
manufacturer
and model.

5. **Using the Manufacturer list box, select the printer's manufacturer.**

6. **Using the Printer list box, select the model of printer, and then click Next.**

If you have questions about how you complete either Step 5 or 6, look at the front of your printer. It should name both the printer manufacturer and model. If you've done this and you're sure that your printer isn't listed, find your printer user manual, use it to determine what other popular printer your printer will emulate (pretend to be), do whatever the user manual says in order to have your printer emulate this other printer, and then select the appropriate manufacturer and printer you want to emulate (as described in Steps 5 and 6).

7. **When the Add Printer wizard displays the fourth dialog box (see Figure 4-5), use it to identify the printer port, or socket, into which you plugged the printer cable and click Next.**

If you don't know which port you used, take a look at the back of your printer and see if the socket is labeled. (It may be.) If this doesn't work, accept whatever port Windows suggests — and then don't be bummed out if you need to come back later and change this specification. (I'll describe how you do this later, so don't worry.)

Figure 4-5:
The Add Printer Wizard dialog box that you use to specify which port, or socket, you plugged the printer cable into.

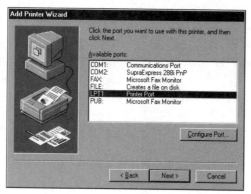

8. **When the Add Printer wizard displays the fifth dialog box, look at the name it suggests using for the printer.**

If this name isn't okay, change it by following these steps:

1. Replace the contents of the Name box.

2. Use the Yes and No buttons to answer the question of whether this printer should be the default printer that Windows uses. (The default printer is just the one that Windows uses unless you tell it otherwise.)

3. When you finish making these specifications, click Next.

9. **When the Add Printer wizard displays the sixth and final dialog box, click the Yes button to indicate that you want to print a test page, and then click the Finish button.**

   Windows adds the printer and then attempts to print a test page.

10. **When Windows asks whether the test page printed correctly, answer the question by clicking the appropriate button.**

    If the test page does print correctly, you're all set. If the test page doesn't print correctly, the Windows Help program starts and displays a window with diagnostic information about your printing problems. You can use the Help program to solve almost every printing problem. (For help with Help, refer to Chapter 3.)

After you successfully add a printer, you can use it with Windows for printing from within Windows programs (as described earlier in the chapter) and for printing from outside of programs. If you open the Printers folder (by clicking Start⇨Settings⇨Printers), you'll also see an icon for the printer. (In the later chapter section, "Working with your printers," I talk more about the Printers folder and about how you can use it to control the way a printer works.)

Adding a network printer

If your computer connects to a network, you can use other people's printers to print your documents. In other words, you can use a printer that's connected to someone else's computer by having Windows use the network to send a printable copy of your document to this other printer. When you use someone else's local printer, you and the copy of Windows running on your computer calls the other printer a *network printer.* Therefore, the process of telling Windows about a network printer that you want to use is called *adding a network printer.*

To add a network printer, you need to have the Windows networking feature installed and working and someone needs to have told this other person's computer that sharing its local printer is okay. Chapter 10 describes how you do this stuff, so if you can't add a network printer by following the instructions provided here, read through Chapter 10. It may just be that the first step you need to take involves setting up your network.

To add a network printer, follow these steps:

1. **Click Start⇨Settings⇨Printers to display the Printers folder.**

2. **Double-click the Add a printer icon.**

   Doing so tells Windows to start the Add Printer wizard.

3. **When the Add Printer wizard displays its first dialog box (the one that says, basically, "Hey, you use this wizard to install a printer") click Next.**

4. **When the second Add Printer Wizard dialog box asks whether you want to install a local printer or a network printer, click the network printer button and then click Next.**

   The Add Printer wizard displays the third Add Printer Wizard dialog box (see Figure 4-6).

Figure 4-6:
You use the
third Add
Printer
Wizard
dialog box
to identify
the printer
as one that
you'll use
over the
network.

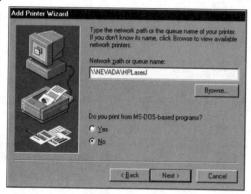

5. **Indicate the path of the printer you want to add.**

   If you know the path of the network printer — and you may if one of your coworkers told you or if you're the person who set up the network — enter it into the Network Path or Queue Name box.

   Otherwise, click the Browse button and then, when Windows displays the Browse dialog box, select the network printer that you want to install. (To see the local printers connected to a specific computer, you may need to click the plus symbol that appears in front of the computer icon.)

6. **Use the Yes and No buttons to indicate whether you want to use this printer to print from MS-DOS programs and then click Next.**

7. **When the Add Printer wizard displays the fourth dialog box, select the printer's manufacturer by using the Manufacturer list box.**

8. **Using the Printer list box, select the model of printer and then click Next.**

If you have questions about how you complete either Step 6 or 7, look at the front of your printer. As noted earlier, it should name both the printer manufacturer and model. If you've done this and you're sure that your printer isn't listed, find your printer user manual, use it to learn what other popular printer your printer will emulate (pretend to be), do whatever the user manual says in order to have your printer emulate this other printer, and then select the appropriate manufacturer and printer.

9. **When the Add Printer wizard displays the fifth dialog box, look at the name it suggests using for the printer.**

   If this name isn't okay, change the name by following these steps:

   1. Replace the contents of the Name box.

   2. Use the Yes and No buttons to answer the question of whether this printer should be the default printer that Windows uses. (The *default printer* is just the one that Windows uses unless you tell it otherwise.)

   3. When you finish making these specifications, click Next.

10. **When the Add Printer wizard displays the sixth and final dialog box, click the Yes button to indicate that you want to print a test page, and then click the Finish button.**

    Windows adds the printer and then attempts to print a test page.

11. **When Windows asks whether the test page printed correctly, answer the question by clicking the appropriate button.**

    The Windows Help program starts and displays a window with diagnostic information about your printing problems if the test page doesn't print correctly. You can use the Help program to solve almost every printing problem. (For help with Help, refer to Chapter 3.)

After you successfully add a network printer, you can use it with Windows for printing from within Windows programs (as described earlier in the chapter) and for printing from outside of programs — as long as the computer to which the printer is connected and the network itself are both working.

Working with your printers

Windows lets you exercise a certain amount of control over the printers you add. You can, for example, start and stop a printer's printing. You can tell the printer not to print some document you've sent it. And you can also tweak some of the technical details about how a printer works.

Getting to first base

To do this sort of stuff with either a local printer or a network printer, click Start⇨Settings⇨Printers. Windows displays the Printers folder. You may remember this folder if you've been reading this chapter from its very start (see Figure 4-7). The Printers folder also provides the Add Printer icon, which you click to describe the local printers and network printers that you want to use.

Figure 4-7:
The Printers folder window.

If you double-click any of the icons in the Printers folder window that represents a printer, Windows opens another window like the one shown in Figure 4-8. This window, which gets labeled with the printer's description that you provide when you add the printer, lists the documents that the printer is supposed to be printing but hasn't yet printed. And that's often kind of handy (especially when you share a printer with a bunch of other people and you wonder where your document is in the queue). But a printer window is also useful for fiddling with a printer.

You can click the column headings shown in a printer window to sort the documents in various ways. For example, if you click the Document name column heading, Windows sorts the documents alphabetically by document name.

Figure 4-8:
This printer
window
shows the
documents
waiting to
be printed
on the TI
microLaser
Pro 600
printer.

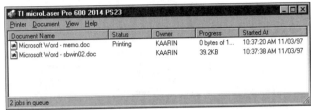

Fiddling with a local printer

You have the most control over a local printer. (Remember that a local printer is a printer that's physically cabled to your computer.) Let me just quickly — in laundry list fashion — tell you about the half dozen or so handiest things you can do:

- ✔ **Pause the printer:** You can tell Windows to stop sending stuff to the printer by choosing Printer⇨Pause Printing. When you do, Windows places a check mark next to the Pause Printing command.

- ✔ **Restart a paused printer:** If you've already paused a printer, you can tell Windows to restart the printer by choosing Printer⇨Pause Printing again. Windows removes the little check mark that appears in front of the command name and then fires up the printer again.

- ✔ **Make a printer the default printer:** You can tell Windows that you want the printer described in the printer window to be the default printer. To do so, choose Printer⇨Set As Default. This setting just means that whenever you tell Windows to print some document, Windows should use this default printer unless you specify otherwise.

- ✔ **Delete everything in the printer queue:** If you have a bunch of documents stacked up in the printer queue waiting to print, you can in one, fell swoop remove all of them by choosing Printer⇨Purge Print Jobs.

- ✔ **Delete a single document:** If you tell Windows that you want to print some document but then later change your mind, click the document name and press the Delete key. (You can also choose Document⇨ Cancel Printing in place of pressing Delete.)

- ✔ **Pause a document:** You can tell Windows that it should wait to print a selected document, too. (Perhaps you have a big document that you want to print at the end of the day, for example.) To do so, click the document name to select it and then choose Document⇨Pause Printing.

> ✔ **Close the printer window:** You probably don't need me to tell you this, but if you choose Printer➪Close, Windows closes the printer window. This command, then, is equivalent to clicking the close box. By the way, closing a printer window doesn't affect the printer. It'll keep on printing. Closing a window just closes the window.

About the other printer commands

Ah, well, yeah, some other commands are available on the printer window's menus. Most people won't need to use these other commands except maybe the Help menu's commands, which work in the usual way (and as described in Chapter 3). You, however? You're interested in a little more detail, which is why you're reading this technical stuff sidebar. So let me quickly give you the birds-eye view by talking about the other two, special commands provided on a printer window's Printer: Work Offline and Properties.

Windows lets you do something called *offline printing,* which is kind of neat. For example, say that you have a little laptop that you take home most nights to do the work you can never get done during the day because of interruptions from well-meaning customers, employees, and vendors. In this situation, you can tell Windows or some Windows program to print a document even though you're at home sitting at the kitchen table, sans printer, wishing you were watching television rather than working.

What happens in this situation is that Windows sends a printable copy of the document to a printer's queue of documents to print, but it doesn't try to print the document. It then places a check mark in front of the Printer menu's Work Offline command to show you that offline printing is turned on. When you later want to print one of the documents, you connect the computer to the printer (if it's a local printer) or to the network (if it's a network printer) and then you choose Printer➪Work Offline again (which turns off the offline printing feature). Let me tell you one other quick thing. You don't have to actually disconnect your computer from its printer or from the network to work offline. You can work offline — say as a way to delay printing some large document — simply by choosing Printer➪Work Offline.

The Printer menu also provides a Properties command. If you choose this command, Windows displays a multi-tabbed dialog box that lets you make all sorts of weird, esoteric changes to the way Windows and your printer work together. I could spend an entire chapter talking about this command, but your best bet is just *not* to use this command unless somebody (like a technical support specialist) or some reference book (like the manual that comes with your new desktop publishing program) tells you to use it. And in these special cases, all you need to do is follow the instructions provided by the special somebody or the special reference.

Fiddling with a network printer

You control a network printer in the same way that you control a local printer. Since I describe how all the local printer control stuff works in the preceding section, I'm not about to bore you to tears by repeating that discussion. However, I should tell you that sometimes — and it depends on how your network is set up — you can't do everything on a network printer that you can do on a local printer. For example, you may be able to delete your printing documents — what Windows calls *print jobs* — but not those of your coworkers: Malcolm, Helmut, or Biff. Similarly, you may be able to pause the printing of your documents, but not the printing of your coworkers' documents.

How much control you have over a network printer and the printing documents in a printer queue depends on the way your network is set up. If you have a great deal of network authority — you're the big kahuna at least in the eyes of the network — you can do pretty much anything you want, and Malcolm, Helmut, and Biff won't be able to stop you. If you don't have much network authority, you may not be able to do squat. I talk more about network security stuff in Chapters 9 and 10. So tune in there if you're interested and you work on a network.

Your Business Image Is Important (About Fonts)

I've told you everything you need to know to print documents. But just very quickly, before I wrap up this discussion of printing, I want to spend a few minutes talking about fonts, including what they are, how they work, and about the ways you can fiddle with them.

What are fonts?

Typographers and designers use the term font in very precise ways. But I'm not going to do that here. I'm going to say that a font is just a character set that looks a certain way:

This font is named Times New Roman.

`This font is named Courier.`

This font is named Berkeley.

Okay, do you see how these characters look different? That's because they're different fonts. Does this make sense? A font is really just a design for characters so they look a certain way: formal, fun, or funky.

Now that you understand what fonts are, you should know three additional things about them. To use a font in a document, Windows needs to have the design information. (This information actually comes in couple of program-like files stored on your hard disk someplace.) In other words, if you want to use the Times New Roman font in a document, Windows needs to have the Times New Roman font design file or files. And if you want to use the Comic font in a document, you need to have the Comic font design file or files.

Windows, I should tell you, comes with a bunch of different fonts that you can use in your documents. And many Windows programs also come with additional fonts. So even though you can't recall ever buying a font, you probably have a bunch of standard fonts already. You can also purchase additional fonts, however, and I'm going to talk about that in a minute.

How fonts affect printing

When you specify that some chunk of document text should use a font, Windows attempts to print the document by using the font, too. This doesn't always work, by the way. While TrueType fonts (one font flavor) and Adobe Postscript fonts (another flavor) print beautifully, not all fonts do. Some fonts are just for display on your screen. (Microsoft actually supplies a handful of display fonts for use in Windows' windows, dialog boxes, and message boxes.)

When you use a font in a document but the font can't be printed, Windows attempts to substitute some font that's close. Usually, this is okay, but you can guess that not all substitutions work well. If you're working with a document and specify that you want to use a font that's only available for display, Windows may freak out when it tries to print the document. In this case, what will probably happen is that Windows will use a default font like Courier.

How to specify a font in a document

You specify which font a document should use with the program you're using to create the document. In Microsoft applications like Word and Excel, the toolbar provides a font drop-down list box (see Figure 4-9). If you activate this list box, you see all the fonts you can use. To specify that you want Windows or the Windows program to use a font, you first select the text (such as by clicking or dragging) and then you choose a font from the font drop-down list box.

Figure 4-9:
The
Microsoft
Word
program
window
provides a
font drop-
down list
box on its
toolbar.

If you look closely at Figure 4-9, you notice that Windows places tiny pictures, or icons, in front of the font names shown in the font list boxes. A little "TT" icon identifies the font as a TrueType font and the printer icon typically identifies the font as an Adobe Postscript font. Both TrueType and Postscript fonts are great because they print the same way they appear on-screen.

Programs that do let you specify a font but that don't provide a toolbar usually provide a Font command (which often appears on the Format menu). When you choose the Font command, the Windows program displays a dialog box that you can use to choose the font as well as to select a font size and any special effects. Figure 4-10, for example, shows the dialog box that Word provides to let you change the font used in a business document.

Figure 4-10:
Many
programs
provide a
Font
command,
which
displays a
dialog box
you can use
to change
a font.

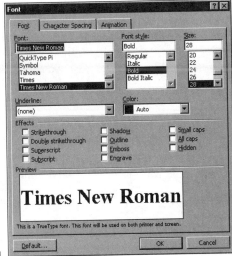

How to use the Fonts Control Panel tool

You can see which fonts you have to work with by using the Fonts tool, which is part of the Windows Control Panel. (The Control Panel is basically just a grab bag of little programs you use to change the way that Windows works.)

To start the Fonts tool, click Start⇨Settings⇨Control Panel. When Windows opens the Control Panel window, look for the icon that's labeled Fonts, and then double-click it. When you do, Windows opens the Fonts folder, which lists the fonts you have available, as shown in Figure 4-11.

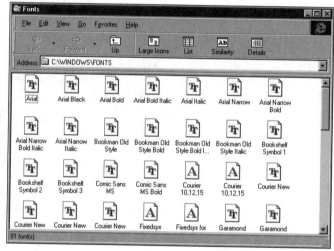

Figure 4-11: The Fonts folder lists the fonts you can use in Windows documents.

After you work with several fonts, you'll become familiar with how the different fonts look. Until that time, what you can do is double-click any font you see listed in the Fonts folder window. When you do, Windows opens a window that shows how text looks when it's formatted by using the font (see Figure 4-12).

Design crimes

The first time you stumble onto this whole font thing, it's easy to go crazy. You suddenly find yourself with dozens and perhaps even hundreds of great fonts. Before you know it, you're using them — all of them — in your documents and creating things that look more like ransom notes than professional, business documents (see Figure 4-13).

Click to print an example document that uses the font

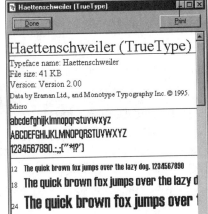

Figure 4-12:
This window describes the Haettenschweiler font.

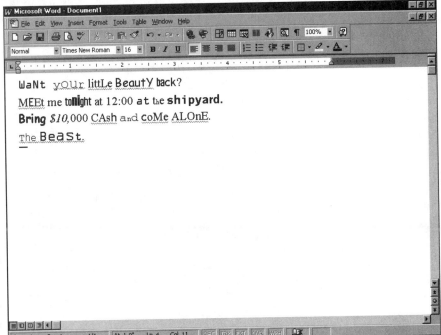

Figure 4-13:
A ransom note for my dog.

Because you're most likely not going to want your documents to look like the one shown in Figure 4-13, you'll want to apply a few basic design rules:

- **Minimize the number of fonts you use in document.** You won't have to worry about the ransom note. And, you'll save printing time. (Documents with lots of fonts take more time to print.)

- **Don't underline text.** <u>Underlining undermines readability. It's really irritating to your readers. Especially if it just goes on and on and on and on, seemingly for no purpose. I mean, you've seen people do this before, right? And it's just as irritating as all get out.</u>

- **Use sans serif fonts for heading text.** They're prettier fonts, and they look much cleaner. (Serifs are those little cross-strokes that get used as pieces of characters.) Take a look at the following to see the difference:

A heading with serifs
A heading without serifs

- **Use serif fonts for body text.** You want to use a serif font for the main body of a document — the stuff people will actually have to take time to read. The reason for this rule is that while serif fonts aren't as pretty, they do enhance the readability of a font.

Part II
Profiting from the
Internet

The 5th Wave   By Rich Tennant

DOYNK SOFTWARE

"It's been reported that we went a little crazy trying to bring this product to market on time..."

In this part . . .

Ah, yes . . . The Internet and the Web. Why write about them in a book on Windows 95? Two reasons. First, as this may be your first computer book, I would be remiss if I didn't get you up to speed on this craze and what it means to your business. Second, and more importantly, Windows 95 works beautifully with a number of programs that make doing business over the Web easy. Some of those programs even come with Windows 95 — and I've included some others with this book's CD. But you have to understand a few basics about the Internet before you can put them to good use with Windows 95. So peruse this part and discover what the Internet and Windows 95 can mean to your business.

Chapter 5

Business on the World Wide Web

· ·

In This Chapter

▶ Getting connected to the Internet

▶ Touring the Web

▶ Finding the information you need

▶ Using Internet Explorer's new Web browsing tools

· ·

*T*his chapter amounts to a crash course on the World Wide Web, the often-talked about and most-hyped piece of the Internet. For the purposes of this chapter, I'm going to assume that you're not some sort of Internet expert — and that you don't want to become one. I am going to assume that you do want to understand the Internet's potential as a business resource.

Let me say one other quick thing. If you're already an experienced Internet user, you can skip much of what this chapter talks about because you already know the stuff. Do, however, take the time to skim the sidebar, "Picking an Internet service provider." (It talks about a handful of issues related to Web publishing.) Make sure that you skim the part, "Using Search Services," if you're not already nice and comfortable with how directory-style search services (such as Yahoo!) and index-style services (such as AltaVista) work. And then read the last section in the chapter, "Channels and Subscriptions," because it describes two nifty new Web-browsing tools that Internet Explorer 4.0 provides. (Netscape Navigator, the other popular Web browsing tool, doesn't work with channels or subscriptions.)

 By the way, I really should mention one other thing here, since I'm just starting out. While I used Internet Explorer for the figures this chapter includes—and, in fact, the companion CD contains Internet Explorer—don't let that throw you if you use Netscape Navigator instead. Although Internet Explorer is so nicely and tightly integrated with the Microsoft Windows operating system, you can use Netscape Navigator or some other Web browser to do business on the Web. For this reason, almost everything this chapter says applies with equal force to any Web browser. The only exception is the part — near the end of the chapter — that talks about channels and subscriptions.

And now it's time to get started.

Making an Internet Connection

You probably know this already, but because the Internet is this big, loosely connected network of networks, you can't actually begin doing Internet stuff until you connect your computer to some other computer that's already connected. (A network, by the way, is just a set of computers somebody has cabled together so the computers that make up the network can share information and resources.) To make this connection, you need to do three things:

1. **Add a modem.**

2. **Pick an Internet service provider (ISP).**

3. **Tell Windows to make what's called a Dial-Up Networking connection.**

Not all that long ago, each one of these three prerequisites was challenging enough to defeat even smart, tenacious geeks. But not now. These days, you do all of this stuff simply by clicking a mouse.

Installing and adding a modem

The first thing you need to do, as just mentioned, is install or add a modem. To do so, purchase the modem (say from the local computer store or through the mail) and then install it according to the manufacturer's directions. The only bit of advice I'll offer you is that you want to get the fastest modem available — probably a 56.6 Kbps modem. (The 56.6 Kbps business just indicates how fast the modem can spew or swallow a stream of 1s and 0s — the raw form that computer data takes. A 56.6 Kbps modem can handle a stream that moves 56,600 of these 1s and 0s every second.)

"Gee, Steve," you may be saying to yourself, "according to the manufacturer's directions? That's a little vague . . . I'd like you to be a bit more specific."

Well, I guess I can try, but really, the procedure is pretty easy. The modem you buy is just a chunk of circuitry, a little circuit board. To install an internal modem (the kind that fits inside your computer), unplug your computer's power, remove the cover, and then plug the little circuit board into a socket on the big circuit board that's inside your computer (and that actually is your computer). If this process — one that involves a screw driver, a little circuit board, and a big circuit board — scares you half to death, don't do it. Just buy your modem at a local computer store and ask them to install it. To install an external modem (the kind that sits outside of your computer), all you have to do is unplug your computer and then plug the modem in to the back of your computer.

If you're about to buy a new modem, let me suggest you also figure out whether you need to purchase a Web browser. If you're going to use a computer that you've very recently purchased, you may already have a Web browser. (If you have Internet Explorer, you'll see an icon for it on your desktop.) If you don't have it, buy your Web browser from the same place you get your modem. (You may even be able to purchase both the browser and a modem together in a starter kit.)

After you or somebody else installs the modem, you need to "add" the modem. *Adding a modem* means that you tell Windows about the modem so it knows it's been plugged into the big circuit board inside your computer. You can add a modem in two ways: the super-easy way and the easy way.

To add a modem the super-easy way, restart your computer. (You can do so by clicking Start⇨Shut Down, and then marking the Restart the computer button when Windows displays the Shut Down Windows dialog box.) When Windows starts up again, watch for a message that says something like, "Hey, hmmm, I see you've installed some new hardware in your computer . . . I'm just trying to figure out what it is . . . okay, cool, it's a modem and you're ready to use it." Okay, Windows won't use these exact words. But it does run a diagnostic test on your computer as it starts and if your modem is plug-and-play (and it is if you purchase the fastest modem available), Windows will see that you've installed a new modem. (*Plug and play* just means that all you need to do is plug some new gadget into your computer in order to play it.)

To add a modem the easy way — and you only do this when the super-easy way doesn't work, you use the Modems tool, which is part of the Windows Control Panel. To do so, take the following steps:

1. **Click Start⇨Settings⇨Control Panel to display the Control Panel window.**

   The Control Panel window displays a bunch of clickable icons you use to start programs that you then use to change the way that Windows works.

2. **Double-click the Modems icon.**

   Windows starts the Install New Modem wizard.

3. **Click Next to have Windows look for the new modem.**

   Windows displays the Verify Modem dialog box as shown in Figure 5-1.

4. **Click Next if Windows detected the correct modem.**

   If Windows did not detect the modem correctly, click Change and specify the correct modem.

5. **Click Finish.**

   Your modem is set up and ready to go.

Figure 5-1:
The Verify
Modem
dialog box.

If Windows can't figure out what it's supposed to do with the modem — this shouldn't happen but it is possible — your best bet is to try the super-easy way again (turn off your computer completely this time) and then, if that doesn't work, try the easy way again. If that doesn't work either, bring the modem back to the store you purchased it at and tell the salesperson that you want your modem money back. Or you can pay the store to install the modem correctly. Or you can read the next section.

When bad things happen to good modems

If you can't get Windows to add a modem automatically or almost automatically, your problem in my painful experience is probably one of two things: Windows either already added the modem or it thinks it's added the modem when it hasn't (or hasn't done so correctly). To deal with this problem, display the Control Panel window (by clicking Start⇨Settings⇨Control Panel) and double-click the Modems tool. If Windows has installed a modem (at least in its mind), it lists the modem in the Modems Properties dialog box. You can check if Windows correctly set up your modem according to the manufacturer's specifications by getting out your modem user manual and clicking the Properties button. Use the tabs, buttons, and boxes in the dialog box Windows displays to make sure that the settings Windows chose for your modem match the settings in your user manual.

If you're fairly sure that the settings are okay, but your modem still doesn't work, try removing the modem and then adding it back again. You can do so by selecting the modem from the list and clicking the Remove button (see Figure 5-2). After you remove the modem, click Add to start the Install New Modem wizard and add the modem back again.

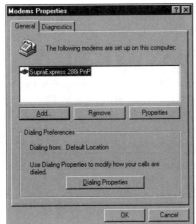

Figure 5-2:
The
Modems
Properties
dialog box.

If you try using your modem and the modem makes noises or its lights blink, but it doesn't dial, your modem is probably correctly connected to your computer. Your problem most likely lies with your modem's dialing properties. Click the Dialing Properties button and make sure that the dialing settings are correct. Also make sure that your modem is firmly connected to your phone line, and the phone line is firmly connected to the wall jack.

Let me tell you one other thing. If you've tried everything I've said so far and still, darn it, nothing has worked, your problem is probably what's called an *interrupt conflict*. Interrupts are basically channels that hardware devices use to communicate with your computer's brain, or CPU. One thing that pretty commonly happens — especially when you have a bunch of gear packed into a computer — is that two hardware devices end up trying to use the same interrupt. Unfortunately, resolving interrupt conflicts isn't something you can do without help from a technical support specialist or the local computer repair shop.

Using the Connection wizard

After you have your modem working — most people don't have any trouble — you need to set up an account with an Internet service provider, or ISP. An ISP lets you connect your computer to their computer for a fee. You happily pay the fee because once you make this connection, you can use the Internet's resources such as the World Wide Web (discussed in this chapter and the next) and e-mail (discussed in Chapter 7).

You set up your ISP account by using something called the Connection wizard. The Connection wizard is part of Internet Explorer 4.0. So, if you don't have Internet Explorer 4.0 and you want to use it, first install Internet Explorer using the companion CD. Then run the Connection wizard by following these steps:

1. Click Start➪Programs➪Internet Explorer➪Connection Wizard.

When you do, the Connection wizard starts and displays its first dialog box, which simply tells you that you've started the Connection wizard.

Even if you're using another Web browser program, you can still use the Connection wizard to describe how your computer and your Web browser should connect to an ISP's network. If you don't want to use the Connection wizard, follow whatever step-by-step instructions your ISP provides.

2. Click Next.

The Connection wizard displays a dialog box that asks what you want to do: set up a new ISP account, modify an existing ISP account, or do nothing. Click the button that indicates that you want to set up a new ISP account.

3. Click Next twice.

The Connection wizard asks you a few questions about your telephone number (so it can suggest local ISP providers), and then it connects to a special computer that supplies updated lists of ISP providers available in your area. When it finishes, it displays the list (see Figure 5-3).

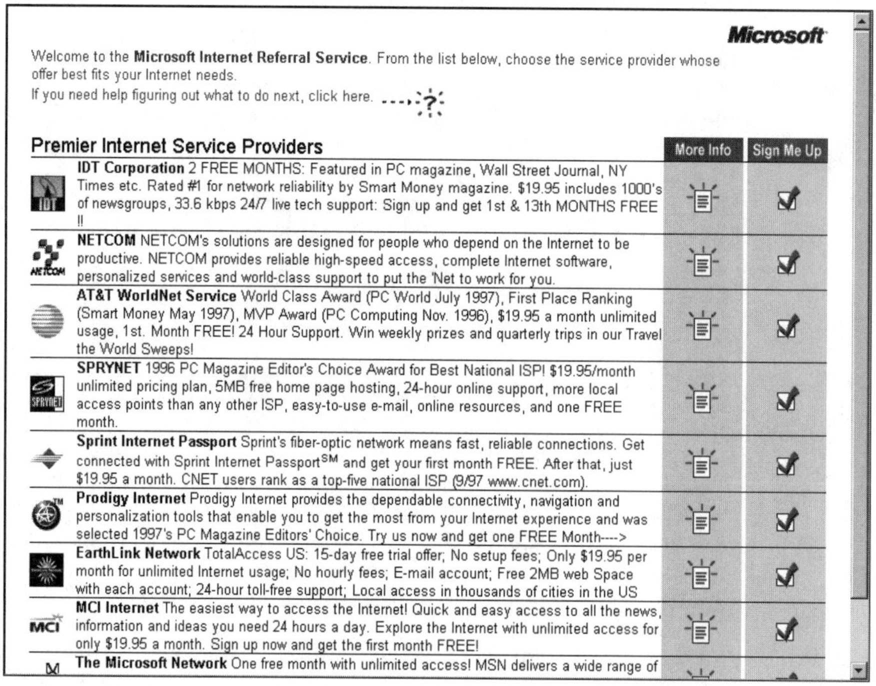

Figure 5-3:
The
Connection
wizard
provides a
list of ISPs
serving
your area.

Microsoft

Welcome to the **Microsoft Internet Referral Service**. From the list below, choose the service provider whose offer best fits your Internet needs.
If you need help figuring out what to do next, click here. ⋯ ⋮?⋮

Premier Internet Service Providers		More Info	Sign Me Up
IDT Corporation 2 FREE MONTHS: Featured in PC magazine, Wall Street Journal, NY Times etc. Rated #1 for network reliability by Smart Money magazine. $19.95 includes 1000's of newsgroups, 33.6 kbps 24/7 live tech support: Sign up and get 1st & 13th MONTHS FREE !!		☑	☑
NETCOM NETCOM's solutions are designed for people who depend on the Internet to be productive. NETCOM provides reliable high-speed access, complete Internet software, personalized services and world-class support to put the 'Net to work for you.		☑	☑
AT&T WorldNet Service World Class Award (PC World July 1997), First Place Ranking (Smart Money May 1997), MVP Award (PC Computing Nov. 1996), $19.95 a month unlimited usage, 1st. Month FREE! 24 Hour Support. Win weekly prizes and quarterly trips in our Travel the World Sweeps!		☑	☑
SPRYNET 1996 PC Magazine Editor's Choice Award for Best National ISP! $19.95/month unlimited pricing plan, 5MB free home page hosting, 24-hour online support, more local access points than any other ISP, easy-to-use e-mail, online resources, and one FREE month.		☑	☑
Sprint Internet Passport Sprint's fiber-optic network means fast, reliable connections. Get connected with Sprint Internet Passport℠ and get your first month FREE. After that, just $19.95 a month. CNET users rank as a top-five national ISP (9/97 www.cnet.com).		☑	☑
Prodigy Internet Prodigy Internet provides the dependable connectivity, navigation and personalization tools that enable you to get the most from your Internet experience and was selected 1997's PC Magazine Editors' Choice. Try us now and get one FREE Month---->		☑	☑
EarthLink Network TotalAccess US: 15-day free trial offer; No setup fees; Only $19.95 per month for unlimited Internet usage; No hourly fees; E-mail account; Free 2MB web Space with each account; 24-hour toll-free support; Local access in thousands of cities in the US		☑	☑
MCI Internet The easiest way to access the Internet! Quick and easy access to all the news, information and ideas you need 24 hours a day. Explore the Internet with unlimited access for only $19.95 a month. Sign up now and get the first month FREE!		☑	☑
The Microsoft Network One free month with unlimited access! MSN delivers a wide range of		

4. Read through the list of local ISP providers.

If you see one that's interesting, click its More Info button it to get another screenful of information about the ISP.

5. When you find the one you want, click its Sign Up button and then follow the on-screen instructions.

You'll be asked to provide personal information, including a credit card number for billing. You'll also be provided with connection information that you want to write down someplace safe, including your username and password. (You may be provided one username and password for connecting to the ISP's network and another username and password for sending and receiving e-mail through the ISP's network.) When you finish with the Connection wizard, you're all set up.

Picking an Internet service provider

Picking the right ISP isn't difficult. In general, you make this business decision the same way you do any other. You look at the costs and benefits of each alternative. You consider the credibility and reputability of your various ISP choices. And, if possible, you validate the data you get from sources like the Connection wizard and double-check your conclusions by talking with other small business users. So I'm not going to talk about this stuff. You already know how to do it.

I do want to mention one wrinkle that you may not be aware of. If you plan to become a Web publisher, you probably want an ISP that lets you use their network to publish your Web pages. I talk more about Web publishing in Chapter 6 and in Chapter 17.

For now, let me say that if you think you do want to become a Web publisher, you want an ISP who lets you store at least a few megabytes of stuff on their computers. (I'm just going to throw out 2 to 5 megabytes here as a suggestion.) If you want to get into Web publishing in a big way, because you want to share information that takes a great deal of space (such as graphic images, program files, or voluminous quantities of text), you want an ISP who provides much more disk space — maybe 20 or even 50 megabytes. If you want to get fancy in your Web publishing — say you want to take orders over the Web, for example, or let people run cool, wizard-like programs on your Web site — you need to make sure that the ISP you choose can do the stuff you need or want to do. (If you're in this situation, you also probably want to learn more about Web publishing.)

Making a Dial-Up Networking connection

Once you install and add your modem and you run the Connection wizard, the hard part is done. To connect your computer to the Internet, you start the Internet Explorer (which is the program you use for working with the World Wide Web). When you do, Windows figures that you want to make a Dial-Up Networking connection and so displays a dialog box like the one shown in Figure 5-4. You supply your username and password.

Figure 5-4:
The Dial-up
Connection
dialog box.

As you can guess, if you check the Save Password box, Windows saves your password information — which means that you don't have to enter it each and every time you log on. Unfortunately, if you choose this option, it also means that anyone with access to your computer can connect to your ISP account and pretend to be you. I wouldn't check this box unless your computer and office are pretty secure.

If you do choose to check the Save Password box, you can also check the Connect Automatically box. If you do, Windows won't prompt you for the username and password when you do something like start the Internet Explorer. It will just make the connection automatically.

How your connection differs from a big business's

Let me mention to you here that the way you connect to the Internet with a regular old modem, the Connection wizard, and Windows Dial-Up Networking isn't the only way to fly. This method is great for small businesses because it's easy (you only have to run a simple wizard). And the ISPs you get when you go this route aren't expensive, relatively speaking. (You're going to pay a few dollars a month in some cases and not much more than about $20 to $30 a month for the unlimited-connection-time plans or the includes-the-option-to-Web-publish plans.)

However, you can connect in a much more sophisticated way. You can ratchet up your expense and complexity and use a special kind of modem and connection called ISDN. ISDN, which probably adds around a $100 a month to your costs, lets you move data twice roughly twice as fast as you can with a 56.6 Kbps modem.

Another option is sometimes available from local television cable companies. Some local cable companies let you use special cable modems to connect to the Internet, and these modems let you move data at rates that are often ten times as fast ISDN. (The specific cable modem speed varies by cable company.)

You can also choose to permanently connect to a local network (like you may already have in your office or may decide to create after reading Chapter 9) by using special, high-speed data lines called *T1 transmission lines*. A T1 transmission line moves data at the rate of 1.5 Mbps, or roughly 1,500 Kbps — which is about 25 times as fast as a 56.6 Kbps modem. The cost for this service probably runs as least several hundred dollars a month, potentially thousands of dollars a month, and probably also requires you to spend several thousand dollars (and maybe more) just to get started.

Despite the fact that you do have these other connection options and that big businesses use these other connection options, I actually think the way the Connection wizard works is really good. I keep saying this, I guess, but it's pretty hard to beat something that's cheap and easy.

Working on the Web

Once you can connect to the Internet, you'll find that working on the Web is easy. I'm not kidding when I say that quite literally all you do is click little snippets of text, pictures, and symbols to jump from one document to another. But I'll start at the very beginning, by explaining (or reviewing) what the World Wide Web is and why it should be interesting to you.

What is the World Wide Web?

In order to explain what the World Wide Web is (and let me just abbreviate this mouthful and start calling it the Web), I need to first define three terms — document, multimedia, and hyperlink — because the Web is actually just a collection of multimedia documents connected with hyperlinks.

A document is just a document. You have zillions of these things floating about your office. Letters to customers. Memos. Invoices that haven't been paid even though they're long overdue. The list goes on and on. As you know, however, while these are all examples of paper documents — heck, they're probably stacked on your desk — you can also have electronic versions of these documents stored a computer's disks in folders. (I talk about all this stuff in Chapter 2.) But these things are still documents. A document is a document is a document. Okay, so now you know the first thing you need to know in order to understand the Web.

So let me move to the next term you need to use: multimedia. A medium is just a method of communication. The written word, for example. A picture. Video. Somebody speaking. This makes sense, right? Each of these is a separate method of sharing information. You already know this. And you maybe also know that you can also have electronic versions of any of these things. You can stick text — written words — in a document. You can draw pictures on a computer by using an illustration program. And you can also store video and sounds in documents. What you may not know is that you can build (assuming you have the right software tools) a document that uses more than one of these mediums. You can create a document that uses words and pictures, for example. You can even stick video clips and sounds into documents. I'm going to show you some pictures of these sorts of documents in just a minute, but for now, the main thing to realize is that you can build documents that use multiple mediums. Or, restated using the current lingo, you can build multimedia documents.

Once you understand what a multimedia document is, you just need to know what hyperlinks are. A *hyperlink* is just a piece of clickable text or a clickable picture that points to another multimedia document — to another Web page. If you click the hyperlink, Internet Explorer grabs and then displays this other multimedia document. (This whole process is not as confusing as it may seem. But don't worry. I'm going to show you how all this works in a just a minute.)

So to quickly review: The World Wide Web is a collection of multimedia documents connected with hyperlinks. And that's the essence of the thing. It really is.

Do you need to know anything else? Oh, probably. You should know that people call the multimedia documents by another name, *Web pages.* You should probably know that these Web pages are stored elsewhere on other computers, called *Web servers,* that send their Web pages to your computer when you ask them to. And you should know that people typically call a collection of Web pages that somebody's created and stuck on a Web server somewhere a *Web site.* But, really, that's all there is. You know what you need to know.

A real-life White House tour

I was thinking about the fact that small businesses like the ones that you
and I work in don't really get the same access to the president of the United
States that big businesses do. And I'm sure that it's not just because our big-
business competitors throw all sorts of money to both parties. I mean, that
wouldn't be right, would it? There must be some other reason. In any event,
because we don't get this access to the president and the vice president, I
thought it'd be nice if you could have a virtual visit via the Web. So come
with me. Along the way, you can pretend to have a coffee schmooze with
George, Bill, or Al — and you won't have to spend, like, $50,000.

Okay, the first thing to do is start your Web browser. If you're using Internet
Explorer, you should be able to do so by clicking Start⇨Programs⇨Internet
Explorer⇨Internet Explorer. If you see an Internet Explorer shortcut icon on
your desktop, you can also double-click that. When you start Internet
Explorer, Windows may prompt you to start a Dial-Up Networking connection. You know what to do. (If you don't know what to do, refer to the earlier
chapter section, "Making a Dial-Up Networking connection.")

If you're using another Web browser, you start it in the same basic way. The
only real difference is that the submenu name and menu command will refer
to this other browser. After you start your browser, it loads a default Web
page — probably one that shows information about your Internet Service
Provider. If you use Microsoft Network as your ISP, for example, you'll
probably see some page from the Microsoft Network Web site. If you use
AT&T as your ISP, you'll probably see a page from AT&T's Web site. (I'm not
going to show you one of these start pages because some people think doing
so constitutes an infringement of the Web publisher's copyright.)

But that's not important. Here's what you want to do next: See that text box
near the top of the screen? The one that's labeled Address box? When you
find this — a five-second task at most — take the following steps:

1. **Click the Address box.**

   Windows selects the box's entire contents, which, yes, do appear to be
   total gibberish.

2. **Type the following gibberish,** www.whitehouse.gov, **into the Address
   box.**

3. **Press Enter.**

   Nothing happens for a few seconds — maybe even for a long minute —
   but after a while, you see the *home page,* or main Web page, of the
   United States White House. Figure 5-5 shows how this Web page looked
   on the day I took this tour, but yours make look different. By the way,
   congratulations. You're now surfing the Web.

Figure 5-5:
The home
page of the
president of
the United
States.

You probably already know this, but your Web browser window is just a regular Windows-interface thing. You can scroll up and down (and sometimes right and left) by using the scroll bars that appear along the right and bottom edge of the Web page.

If you see an underlined chunk of text, a chunk of text that appears in different color, or a little picture, you can usually click it to move to another Web page. For example, if while viewing the White House home page you scroll down a bit, you'll notice a hyperlink for the president and vice president of the United States. If you click this hyperlink, you move to another Web page, like the one shown in Figure 5-6. And you can keep on clicking hyperlinks to move to new Web pages, one after the other.

You can also tell when you're pointing to one of these hyperlinks because the mouse pointer changes to a pointing finger.

Do I need to tell you anything else? Oh yes. To move back and forth between Web pages you've already viewed, you can click the Back and Forward buttons. Back moves you to the page you were just viewing and Forward — well, you get it, right? You can click the Stop button to tell Internet Explorer to give up trying to display some Web page (say because things are taking too long). And you can click the Refresh button to tell Internet Explorer to

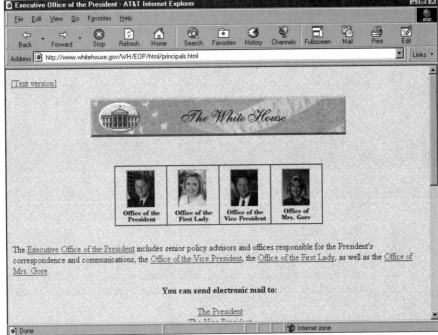

Figure 5-6:
Another
Web page
from the
White
House Web
site.

grab a new copy of the Web page (you may do this if a Web page changes frequently or if something didn't work right the first time you told Internet Explorer to grab the page). And that, pretty much, is everything you need to know about navigating the Web.

For a list of other useful business World Wide Web sites that you may want to explore, take a look at the Small Business Internet Resource Library on the companion CD. Or check out *Small Business Internet Directory For Dummies,* by Esau Barchini and Lee Musick (IDG Books Worldwide, Inc.).

Downloading and printing pages

You can print a Web page by clicking the Print button, which probably appears on the Internet Explorer's toolbar. You can also choose File⇨Print. If you have questions about printing, you can refer to Chapter 4.

You can save a copy of Web page (so you can later view it or reuse some portion of its information) by choosing File⇨Save As. I describe how the Save As command works in Chapter 2, so I won't repeat that discussion here. If you have questions, of course, feel free to flip back.

Understanding how URLs work

Much of the time you really can navigate the Internet by clicking hyperlinks. But you should know that you don't have to move to Web pages by using hyperlinks. You can also tell your Web browser, "Hey, I just want to see this specific page I already know about." To do so, you provide the Web page's address or *uniform resource locator (URL)*. You type this bit of information into the Address box of the Web browser window. In fact, in the earlier chapter discussion of the White House's Web site, that's exactly what you did. When you typed www.whitehouse.gov, that gibberish is actually part of a URL.

URLs, in other words, are like people's addresses. With a person's address — assuming you know your way around town — you can find a friend's house or a business's office. With a URL, your Web browser can find a Web page.

URLs consist of four parts: the protocol name, the server name, the pathname, and then the Web page name. This sounds really complicated, but it's not. For example, one of the Web pages at the White House Web site is this:

```
http://www.whitehouse.gov/WH/html/library.html
```

While this URL looks terribly complicated, it actually isn't if you break it down into its four component pieces. Let me explain what each of these items is.

Protocol names

The protocol name identifies the Internet protocol. (In the world of computers, *protocol* refers to a set of rules and conventions, but you can think of Internet protocols as methods of sharing information.) World Wide Web pages use the protocol http://. But the Internet does support other protocols. Table 5-1 lists a few of them.

Table 5-1	Commonly Encountered Protocol Names
Protocol	*Description*
ftp://	The ftp, or file transfer protocol, lets you move files between computers.
gopher://	The gopher protocol lets you view Internet resources via menus, submenus, and menu items.
http://	The http:// protocol lets you move Web pages between computers.
telnet://	The telnet protocol first turns your computer into a dumb terminal (basically a screen and a keyboard) and then connects this "terminal" to another computer by using the Internet.

Server names

The second part of a URL is the name of the server. The server is just the name of the computer on which the resource such as a Web page resides. Web server names typically (although not always) start with the acronym www to identify the Web site as a World Wide Web server. Then they typically name the company or organization owning the site. They end with a three-letter domain identifier. This all sounds pretty darn complicated, the first time you read it, but in the case of the White House's Web server, the server name is just:

```
www.whitehouse.gov
```

The *www* part of this name identifies the server as a Web server. The *whitehouse* part of the name identifies the owner of the Web site. And the *gov* part of the Web server name identifies the type of domain as a government organization. Table 5-2 identifies some other common domain identifiers. (A *domain* is just a network that's been connected to the Internet.)

Table 5-2	Common Domain Names
Domain	*Description*
com	A commercial organization such as Microsoft, Boeing, or IBM
edu	An educational organization such as the University of Washington or your local high school
net	An administrative network or, sometimes, an Internet service provider
org	A not-for-profit organization such as Public Broadcasting Service or United Way

If you think this all sounds way, way too complicated to make sense of, don't give up quite yet. With what you now know, you can understand the URLs that television advertisers always seem to include in their ads these days. Microsoft, for example, looks like this:

```
http://www.microsoft.com
```

And Boeing looks like this:

```
http://www.boeing.com
```

The folks at PBS have a URL that looks like this:

```
http://www.pbs.org
```

And if you have a kid going to college and you haven't yet saved a ton of money, I hope your young scholar avoids this URL:

```
http://www.harvard.edu
```

All of the preceding URLs use the Web's protocol, `http://`, and a server name that includes the www acronym, but as I mentioned earlier, you can share information over the Internet in other ways. For example, as mentioned earlier, ftp sites let you grab useful files (like text files of information and program files that do cool things). The ftp protocol uses a different protocol name, `ftp://`, and ftp servers also typically use the acronym *ftp* in their names. For example, Microsoft Corporation also maintains a neat ftp site with files that people can grab. The Microsoft ftp site's URL is:

```
ftp://ftp.microsoft.com
```

Path names

As you can guess, a Web server may store hundreds of pages. Not surprisingly, then, a Web publisher organizes a Web server's information into directories, or folders, in the same manner as you organize your hard disk. A URL, therefore, typically includes directory names or folder names. In the following URL, for example,

```
http://www.whitehouse.gov/WH/html/library.html
```

the part that comes after the server name is the directory path:

```
/WH/html/
```

In essence, this directory information tells your Web browser that the Web page it wants is stored inside a subdirectory named *html,* which in turn is stored in directory named *WH.*

Web servers use directories to organize their Web pages in the same basic way that you use folders to organize your hard disk.

Document names

The very last part of a URL is the actual document name. In the White House URL, `http://www.whitehouse.gov/WH/html/library.html`

The document name comes at the very end:

```
library.html
```

Partial URLs work okay

I should tell you that you can often enter just a partial URL and still get the resource you want. For example, if your Web browser can look at the server name and figure out that what you're asking for is a Web page, you don't need to enter the `http://` part of the URL. Similarly, if your Web browser can look at the server name and figure out that what you're asking for is really an ftp site, you don't need to enter the `ftp://` part of the URL. What's more, Web servers all have a default page called a *home page* that they display if you don't specify some other Web page. This means that you can get a Web page from a server even if you don't include a path name and document name. By the way, this ability of a Web browser and server to accept partial URLs is why earlier in the chapter, you could enter just **www.whitehouse.gov** in order to get a Web page from the White House. Note that this Web page doesn't include the protocol name `http://`. Nor does it include a directory or path name or a document name.

Document names often use *htm* or *html* as their file extension, but not always. Some Web pages on some servers use other, rather kooky file extensions. You'll often see document names that use the file extension *asp* on Microsoft Corporation Web servers, for example. The *asp* file extension identifies a Web page as one that uses some of Microsoft's proprietary ActiveX technology and comes from an ActiveX Server. (You don't need to know anything about ActiveX, by the way. You can think of it as a sort of specialty flavor of the `http://` protocol.)

Using Search Services

One of the big problems with the Internet in general — and the World Wide Web in particular — is that finding stuff is tough. Oh sure, you can browse a bunch of different Web pages by clicking hyperlinks or by plopping URLs into the Address box. That's all fine and good, but if you want to find some specific bit of information — information about some new technology your competitor is using or about some quirky income tax law that now applies to small businesses — you're in a bit of pickle. Quick: How do you find information about virtual private networks? Or how do you find out about Irish income tax laws?

You use a search service. Search services catalogue (or attempt to catalogue) Web servers and Web pages. How they do so — in terms of mechanics and all that — is beyond the scope of this book. But that they do it is extremely important to you if you're to begin using the Internet as tool.

Two types of search services exist: directory-style search services and index-style search services. *Directory-style search services* create what amounts to a directory. Within a directory, the search service organizes Web server and Web page descriptions by category, subcategory, sub-subcategory, and so on. One popular directory-style search service is Yahoo!, which you can use by entering its URL, www.yahoo.com, into the Internet Explorer Address box. When you see the main Yahoo! directory, you select a category of information (by clicking a hyperlink) to display another Web page that lists subcategories within the category (see Figure 5-7). When you see this Web page, you select a subcategory (again by clicking a hyperlink) to display another Web page that lists sub-subcategories within the subcategory. You continue your searching until, ultimately, you end up with a list of Web servers or Web pages that provide (or at least hopefully provide) information you're interested in.

An *index-style search service* maintains a huge index of Web servers and Web pages. What you do is supply a word or phrase that you want to look up (see Figure 5-8). The index-style search service then looks up the word or phrase in its index and displays an index Web page that lists a bunch of other Web pages that use the word or term. (Actually, this description isn't quite accurate. Usually, an index-style search service finds thousands of Web pages that use the word or phrase you supply and, therefore, creates a list of Web pages hundreds of pages long. The index-style search service, however, attempts to list the Web pages first that match your search argument.) When you see the index Web page, you select the Web page you want to move to by clicking its hyperlink.

People (usually businesses) have created a bunch of different search services. They all work a little differently, so I'm not going to describe any in specific detail. I do, however, want to share two tips for working with these things:

- **Experiment with different search services.** Different services, big surprise, work differently. You may find that you tend to have more luck if you use a particular service. AltaVista works really well for me. My wife likes Yahoo! But you may find that Magellan (www.mckinley.com) or Lycos (www.lycos.com) or some other service works best for you.

- **Learn to use at least one service well (preferably after you've experimented with all of them for a bit).** Instructions for using any of the search services is provided either on the search service's main Web page or on another Web page that you can easily get to from the main Web page. (You may need to click a hyperlink that's labeled something like "Help" or "More Information.")

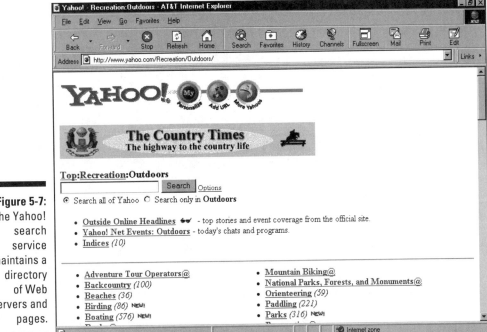

Figure 5-7:
The Yahoo!
search
service
maintains a
directory
of Web
servers and
pages.

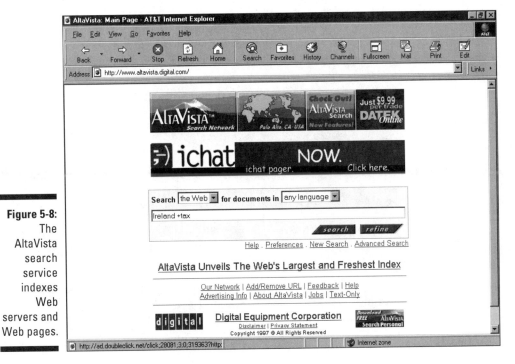

Figure 5-8:
The
AltaVista
search
service
indexes
Web
servers and
Web pages.

Channels and Subscriptions

In the preceding section on search services, I mention that one problem of the Internet is finding stuff. A great deal of neat content is available through the Internet, but you often can't find it unless you either luck out, get a tip from someone else, or know how to use a search service.

The Internet also has another problem: Moving Web pages from Web servers to your computer takes too long. Even if you have a fast modem, you'll often find that most of the time you spend browsing is just wait time. You wait to connect to some Web server, to retrieve some page, and to retrieve the page's images. Then you move to the next Web server or Web page and repeat the process. And so it goes.

To deal with this problem, Internet Explorer 4.0 (with the help of Windows) lets you perform a couple of neat tricks. You can ask special, really smart Web servers — called *channel sites* — to automatically deliver their content to your computer. And you tell Internet Explorer that it should go off and at regularly scheduled times grab new copies of Web pages (if the Web page has changed since you last viewed it), a process called a *subscription*. These two tricks may not seem all that neat — and, true, they probably don't warrant the marketing hype they receive — but they do mean that you can have your computer sit around and wait while it grabs Web pages, and not you. Your computer can grab Web pages during the middle of the night or while you're out for lunch, which saves you time and frustration.

Channels

If you want to ask a channel site to automatically send you new copies of the Web site's pages, you view the Web site's home page and follow these steps:

1. **Locate and then click the Web page's Add Active Channel command button (see Figure 5-9).**

2. **When Internet Explorer displays the Modify Channel Usage dialog box (see Figure 5-10), mark the "Yes, notify me of updates and download the channel for offline viewing" radio button.**

If you don't want to retrieve a new copy of a Web page but do want Internet Explorer to notify you of changes on a Web page, you can mark the "Yes, but only tell me when updates occur" button.

After you follow these steps, the channel regularly delivers new pages to your computer. Note that your computer needs to be connected to the Internet, of course. However, while this may seem like a problem (because as a small business you're going to use a Dial-Up Networking connection), you can also tell your computer to connect to the Internet at some regular interval (perhaps in the middle of the night), too.

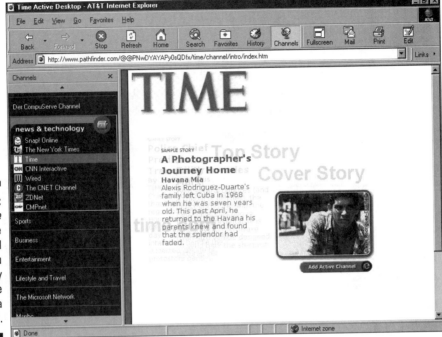

Figure 5-9:
The *Time*
magazine
channel
lets you
automatically
receive
Time via a
channel.

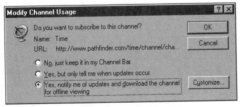

Figure 5-10:
The Modify
Channel
Usage
dialog box
lets you
describe
how a
channel
should work.

Subscriptions

With a channel the Web server automates the process of scheduling when a
Web page gets moved to your computer, but subscriptions work differently.
With a subscription, your browser (Internet Explorer) schedules when a
Web page is retrieved. In other words, rather than having you manually
request a Web page (by clicking a hyperlink or by entering a URL into the
Address box), with a subscription, Internet Explorer just maintains a list — a
subscriptions list. It then uses this list to figure out when it's supposed to
grab Web pages for you.

A subscription doesn't cost you money. When you subscribe to a Web page, all you're doing is telling Internet Explorer that it should regularly retrieve the Web page.

To subscribe to a Web page, follow these steps:

1. Display the Web page you want to subscribe to.

2. Choose Favorites⇨Add to Favorites.

Internet Explorer displays the Add Favorite dialog box (see Figure 5-11).

Figure 5-11:
The Add
Favorite
dialog box
lets you
subscribe
to Web
pages.

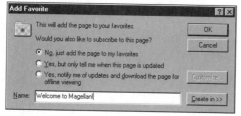

3. If you want Internet Explorer to regularly check a page to see if it's changed and, if it has, to download a new copy of the page, mark the "Yes, notify me of updates and download the page for offline viewing" button.

If you don't want to retrieve a new copy of a Web page but do want Internet Explorer to note when a Web page changes and then notify you of changes, you can mark the "Yes, but only tell me when this page is updated" button. If you merely want Internet Explorer to memorize the Web page's URL and then save this information in its Favorites folder, mark the "No, just add the page to my favorites" button.

4. Click OK.

Getting more specific help

This chapter talks about the Internet and the World Wide Web in a general way. And with what you know, you'll be able to do most of what you need to do with the Internet.

You should know, however, that if you want to immerse yourself in the details of Netscape Navigator or in Internet Explorer, you can get other books. IDG Books Worldwide, Inc., publishes *Internet Explorer 4.0 For Windows For* *Dummies,* by Doug Lowe. And they publish *Netscape Communicator 4 For Dummies.* Both of these titles go into much greater detail about how these Web browser programs work. Oh, shoot, and I almost forgot. If you want a great deal more information about the Internet in general, I'll also point out that IDG's *Small Business Internet For Dummies,* by Greg Holden, is a really good resource.

Chapter 6

A Web Publishing Primer

So, you've decided that you want to publish on the Web. Perhaps you've concluded that becoming a Web publisher will provide your business with substantial benefits or open the door to interesting opportunities. This chapter discusses exactly what Web publishing with Windows 95 programs entails and describes the different options you have for publishing Web documents.

You have two ways of creating HTML documents, a hard way and an easy way. The hard way is to learn HTML and then code the stuff yourself. The beginning of this chapter describes how you create a bare bones HTML file and how you add basic Web page elements to the file. This approach, while tedious, actually produces some benefits, as any professional HTML coder can tell you. Most notably, your Web pages load faster because they don't include any extraneous and unnecessary codes. (Remember that HTML is really a set of instructions to your Web browser, so the more tightly these instructions are written, the more quickly a Web page loads.) But in order to create professional Web pages for your business, you need to become fairly proficient in using HTML. The time cost of this is probably more than you can afford. After all, you have a business to run.

Later on, this chapter describes the easy way of creating an HTML document — by using a WYSIWYG (What You See Is What You Get) Web authoring program like FrontPage Express (included on the companion CD as a part of Internet Explorer) that doesn't require you to know any HTML. The easy way works just as well, if not better, for most small businesses and individuals. With a WYSIWYG Web authoring program, you just supply the text, pictures, and URLs. The program adds all the HTML tags for you.

After you read this chapter, you may want to quickly peruse Chapter 17.

What is a Web Page Made Of?

If you browse the Web very much, you've seen a sampling of the impressive things people can do with Web pages. Okay, so here's the deal: Web pages and all of the different, fun stuff they include are all made possible by HTML.

You may have noticed that when you display a Web page in your Web browser, the last part of the Web page's URL ends in the letters htm or html. This is because Web pages are HTML files. (For more information about Web pages and URLs, refer to Chapter 5.)

HTML stands for Hypertext Markup Language, a language that tells a browser how to display information. All Web pages are made up of a series of codes written in HTML. You don't see these codes when you display the Web page in your browser, thank goodness, but they're there. These codes, called *tags,* mark the elements of a Web page. They mark where headings, tables, paragraphs, and other elements begin and end. Some tags also include attributes about the elements. For example, some tags tell the Web browser what background color a page should have, still other tags describe what font and point size the text should be in, and then other tags specify how pictures should be aligned.

The basic elements of an HTML document

Web pages are made up of three basic elements: text, pictures, and hyperlinks. Web pages can also and often do include fancier elements such as video or sound clips, special little programs, or various animated features.

Text, the foundation

While you don't need extensive amounts of text on each page in your Web site, you need text on almost all of the pages. You need to describe your business and the products or services you sell. You most definitely also want to include your address and telephone or fax numbers so that customers can contact you. You can probably think of some other things that you want to share as well.

Coming up with the text

Adding textual content is probably one of the most difficult (and definitely the most time-consuming) parts of Web publishing. Not because telling Web browsers how to display text is difficult. It isn't. Writing this HTML code is as simple as it gets. But because coming up with and organizing content is not always as easy as it sounds. I don't mean to stress you out here right from the start, but keep in mind that the message you're publishing is the most important part of your Web site. Publishing on the Web is much like publishing a newsletter — first and foremost you need to figure out what you want to say. Your message needs to be clear and concise. You don't want it to include embarrassing errors, or to mislead or offend people. Oftentimes, when people get swept up by the fervor of Web publishing, they spend more time making their Web site pretty than they do making it informative and useful. Don't fall into this trap.

After you have your message written and organized, having it professionally edited isn't a bad idea. I'd suggest this even if you got an "A" in composition. The time and money is almost always worth it. You don't want to publish spelling or grammar errors for all of the world to see.

If you live in a large city, you may be able to find a list of editors in your phone book. If you live in a rural area, you may have to send your Web page text to an editor in another city. To locate a professional editor, try conducting an Internet search of the word "copy editor" or "editorial service."

Adding text to an HTML document

After you have your Web page text or know exactly what you want to say, you create an HTML document and include the text in the document. If you want to code the HTML document yourself, you need to know HTML. That sounds scary, but it's actually a fairly simple language. You can download an HTML tutorial from the Web for free to get you started (a good tutorial is available at www.ncsa.uiuc.edu/General/Internet/WWW/HTMLPrimer.html). For more help and information writing HTML, conduct a search on the word "HTML" by using a search engine. Just to calm your anxieties, I'll let you know that after downloading a tutorial from the Web, most people can create a simple (very simple) HTML text document within an hour or so.

You can write an HTML document by using a bunch of different programs. You can use WordPad, which comes with Windows. You can also use an HTML editor, a special program that includes commands and buttons specifically for formatting HTML documents.

Several HTML editors are available. You can either purchase one at a local software store or you can download one from the World Wide Web.

Another way in which you can create HTML documents (oftentimes without even needing to know the language) is by using your word processor. Microsoft Word 97, for example, allows you to save documents as HTML files. Word then adds the HTML tags for you. (If your word processor doesn't include this function, you can still write the HTML document with your word processor; you just need to remember to save the document as a text only file when you're done.)

I'm going to assume, however, that you're using WordPad. To build your HTML document in WordPad, follow these steps:

1. **Start WordPad by clicking Start⇨Programs⇨Accessories⇨WordPad.**

2. **Enter the following required elements on a blank document:**

```
<html>
<head>
<title> </title>
</head>
<body>
</body>
</html>
```

3. **Add your textual content as shown in Figure 6-1.**

   The title of the Web page goes in between the two title tags, and the individual paragraphs of textual content go in between the body tags. If you want to add headings, you can use <h1> and </h1> for beginning and ending a level-one heading, <h2> and </h2> for beginning and ending a level-two heading, and so forth.

   HTML is not case sensitive. It doesn't matter whether you type <head> or <Head> or <HEAD>.

4. **Save the document by choosing File⇨Save As.**

   Enter a name for the document in the File Name text box and then add the file extension .htm to the file name. From the Save As Type drop-down list box, select Text Document and then click the Save button.

5. **Confirm that your HTML tags were entered correctly by displaying the document in your Web browser (as shown in Figure 6-2).**

   To do so in Internet Explorer, choose File⇨Open and then click the Browse button. Use the Open dialog box to locate the file and then click Open.

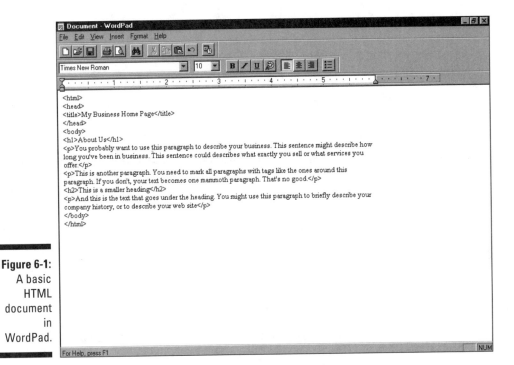

Figure 6-1:
A basic
HTML
document
in
WordPad.

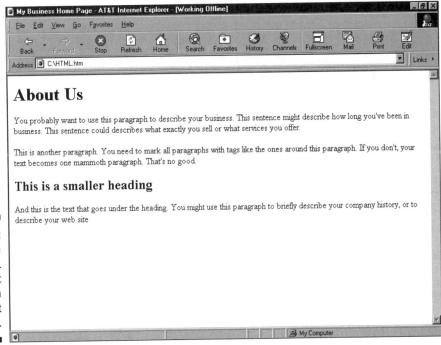

Figure 6-2:
What the
HTML
document
looks like in
Internet
Explorer.

Graphics

While the textual content of your Web page may be the most important part, you shouldn't neglect graphical elements. Graphics add pizzazz to your Web page. They catch the visitor's attention and make your Web page look more professional.

The first step in adding graphics to your Web page is deciding what you want to add. Because graphic files tend to be rather large, you should limit the number of graphics you display on each page. If you don't, your pages will take a long time to load and this wait will turn away potential Web site visitors, such as customers. People just don't like waiting around for pages to load.

When you're deciding which graphics to include and which to leave out, you probably want to put your business logo on each page to clearly identify your business and make each page look official and consistent with the other pages in the Web site.

After you decide which images you want, you need to create electronic files of the images if you have not already done so. You may have to scan a photograph or use a graphic editing program to draw a logo or symbol. (You may want to consult a professional graphic designer if you don't consider yourself artistically-inclined.)

After you have the graphic image in an electronic format, you need to save it as a JPEG or GIF file. JPEG and GIF are two image file formats commonly used on the World Wide Web because they compress image files, reducing the size of images so that they take less time to load. To convert an image file to JPEG format by using Paint Shop Pro (included on this book's CD), follow these steps:

1. **After you install Paint Shop Pro (see Appendix A for instructions), click Start⇨Programs⇨Paint Shop Pro.**

2. **Choose File⇨Open.**

   Doing so brings up a dialog box that you can use to locate the file.

3. **When you find the image file that you want, double-click the image file to open it.**

   The file opens in Paint Shop Pro.

4. **After the image file opens, choose File⇨Save As.**

   The Save As dialog box appears, as shown in Figure 6-3.

Figure 6-3:
Saving a
graphic as
a JPEG file.

5. **Click on the item next to the line that reads "Save as type" and pick the GIF or JPG extension.**

6. **Use the Save As box to open the folder where you want to store your image.**

7. **Click on Save.**

8. **Choose File⇨Exit.**

After you have your graphics in GIF or JPEG format, you're ready to add them to your HTML document. To add a graphic to your HTML document, use the tag `<img src=imagename>` where imagename is the URL of the image file in quote marks, including the file extension .gif or .jpg. (See Figure 6-4.)

Hyperlinks

The last basic element that your Web pages need is *hyperlinks.* Hyperlinks link all of the pages in your Web site together. So if your Web site includes a home page, a separate page that lists the products you sell, another page that lists the latest news and happenings at your business, and so forth, the hyperlinks connect all of these pages so that visitors can freely move between them. If you think of your Web site as subway system, hyperlinks are the tracks. Without the tracks, it doesn't matter how great the stations are, because nobody can get to them. Hyperlinks not only link your own little city of pages together, but they also ideally connect people to other destinations. If you don't add hyperlinks to other Internet resources, your Web site becomes a lonely, isolated village.

Web browsers replace this tag with the image file.

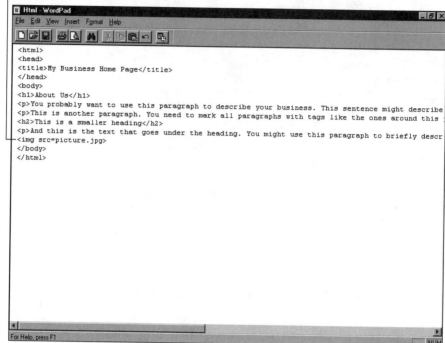

To add hyperlink tags to your HTML document, use the tag

```
<a href="filename">link text</a>
```

where filename is the document you want to link to and link text is the text you want displayed as the link. If you want to link to a document in a different directory, you need to include the complete pathname. If you want to link to another Internet resource, you need to include the complete URL including the protocol (such as `http://` for a World Wide Web page), as shown in Figure 6-5.

HTML fancy stuff

After you add the basic HTML elements, you can begin formatting your HTML document so that it looks pretty. You can specify which colors you want to use for the text and the background, and you can add other character and paragraph formatting. I can't possibly explain all of the various formatting options in this book, so refer to an HTML tutorial or to your HTML editor's Help file.

This hyperlink points to a document in the same folder as the Web page.

```
Html - WordPad
File  Edit  View  Insert  Format  Help

<html>
<head>
<title>My Business Home Page</title>
</head>
<body>
<h1>About Us</h1>
<p>You probably want to use this paragraph to describe your business. This sentence might describe
<p>This is another paragraph. You need to mark all paragraphs with tags like the ones around this
<h2>This is a smaller heading</h2>
<p>And this is the text that goes under the heading. You might use this paragraph to briefly descr
<img src=picture.jpg>
<a href="prdctlst.html">Product List</A>
<a href="http://www.ncsa.uiuc.edu/General/Internet/WWW/HTMLPrimer.html">A great HTML guide</A>
</body>
</html>

For Help, press F1                                                                    NUM
```

Figure 6-5:
An HTML
document
with a
couple of
hyperlinks.

This hyperlink points to a page on the World Wide Web.

Some Web-design no-nos

I should probably stop here and share some candid comments with you, to help you avoid common mistakes in Web authoring.

Don't go overboard

Beginning Web designers have a tendency to try to put too much stuff on a page: extraneous graphics, background sounds and patterns, and animated elements. These features only distract, confuse, and annoy visitors. Keep in mind that the average computer user can only receive 28,800 bits of information per second, which isn't all that fast. (A rather standard-sized Web page of 100 Kbps takes about a half a minute to retrieve assuming that all goes well.) People, for obvious reasons, don't like to wait around for pictures of your storefront, your employees, and your family dog to load. As a general rule, only include elements that add valuable content to a Web page. And also divide the content you wish to publish among several Web pages, so that each individual Web page takes a shorter time to load. Nobody wants to scroll through your company history, your last year's sales, and your personal profiles to get to your product list. Put each of these items on its own page.

Don't forget legibility

Make sure that you keep color contrasts in mind. Even if your company's logo is in yellow and white, don't use yellow text on a white background. Choose a text color that is easily legible on top of your background color and that can be easily distinguished from hyperlink text colors. Choose a simple font and limit the number of fonts you use to one or two. You don't want your Web page to look like a ransom note. Also make sure that your font is not too small or large. A 12 point font usually works well. It is large enough to be easily read but small enough so that you can fit a good amount of text on a page. Choosing a larger font doesn't make you look like you have more to say, nor does it make your message look more important. It just looks big.

Don't forget the limitations of various browsing software

Not everyone browses the Web with the same software you used to preview your Web site. Some people prefer to use a text browser to save time. Other people may use older browsers that don't support features such as frames or active elements and scripts. Don't rely on these types of features to convey important information. Be aware of the various browsing styles when you create your Web site and try to preview your Web site by using as many different browsers as you can to make sure that you aren't leaving some visitors in the dark.

Don't forget to maintain your Web site organization

When you decide to publish to the Web, your work is not completely done the second you publish your site to a server. A Web site requires periodic maintenance like just about anything else. When you're creating your Web site, make sure that you include a hyperlink back to your home page on every Web page in your Web site. After you publish the Web site, periodically test your links to make sure that they are functioning properly, and that each page loads the content you expect it to.

Starting FrontPage Express

To start FrontPage Express, click Start⇨Programs⇨Internet Explorer⇨ FrontPage Express. Doing so opens the FrontPage Express application window, which displays a blank Web page.

Adding text to a Web page

To add text to a page, you can either type the text directly onto the page (you don't need to add the HTML tags — FrontPage does this step for you), or you can simply copy and paste the text from your word processor. The biggest advantage of using FrontPage Express over writing your own HTML document in, say, WordPad is that FrontPage Express lets you format text with the click of a button, much as you would by using a word processor. Figure 6-6 shows what formatted text looks like on a page. You don't need to memorize all of the HTML tags for formatting text. You use the Format toolbar. (If this toolbar isn't displayed, choose View⇨Format toolbar.) Table 6-1 lists the Format toolbar's buttons and what each one does.

Table 6-1	The Format Toolbar
Button	*What It Does*
Heading 1 ▼	The Change Style drop-down list box lets you create headings and lists.
Comic Sans MS ▼	The Change Font drop-down list box lets you change the font.
A↑	The Increase Text Size button increases the point size of the text to the next largest size.
A↓	The Decrease Text Size button decreases the point size of the text to the next smallest size.
B	The Bold button boldfaces text.
I	The Italic button italicizes text.
U	The Underline button underlines text.
🎨	The Text Color button allows you to change the text color.
≣	The Align Left button aligns the paragraph along the left side of the page.
≣	The Align Center button centers the paragraph in the page.
≣	The Align Right button aligns the paragraph along the right side of the page.
≝	The Numbered List button lets you create a numbered list.

(continued)

Table 6-1 *(continued)*

Button	What It Does
	The Bulleted List button lets you create a bulleted list.
	The Decrease Indent button un-indents the selected line or paragraph.
	The Increase Indent button indents the selected line or paragraph.

Don't use the Underline button for emphasis in your Web page text. Underlined text is usually reserved for hyperlinks.

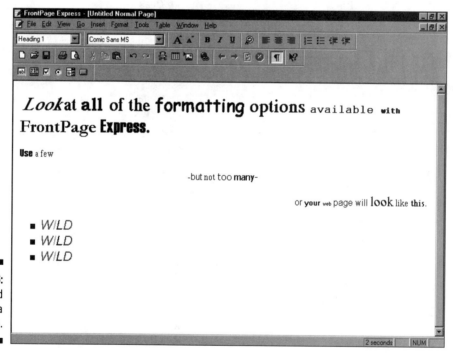

Figure 6-6:
Formatted
text on a
Web page.

Adding pictures

Adding graphics to your Web pages is a snap with FrontPage Express. FrontPage Express even comes with a collection of clip art images you can use to add flavor to your Web pages. To add a graphic to your Web page, follow these steps:

1. **Place the insertion point where you want to add the graphic.**

2. **Click the Insert Image button to display the Image dialog box.**

3. **Click the Other Location tab if you want to add your own image.**

   Alternately, if you want to add a Clip Art image, click the Clip Art tab (as shown in Figure 6-7).

4. **Click the Browse button to display another Image dialog box.**

   Use this dialog box to locate the image you want to insert. When you have found the image, select it from the list box and click the Open button. FrontPage Express inserts the image.

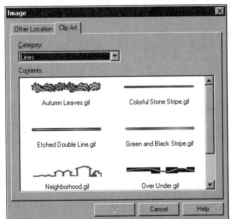

Figure 6-7:
Inserting a
Clip Art
image.

Adding hyperlinks

The last thing your Web page absolutely needs is hyperlinks. Luckily, with FrontPage Express, adding hyperlinks is a piece of chocolate cake. To add a hyperlink, follow these steps:

1. **To add a hyperlink to another Web page in your Web site, open the Web page to which you want to link by clicking the Open toolbar button.**

2. **Display the Web page to which you want to add the hyperlink.**

3. **Type some text or insert a graphic that you want to use as a hyperlink.**

4. **Select the text or graphic image.**

5. **Click the Create Or Edit Hyperlink button.**

   FrontPage Express displays the Create Hyperlink dialog box (see Figure 6-8).

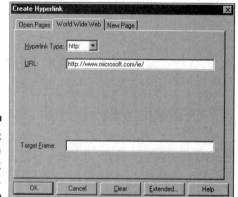

Figure 6-8:
The Create Hyperlink dialog box.

If you want to link to a Web page you currently have open, click the Open Pages tab and select the Web page from the list box. If you want to link to a Web page on the World Wide Web, click the World Wide Web tab and enter the Web page's URL in the URL text box.

6. **Click OK to create the link.**

   FrontPage Express underlines and changes the color of a text link, as shown in Figure 6-9.

To see where a hyperlink points, move your mouse over the link. The link's destination appears in the lower-left corner of the FrontPage Express application window.

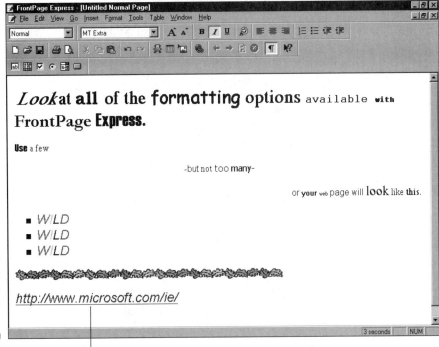

Figure 6-9:
A Web
page with a
hyperlink.

This hyperlink points to an Internet Explorer Web page on Microsoft's Web site.

FrontPage Express' fun stuff

If you've been following along here, you have probably noticed that I haven't explained the majority of the commands available in FrontPage Express. There are just too many to cover here. Once you get the basic elements on your Web pages, feel free to experiment around with some of FrontPage Express' more advanced features. FrontPage Express includes dozens of tools you can use to easily spice up your Web pages. For example, you can use Format➪Background to change the background color to your Web page or to add a background wallpaper. The Insert menu also has several commands for adding special elements to your Web pages, such as marquees (scrolling text), programming scripts, videos, sounds, animations, horizontal lines, and form fields for form pages.

So what's the full-blown version of FrontPage like?

As you may know, another version of FrontPage is available, called FrontPage 98. If you like how FrontPage Express works and you want to create a more elaborate Web site, you may want to upgrade to FrontPage 98. FrontPage 98 has three major benefits over FrontPage Express.

✔ FrontPage 98 includes several more wizards that you can use to create a complete Web site for your business. (All you do is tell FrontPage which pages you want to include, as shown, and which design scheme you want to use, and FrontPage creates and links all of your pages, and then tells you what information should go where. You only have to fill in the blanks.)

✔ The second major benefit of FrontPage 98 is a program called FrontPage Explorer, which lets you view and work with all of the Web pages in your Web site at once. (This feature becomes essential if your Web site includes more than a couple of pages.)

✔ FrontPage 98 lets you add even more advanced components to your Web pages, which you need if you want your Web site to include such things as elaborate forms.

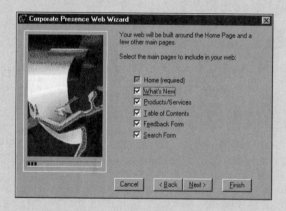

Publishing Your HTML Documents

After you create your Web site, the next step is putting it on a Web server so that other people can view it. Internet Explorer 4.0 comes with a Web Publishing wizard you can use to move HTML documents to a Web server.

Finding a place to publish

The first step in getting your Web site onto a Web server is finding a server to put it on. Not all Internet service providers offer space for publishing Web sites, and some offer more space than others. Contact your Internet service provider if you don't know whether you are allotted space for posting Web pages. (For more information on finding an Internet service provider, see Chapter 5.) If your Internet service provider doesn't offer space for posting Web pages, you may want to purchase an account with a Web presence provider. Web presence providers are just like Internet service providers except they specialize in Web publishing and are often able to provide more technical support for Web publishing.

If you are planning on upgrading to FrontPage 98 (see the sidebar "So, what's the full-blown version of FrontPage like?" earlier in this chapter), you should choose a Web presence provider that has FrontPage Server Extensions installed on its server. FrontPage Server Extensions allow you to include FrontPage's more advanced elements in your Web pages. For a list of Web presence providers that have FrontPage Server Extensions, visit the site http://microsoft.saltmine.com/frontpage/wpp/list.

Using the Web Publishing wizard

After you have a place on a server to publish your Web site, you're ready to use the Web Publishing wizard. To run the Web Publishing wizard, click Start⇨Programs⇨Internet Explorer⇨Web Publishing Wizard, and then follow these steps:

1. **Click Next to begin publishing your Web site.**

2. **In the next dialog box, enter the name of the HTML file or the folder of files you want to publish and click Next.**

3. **Enter a name for your Web server and click Next to continue.**

   For example, you may name the server simply "My Server." Or you can name it Joe. Or Betty. As you like.

4. **Enter the URL of your Web site and click Next.**

   Your Web presence provider should provide you with this information.

   If you're currently working offline, the Web Publishing wizard prompts you to connect to the Internet. It also requests that you enter in a password for accessing the Web server.

   If the Web Publishing wizard requests that you enter the protocol your Web server uses, select the protocol from the drop-down list box and click Next. If you don't know this information, contact your Web presence provider.

5. In the next dialog box, describe the protocol you selected and click Next.

6. Click Finish to post your files to the Web server.

Achieving visibility after you're on the Web

You aren't the first business to publish to the Web. You have plenty of company out there. So how do you get your customers or whoever else you want visiting your Web site to find you among the millions of other Web sites?

Getting listed with a directory-style search engine

Within a couple of weeks after you publish your Web site, index-style search services such as AltaVista may already include you in their databases if an existing indexed Web page links to your site or if you have registered a domain name. But you want to show up on as many search engines searches as possible, right? Then you need to actively request being added to their databases. For example, if you want to suggest to Yahoo! that they add your site, follow the instructions listed on this Web page: www.yahoo.com/docs/info/include.html. You can add your Web site to each individual search engine database, or you can also pay a company to add your site to several search engine databases. You can get information about companies that do this from your Internet service provider or your Web presence provider.

Registering with InterNIC

If you choose to publish a Web site under your company's own domain name, (instead of as a Web site on your Web presence provider's domain name) you need to register the domain name you choose with InterNIC. InterNIC just makes sure that no two Web pages share the same address. Usually, registering with InterNIC comes as a part of the set up fee when you purchase an account with a Web presence provider. If not, you need to register the Web site yourself. You can find more information on doing so at the InterNIC Web site: www.internic.net

---

Publicizing your URL

This step is probably obvious, right? One of the best ways to get traffic on your Web site is by publicizing your URL. Have it added to your letterhead and business cards. Include it in your advertisements in the phone book and the newspaper. Mention it on your radio or television commercial. You can also take advantage of the World Wide Web to advertise your Web site. If your community has a popular site, advertise your Web site there. You can usually get advertising rates and other information about how to advertise on a page by clicking links.

Getting people to come back

So you created a great site. Everyone is impressed, including your mother-in-law. But how do you keep up the traffic? Some sites use prizes or promotions to get visitors to return. This tactic works well, but most importantly, you need to constantly provide new and exciting information on your Web site. If you don't frequently update your Web site, you won't have people coming back for seconds. As the saying goes, "old news is no news."

For more tips and tricks on setting up, designing, and maintaining a Web site for your small business, take a look at a copy of IDG's *Small Business Web Strategies For Dummies*, by Janine Walker.

Chapter 7

Electronic Business Correspondence

*E*lectronic correspondence has gained a great deal of popularity over the past couple of years. This popularity stems in part from the simple fact that e-mailing is fun. But electronic correspondence is more that just fun and games for small businesses. It is also an inexpensive and efficient way for businesses large and small to communicate. If you need to send documents across the country and have them arrive by the next morning, you can either spend around $15 to overnight them or you can spend pennies to send them electronically. If you need to send one hundred letters through the mail, you can spend 32 cents on stamps, plus the cost of paper, envelopes, ink, and your time, or you can spend about five minutes to have them delivered immediately. If you do business internationally, you can save even more. A half ounce airmail letter costs 60 cents to mail and takes about a week to get most anyplace. A telephone call can cost around $1 a minute. An e-mail costs next to nothing and can get there within a matter of seconds.

With Windows 95, you can use several different programs for e-mailing. Because I can't possibly know which one of these programs you have, nor can I describe how each and every one of these programs work, I'm just going to tell you how e-mailing works in Outlook Express (a nifty little e-mail program that comes with Internet Explorer 4.0 on the companion CD). If you choose to use a different program, most of what I say here still applies, because e-mailing programs for Windows 95 usually work in just about the same way.

This chapter assumes that you use a dial-up connection to send and receive all of your e-mail. It doesn't talk about configuring e-mail on a local area network (or LAN). I'm assuming that you don't have an internal mail system on a LAN. Client-server networks (the kind you need to send mail across) just don't make sense for most small businesses. They're too expensive and require too much maintenance. Unless you have the time and the patience to read thousands of pages of networking manuals, or unless you have a degree in computer science, maintaining a network can be a regular nightmare. And if you're not up to doing it yourself, paying for a network technician's expertise can cost you an arm and a leg. (For more information about the different types of networks and about setting up a simple peer network, see Chapter 9.)

Starting Outlook Express

Once you install Outlook Express from the companion CD, you can start by clicking the Launch Outlook Express button on the Quick Launch toolbar (you can find this toolbar on the left side of the Windows taskbar). Or click Start⇨Programs⇨Internet Explorer⇨Outlook Express. Outlook Express prompts you to connect to the Internet if you aren't currently working online. If you want to see if you have new mail, you can go ahead and connect. But if you want to write a message first, click the Work Offline button to compose the message offline.

If you have an unlimited usage account, it really doesn't matter how long you spend online. You can theoretically stay online 24 hours a day, or at least whenever you're working on your computer. But if you have an account that charges you for your hourly usage, or if you have to make a long-distance call to access your Internet service provider, you probably want to limit the time you spend online. Another reason you may want to limit the time you spend online is if you have a fax machine or voice number that shares the same line as your modem. You probably want to keep this line free for people (like customers) to contact you. One way you can limit your online time is by composing new messages and reading received messages offline. By doing so, you need to only briefly connect when you want to send and receive messages.

After you close the logging-on screens, take a look at the Outlook Express home screen shown in Figure 7-1. This screen provides shortcuts to all of the things you can do in Outlook Express, and also gives you a tip of the day for using the program. You don't really need this screen, however, so go ahead and check the When Starting, Go Directly to My Inbox box.

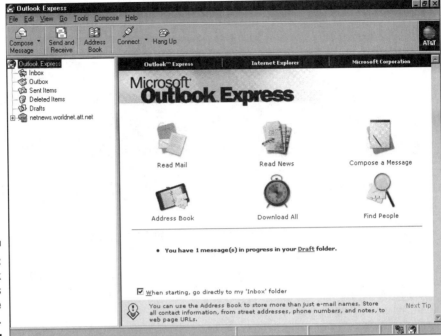

Figure 7-1:
The Outlook
Express
home
screen.

To send and receive mail electronically, you need to have an account with an Internet service provider. If you don't already have one and you have Internet Explorer, start Internet Explorer and choose View⇨Internet Options. When Internet Explorer displays the Internet Options dialog box, click the Connection tab and then click Connect to run the Connection wizard. When the Connection wizard asks, tell it that you want to choose a new Internet service provider and set up a new account. When you give the Connection wizard your area code and prefix, it will give you a list of Internet service providers in your area. You can read about the different plans offered by these companies and then set up a new account immediately. (For more information about the Connection wizard or Internet Explorer, refer to Chapter 5.)

Writing e-mail messages

To write and send a message to someone, follow these steps:

1. **Click the Compose Message toolbar button.**

   Outlook Express displays a blank new message window.

2. **Click the To text box and enter the person's e-mail address.**

E-mail client choices

This chapter talks about using Outlook Express for sending and receiving e-mail, but as I mentioned before, many other popular e-mail programs are available. Most of them work much like Outlook Express, but each has its own special benefits. Here's the rundown on some of the most popular e-mail programs.

Netscape Communicator, the latest version of Netscape's Web browser, comes with an Internet news and mail program called Netscape Messenger. It differs a little from Outlook Express in that it has separate windows, one that displays your mail folders and another that displays a message list and a preview pane message next.

Many people use Eudora, either in the free version called Eudora Light or the complete version called Eudora Pro. Eudora Pro is a powerful e-mail program that has extensive options. For example, it allows you to encode messages in several different ways. It also has superior drag-and-drop abilities. With Eudora Pro, you can create a different signature (like electronic letterhead) to attach to the messages you send from a specific account. If you know that many of your clients or vendors use Eudora, it may be a good choice for you because you can view Eudora formatting that you wouldn't otherwise be able to.

Pegasus Mail is another popular e-mail client. Not only is the program free, but it is also powerful and easy to use. It has several features that allow you to customize and set options for the way your messages are sent and handled. If you receive lots of mail, this client is a good choice.

3. Click the Subject text box and type a short subject.

Don't try to type the whole message in this box. Just limit it to a couple of words or a short phrase, such as "Meeting Thursday."

4. Press the Tab key and begin writing your message.

Figure 7-2 shows an example message. Don't worry if you think you have more to say than what fits in the box you see. As you type, the box scrolls down, so you can just keep writing. Your message can be dozens of pages long.

Don't learn the hard way (like I did). If you're writing a lengthy message (or if you think you've just composed a literary masterpiece), save it every few minutes just like you would if you were typing in a word processor. Outlook Express is a reliable program, but you can't count on it never crashing. And it can't protect you against power outages, or the people in the office next door flipping the circuit breaker to wire new lamps. To save a message you're working on, choose File⇨Save. Doing so stores the message in your Drafts folder.

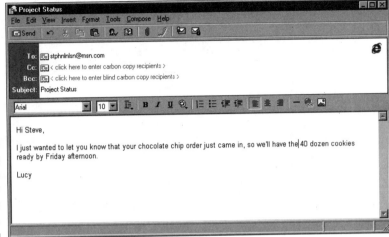

Figure 7-2:
A message
in the New
Message
window.

5. **When you finish typing the message, click the Send button.**

   If you are working online, Outlook Express sends your message on its way. If you're working offline, Outlook Express moves your message to your Outbox folder. You need to connect to the Internet to deliver your message. To do so, choose Tools⇨Send and Receive and then choose the account you want to use for delivering the message. (If you only have one account, you only have one choice here.)

6. **Make sure that your message delivery worked by clicking the Sent Items icon on the left side of the Outlook Express window.**

   Your sent message should show up in the list on the right (as shown in Figure 7-3).

Reading messages

With any luck, after you write a few e-mail messages, you begin receiving e-mail messages. To check your mailbox and read incoming mail, follow these steps:

1. **If you're currently working offline, choose Tools⇨Send And Receive.**

   Choose the account that you want to download messages from the submenu. (If you have only one account, you have only one choice here.)

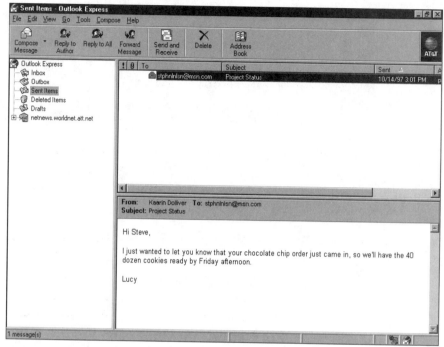

Figure 7-3:
Sent items
appear in
the Sent
Items
folder.

The scoop on e-mail addresses

If you're new to the world of electronic mail, you may find e-mail addresses kind of confusing, so let me give you the run-down on them. When you want to send a message to someone electronically, you need to know the person's e-mail address. This address is different than the person's street address. If you don't know a person's e-mail address, and you want to send her an e-mail, the easiest way to get her e-mail address is to call and ask for it. Make sure that you have this person spell it out for you, because if you get a single character incorrect, it won't work. For example, if you have a friend named Henry Smith who has an e-mail address with the Acme Corporation, he may tell you that his address is "hsmith at acme dot com". When Henry says "at" he means that you're supposed to use the @ symbol. And by "dot" he means a period. So, you would type the address as **hsmith@acme.com** in the To box. You can type the address in uppercase or lowercase, but don't add any spaces.

Just in case you're wondering, the part of the address before the @ is called the *username*. People usually get to choose their own username, depending on their Internet service provider's policy. A username identifies who you are. The part of the address after the @ is the *domain name*. It identifies the server that delivers and receives your messages.

Unless your business has a permanent connection to the Internet (and I'm assuming that it doesn't because a permanent connection is mighty expensive), your computer connects to the Internet via your modem and your phone line. So, in order for e-mail messages to arrive at your computer and for outgoing messages to leave your computer, you need to initiate a physical connection. Messages can't just magically show up on your computer screen out of thin air. Whenever you want to deliver or receive messages, you need to make a dial-up connection to your Internet service provider by choosing Tools⇨Send and Receive. Keep in mind that unlike with traditional mail, you can receive electronic mail several times during the day, and at any time of the day. So if you want to use e-mail as a medium for customers and vendors to reach you, you need to check your mail periodically throughout the day.

2. **Click the Inbox icon from the list on the left if your Inbox isn't already currently displayed.**

   The contents of your Inbox are listed in the list on the right. New, unread messages are boldfaced (see Figure 7-4).

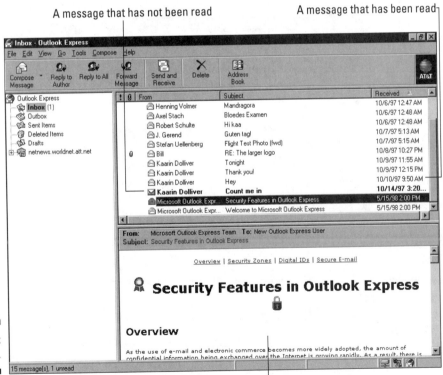

Figure 7-4:
The Inbox.

3. To read a message, select it from the list on the left.

Outlook Express displays the message text in the lower-right frame. To read a message in its own window, double-click the message header in the list on the left.

Forwarding and replying to messages

To forward a message, select the message in the Inbox and click the Forward Message button. If you already have the message displayed in its own window, just click the Forward button. Outlook Express opens a new message window, shown in Figure 7-5, so you can describe whom you want to forward the message to and so you can add your own two cents to the forwarded message.

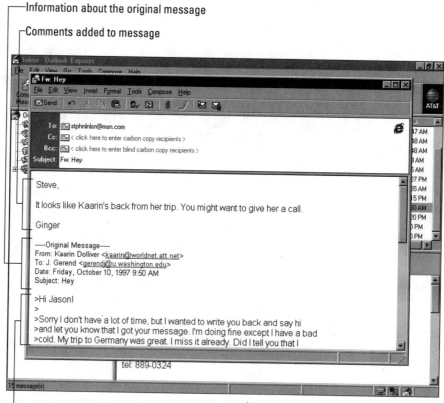

Information about the original message

Comments added to message

Figure 7-5:
Forwarding
a message.

The original message text

Replying to messages works in much the same way. To reply to the message sender, select the message in the Inbox and click the Reply to Author button. If the message was sent to multiple recipients, you can reply to all of the people who received the message by clicking the Reply to All button. If you have the message displayed in its own window, click the Reply to Author button to reply to only the message sender or click Reply All to reply to all of the message recipients.

TIP

You can usually identify forwarded messages or replies to messages just by looking at them in your Inbox. Forwarded messages begin with the letters FW in the Subject line and replies to messages usually begin with the letters RE.

Attachments

You can send more in an e-mail message than just text. You can send word-processing documents, spreadsheets, scanned pictures, and all sorts of other files. These other files attached onto messages are called *attachments*.

To attach a file to a message you're writing, follow these steps:

1. **Place the insertion point in the body of the message and click the Insert File toolbar button (the one that looks like a little paper clip).**

   Outlook Express displays the Insert Attachment dialog box shown in Figure 7-6.

Figure 7-6: The Insert Attachment dialog box.

2. **Use the Look In drop-down list box and the Look In list box to locate the file you want to attach to the message.**

3. **Check to make sure that the Make a Shortcut to this File box is not marked and then click Attach.**

   Outlook Express attaches the file to the message and displays an icon for the file in the message body. That's it. You can now send the message like you would any other message.

You can usually tell that an incoming message has an attachment because Outlook Express puts a tiny paper clip icon beside it in your Inbox. Double-click the message to display it in its own window. The attachment should appear in the lower part of the window (see Figure 7-7). To view the attachment, double-click it.

Double-clicking the attachment launches whatever program you regularly use to work with such files. For example, if you receive an invoice attachment written in Word, double-clicking the attachment launches Word. If you receive an image file attachment, double-clicking the file launches whatever image editing program you have on your computer. After you display the file, you can work with it as you normally would and save it to your computer like any other file.

If instead you don't want to view the attachment, but want to save it directly to your computer, right-click the file attachment icon and choose the shortcut menu's Save As command. In the Save Attachment As dialog box, you can specify a name and location for saving the file.

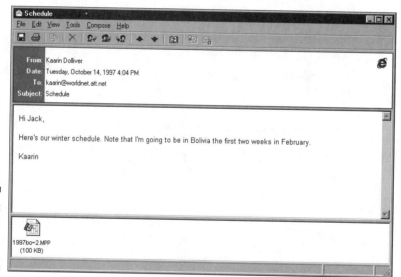

Figure 7-7: A message with an attachment.

The attachment blues

If you find that receiving attachments doesn't work as smoothly as I make it sound, don't feel bad. You're not alone. Attachments are tricky little critters. Even if you do everything right, they just don't always work. There are no sure-fire solutions to the multitude of attachment problems lurking out there, but you can take a couple of preventative measures to decrease your chances of having attachment troubles.

Don't try to attach more than one file to a message. If you have more than one file to send, attach each file to its own separate message. Many mail servers and e-mail programs don't accept multiple attachments. Be sure to indicate in the message subject or body that the message is only one part of a set. For example, you might write "Employment contracts, part 1/3" so that people know that it is the first part of a set of three messages.

Keep the attachment size down. If you have to attach a large file (graphic image files or any files that include graphics tend to be quite large), zip the file up before attaching it. Zipping a file compresses the size of the file.

Zipping also lets you put several files together into an archive so that you can send them all in one message. If you don't have zipping software, you can install the program WinZip from the companion CD.

Make sure that you let people know that you've sent an attachment. Don't assume that the attachment arrived properly just because the recipient received the message. If you add a line in the body of the message to the tune of "I'm attaching the file for our summer project schedule to this message," the chances are much greater that you'll hear from the message recipient if something goes afoul. The same applies if you forget to attach something.

If you receive a message that has a bunch of garbeldy-gook attached to it, don't panic. All is not lost. This just means that somewhere along the line, the servers and programs handling the e-mail message didn't speak the same language, and so the message arrived in a different code.

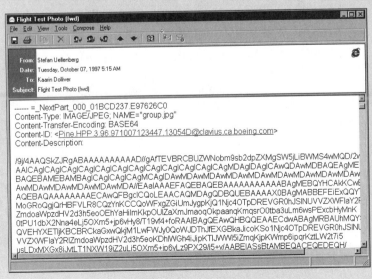

(continued)

(continued)

Luckily, programs exist that translate this code back into something you can recognize. WinZip is one of them. To decode an attachment using WinZip, follow these steps:

1. **Select the message with the messed-up attachment from your Inbox.**

2. **Choose File⇨Save As.**

3. **Enter a name for the file in the File Name text box.**

4. **Select text files from the Save As Type drop-down list box.**

5. **Start WinZip and open the text file.**

   With any luck, WinZip displays a list of the contents of the message. The first few items list the message text, and the last items list the message attachments.

6. **Double-click the attachment file to open it.**

   If all else fails, contact your Internet service provider for help. They can tell you which protocols their server supports and can give advice for attaching files.

Using the Address Book

Outlook Express provides a handy little tool called the Address Book for storing all of the e-mail addresses you collect. As a matter of fact, using the Address book, you can store more than just e-mail addresses, you can store just about any contact information for a person — his home and business addresses, telephone, fax, cellular phone and pager numbers, his job title and department, and so forth.

To add a new contact to the Address Book, follow these steps:

1. **Click the Address Book toolbar button to display the Address Book.**

2. **Click the New Contact toolbar button.**

3. **Click the Personal tab and enter the contact's name and e-mail address (see Figure 7-8).**

4. **Click the Home or Business tab to enter contact information about the person.**

5. **Click the Other tab to add notes about the person, such as his or her birthday.**

6. **Click OK to return to the Address Book list.**

To send a letter to a contact in your Address book, just type the first few letters of the person's name in the To box of the New Message window. Outlook Express looks for matching entries in your Address Book (as shown in Figure 7-9). If the match it finds is correct, click Enter to accept it. Note that once you enter a contact's e-mail address into the Address Book, you no longer need to enter the person's e-mail address into the To box. Just enter the person's name and Outlook Express grabs the e-mail address information from the Address Book.

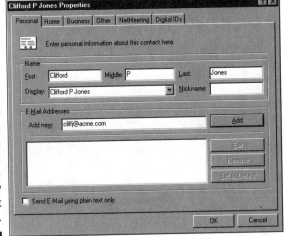

Figure 7-8:
The
Personal
tab of the
New
Contact
dialog box.

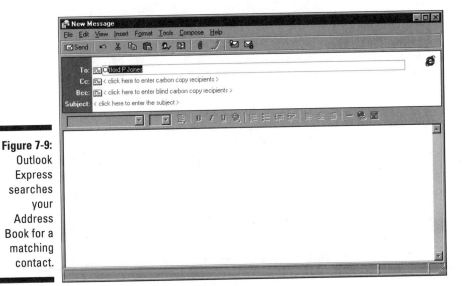

Figure 7-9:
Outlook
Express
searches
your
Address
Book for a
matching
contact.

Subscribing to Mailing Lists

In addition to using e-mail to send and receive personal letters, you can also use it to subscribe to and receive regular newsletters from organizations or clubs. For instance, you can join a mailing list for accordion enthusiasts, for unicyclists, or for soapmakers. Electronic mailing lists work just like their real-life counterparts. You sign up to join a mailing list, and the organization sends you its newsletter in regular installments.

Several different mailing lists may interest you or relate to your field of business. To see a list of publicly accessible mailing lists, check out the following web site: www.liszt.com/. If you find a list that interests you, copy down the instructions for subscribing to the list.

To begin receiving regular mailings, you need to join the mailing list. The instructions for subscribing to mailing lists vary from list to list, so you need to make sure that you write them down for each list and follow them carefully. Even if it seems unfriendly, you need to type only what the instructions say, nothing more and nothing less. Mailing list request letters are processed by a computer instead of a human being, and the computer just gets messed up when you add text to your mailing list request like "Hi, my name is Bob and your mailing lists sounds really interesting. Please sign me up. Thanks."

Try out a couple of mailing lists first before signing up for more. Mailing list messages can rapidly fill up your mailbox, so test out a couple first and then cancel the ones that don't interest you before subscribing to new ones.

Here are a few general lists that may be of interest to small businesses:

- **Self-Employment Digest:** This list provides a forum for self-employed people to share tribulations and offer suggestions. To join, send a message to sed@ultranet.com with the subject SUBSCRIBE DIGEST. Leave the body of the message blank.

- **Top Ten List of Small Business Successes:** This list highlights ten business success stories daily and provides strategies for several aspects of running a small business. To subscribe to this list, send a message to majordomo@topten.org with the body subscribe toptenbusiness-list.

- **Small biz software showcase:** This list allows small business owners to discuss and describe business applications that they have found helpful. To subscribe, send a message to jricord@nucleus.com with the subject subscribe small biz.

- **The Global Profit$ Email Newsletter:** This list describes how you can increase your profits both online and off. To subscribe, send a message to list-request@lotcom.com with the body SUBSCRIBE GLOBALPROFITS.

- **Work at home moms:** This list allows mothers running home businesses to share advice and ideas. You can sign up for this list at the following Web page: www.wahm.com/join.html.

Reading and Posting to Newsgroups

Another way of communicating with several different people who share your same interests is through newsgroup postings. Newsgroup postings differ from mailing list messages because they do not take up space in your Inbox. With newsgroups, people post messages to a server, and you choose which messages you want to read by looking at the message headings. To use Outlook Express for reading and posting to newsgroups, follow these steps:

1. **Choose Go⇨News.**

   If this is the first time you're using newsgroups, Outlook Express may ask you for the name of your news server or it may tell you that it needs to download the current list of active newsgroups. If you don't know the name of your news server, contact your Internet service provider.

2. **To display a list of available newsgroups available through your Internet service provider, click the News groups button.**

   The Newsgroups dialog box is displayed (see Figure 7-10).

3. **To find a newsgroup that relates to a topic that interests you, enter a keyword in the text box.**

   Outlook Express displays a list of all newsgroups that contain this word.

4. **To preview a newsgroup that sounds interesting and to find out if it's really about what you think it's about, select the newsgroup from the list and click the Go To button.**

   If you're working online, Outlook Express displays the list of article headers people have posted to that newsgroup. If you're working offline, you need to click the Connect button and go online, and then you need to choose Tools⇨Download 'news server' command (where news server is the name of your ISP's news server).

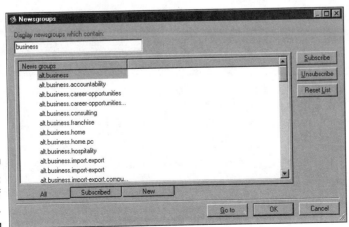

Figure 7-10:
The list of
newsgroups.

5. To read a newsgroup posting, select the article heading from the list on the right.

Outlook Express displays the article text in the lower-right pane. If you want to view the article in its own window, double-click the article heading.

6. To subscribe to a newsgroup, select the newsgroup from the list on the left and choose Tools➪Subscribe to this Newsgroup.

The next time you want to read the articles posted to this newsgroup, all you have to do is select the newsgroup from the list on the left. Figure 7-11 shows some newsgroups I've subscribed to and the articles posted to the newsgroup selected.

After you monitor a newsgroup for a while, you are ready to begin posting your own articles to the newsgroup. To post an article to a newsgroup, follow these steps:

1. Select the newsgroup from the list on the left and click the Compose Message Button.

Outlook Express displays the New Message window and fills in the Newsgroup line for you.

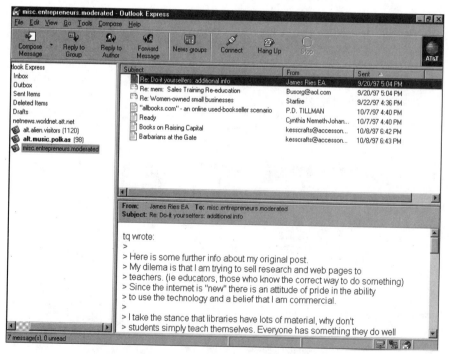

Figure 7-11:
A
newsgroup.

2. **Type a Subject and the message body like you do for a regular e-mail message.**

3. **When you finish, click Post to post the message.**

You can reply to newsgroup postings just as you can reply to e-mail messages. To post a reply to an newsgroup article for the whole newsgroup to read, click the Reply to Group button. Or click the Reply to Author button to send an e-mail message only to the author of the newsgroup article (Outlook Express fills in the person's address from the newsgroup posting).

Here's a list of newsgroups that may be of interest to small businesses:

- ✔ Misc.entrepreneurs.moderated
- ✔ Misc.taxes.moderated
- ✔ Misc.legal.moderated
- ✔ Misc.business.marketing.moderated
- ✔ Misc.business.moderated

All of the newsgroups I recommend here are *moderated*. To find out why, take a look at a few of the newsgroups that aren't moderated. If your experience is like mine, you won't see a single posting that isn't an advertisement. If you're looking to ask and answer questions in an open forum, you may want to subscribe to moderated newsgroups to filter out the advertising.

To unsubscribe to a newsgroup, select the newsgroup from the list on the left and choose Tools⇨Unsubscribe to this Newsgroup.

Part III
Teamwork

In this part . . .

If you're in business, you work with people. So this part talks about how you can share the information you create and store on your computer with other people and their computers.

Chapter 8

Sharing Information

• •

In This Chapter

▶ Moving and copying information between programs

▶ Exporting information in other formats

▶ Faxing information with Microsoft Fax

• •

*A*fter you begin using your computer to create and store information, you will also want to begin sharing that information with coworkers, vendors, and customers. Fortunately, Windows makes this task really easy. With Windows, you can create documents that include a bunch of different types of information. And you can share information by distributing documents. With Windows, you can easily distribute electronic versions of business documents — even to people using different programs and different computers.

Note: If you're working on a network, you can also use the network to share information. Chapter 9 explains how you set up a Windows network. Chapter 10 describes how you work on and share information over a small network.

Sharing Information between Windows Programs

The neat part about Windows is that it lets you share information between all sorts of different programs. If, for example, you have a chunk of text in a word-processing document that you want to insert into a spreadsheet, you can easily do so. Or if you have a table in a spreadsheet application that you want to insert in a word-processing document, you can do this as well. You can copy and move data between applications in two ways, by dragging and dropping it directly or by cutting it to the Clipboard and copying it from there. I'll tell you about both ways, and then you can decide for yourself which one you like best.

The dragging and dropping method

This method of moving stuff doesn't sound very pretty. It may remind you of the way your little sister used to drag her favorite doll along the sidewalk until its toes wore off. But dragging and dropping by using the mouse is a pretty nifty little trick. To copy or move information between two applications using the mouse, follow these steps:

1. **Open the file with the selection you want to cut or copy.**

   This is called the *source file.*

2. **Open the file into which you want to paste the selection.**

   This is called the *destination file.*

3. **If you don't already have the applications for these files running, you need to start them, of course.**

   You can start applications by clicking the Start button and choosing the name of the application from the Programs menu. (If the program you want to run isn't on the Start menu, see Chapter 12 for information on adding programs to the Start menu.)

4. **Close any open programs that you're not working with.**

   I tell you why in the next step.

5. **Right-click the Windows Taskbar and choose either the Tile Windows Horizontally or the Tile Windows Vertically command.**

   The choice is yours. The Tile Windows Horizontally command stacks open application windows on top of one another. The Tile Windows Vertically command places them side by side, as shown in Figure 8-1. But you probably guessed that. Now you can guess why I told you to close any extra application windows? If you're a power-multitasker and have, say, five or six applications running at once, Windows tiles all five or six application windows, turning your screen into a bunch of skinny strips that you can't begin to work with.

6. **Select the information you want to move or copy.**

   If you want to copy the selection, hold down the Ctrl key. If you want to move it, don't touch the Ctrl key.

7. **Click on the selection and drag it to the destination file.**

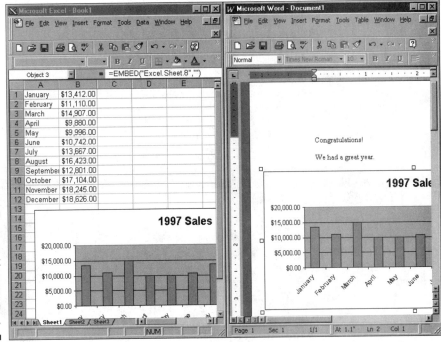

Figure 8-1:
Copying
text
between
tiled
application
windows.

Moving information via the Clipboard

Another way you can move information around on your computer is by using the Clipboard. The Clipboard is just like a secret storage space on your computer that keeps whatever you cut or copy until you paste it.

When you place something on the Clipboard, it wipes out whatever was formerly on the Clipboard. So if you cut something but haven't yet pasted it anywhere, make sure that you paste it somewhere before you cut or copy anything else.

Cutting, copying, and pasting using menu commands

You can move text between applications by using the Edit menu's Cut, Copy, and Paste commands (see Figure 8-2). To do so, follow these steps:

1. **Select the information you want to copy or move from the source file.**

2. **Choose Edit⇨Cut if you want to move the selection or choose Edit⇨ Copy if you want to copy the selection.**

3. **Display the destination file.**

4. **Place the insertion point where you want to paste the selection.**

5. **Choose Edit⇨Paste.**

Dragging stuff to the desktop

You can also store just a portion of a file on your desktop so that you can paste it later. This file portion is called a *scrap file.* To create a scrap file, arrange your application windows so that a corner of your desktop peeks through. Then drag the selection to the desktop. You can later drag the selection from the desktop into a file in another program.

A scrapfile on the desktop

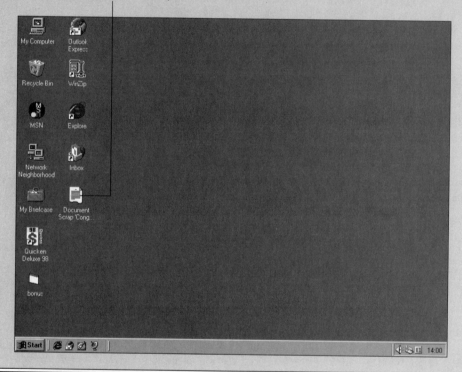

Figure 8-2:
The Edit
menu lists
commands
for cutting,
copying,
and pasting.

Cutting, copying, and pasting with toolbar buttons

Another way you can cut and copy information to the Clipboard and then paste it from the Clipboard into another application is by using toolbar buttons. Most programs have Cut, Copy, and Paste toolbar buttons. The Cut button usually looks like a little pair of scissors, the Copy button looks like two pieces of paper, and the Paste button looks like a piece of paper on a clipboard.

Cutting, copying, and pasting with keyboard shortcuts

The quickest way to cut, copy, and paste is by using keyboard shortcuts. To cut the selected information, hold down the Ctrl key and press the letter x. To copy the selected information, hold down the Ctrl key and press the letter c. To paste the contents of the Clipboard, hold down the Ctrl key and press the letter v.

Viewing the contents of the Clipboard

To view the contents of the Clipboard, you use the Clipboard Viewer. Just click Start⇨Programs⇨Accessories⇨Clipboard Viewer, to display the Clipboard Viewer, as shown below.

(If you don't see this program listed in the Accessories folder, it is because it doesn't usually come installed with Windows. See Chapter 11 for information on installing Windows Accessories.)

Clipboard Viewer	□ ×
File Edit Display Help	

```
January $13,412.00
February     $11,110.00
March   $14,907.00
```

Saving Information in Other Formats for Exporting

When you move information on your own computer, you generally don't need to save it in another format, because you can usually just cut, copy, and paste as described in the previous section. But sometimes you do need to first translate information so that another program on your computer can read and understand it. And often times when you share information with other people, you need to save it in another format so that their computer and software can read and understand it.

Saving a file in another format works the same way in just about all applications. I'm going to use Microsoft Word as an example, though, because it has many options for saving in other formats, but you'll find the steps similar in other programs.

To save a Word document in another format, follow these steps:

1. Choose File⇨Save As to display the Save As dialog box (see Figure 8-3).

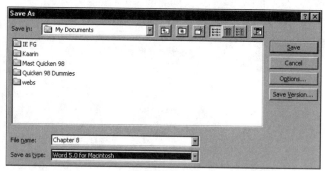

Figure 8-3:
Saving a
word
processing
document
in another
format by
using Word.

2. Use the Save in drop-down list box and the list box below it to tell Windows where you want to save the file.

If, for example, you want to save the file to your floppy disk so that you can mail it to someone, select your floppy disk drive from the Save in drop-down list box.

3. Type a name for the file in the File name text box.

Although Windows 95 lets you use really long file names, if you're planning on sharing information with other people (who may or may not be running Windows 95), you should keep the file name to a maximum of eight characters, just to be sure. You can use any combination of numbers and letters, but don't use spaces.

4. In the Save as type dialog box, select the file format you want to use for saving the file.

As mentioned before, Word gives you several choices here. Picking the right one isn't always easy. In order to do so, you need to know what operating system the person on the receiving end has, which software she's running, and possibly even which file formats this software can read. To make less room for error, your best bet is to just call up the person you're sharing information with and ask her exactly what software she has and which version of this software she's running.

5. Click the Save button to save the file.

Word may tell you that some of your formatting will be lost if you save the file in the format you chose. Don't worry if you get this message. Word almost always gives this warning if you choose to save a file in another format, and the formatting is almost never lost. It simply warns you just in case.

Figuring out the right format for saving a file

If you can't get all of the information you need to save the file in the right format, you can make a couple of assumptions. By following the next two tips, the person receiving the file should be able to read the file, but he may have to convert it on his end first.

- ✔ If you know which software program a person is using, you don't absolutely have to know the version. For example, if you know that a customer uses Word on the Macintosh, you don't have to know whether he uses Word 3.0 or Word 4.0. If you're unsure, pick the smaller number (which is the earlier version). You can almost never go wrong here, because later versions of software can always read earlier versions, but not vice versa.

- ✔ If you know a person has a PC, but you don't know whether she uses Word, WordPerfect, or Works, you can save the word-processing document as a rich text format (RTF) file. Doing so preserves almost all of your formatting and is readable by all word-processing programs running Windows.

For more information on saving files and formatting floppy disks, see Chapter 2.

Using the Paste Special command

Some programs have a command called Paste Special. The Paste Special command allows you to reformat the information before you paste it. This feature is really useful if you're working with two different types of applications (such as a spreadsheet and a word processor). The Paste Special dialog box gives you a choice of how you want to paste the selection. Sometimes it also allows you to link the information you've pasted to its source file. (The advantage of this link is any changes you make to the original selection are automatically reflected in the destination file.)

Sharing Data with Mac Users

As I hinted at earlier, you can save files in special formats so that you can export them to the Macintosh. Although sharing files with Macintosh users should work without a hitch in most cases, sometimes it won't work at all. If the person you want to share information with has an older Mac, his or her Mac probably won't be able to read PC disks. Unfortunately, your PC can't read Mac disks either. Luckily, however, this ailment can be remedied.

Check out the Ziff Davis Web site page for Macintosh software at www.zdnet.com/mac/software/browse_default.html. They have several different utilities you can download to make file transfers with the Macintosh run more smoothly. For instance, you can download programs that allow your PC to format and write to Mac floppy disks. You can also download programs that fix file names for the Mac user or for you (Macintosh and Windows have different ways of naming files).

Using Microsoft Fax to Send Information

A quick way of sharing information with others, and a way that poses fewer compatibility problems, is to fax files by using Microsoft Fax, an accessory that comes with Windows 95. With Microsoft Fax, you can turn your computer and modem into a fax machine and send files to anyone who has a fax machine.

To use Microsoft Fax within an application such as Word, follow these steps:

1. **Choose File⇨Print.**

2. **From the Printer Name box, choose Microsoft Fax.**

   If Microsoft Fax isn't included in the list, see the sidebar "Setting up Microsoft Fax."

3. **Specify the pages that you want to print in the Page Range box and click OK.**

If Microsoft Fax displays the log on screen for your Internet service provider, don't log on. Mark that you want to work offline.

4. **The first Compose New Fax dialog box asks you where you're dialing from.**

If you're using a laptop and are on the road, click the Dialing Properties button to tell Microsoft Fax where you're calling from. If you're using a laptop at home, click Next. If you're working on a desktop computer, check the I'm Not Using A Portable Computer box and click Next.

5. **The next dialog box, shown in Figure 8-4, asks you a few questions about where and to whom you want to send the fax.**

Enter the fax recipient's name in the To box or click the Address Book button to grab the person's contact information from your Address Book. Then enter the person's fax number in the Fax # box. When you finish, click Next.

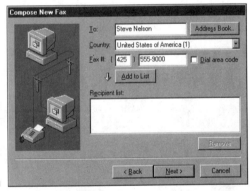

Figure 8-4:
Describing
the fax
recipient.

6. **Click either the Yes or No button to tell Microsoft Fax whether you want to send a separate cover page.**

If you want to include a cover sheet in your fax, choose the type of cover sheet from the list box.

7. **If you don't want to send your fax immediately, but instead want to specify a certain time at which you want to send it, click the Options button.**

8. **Enter a subject for the fax in the Subject box and optionally, enter any notes about the fax in the Notes box.**

If you chose to create a cover page, Microsoft Fax asks you whether you want the subject and notes to go on the cover page or on the file itself. Click Next to continue.

9. **Click Finish to send the fax.**

   Microsoft Fax dials the fax number and displays the status of the fax in the upper-left corner of your screen so that you can see if it goes through.

If the program you're using doesn't have options for printing to Microsoft Fax, you can create a fax and then attach a file to it by clicking Start⇨Programs⇨Accessories⇨Fax⇨Compose New Fax. The Fax menu also has two other commands you can use for creating cover sheets and another for calling an information service to request a file as a fax. You can also set up Microsoft Fax to receive incoming faxes by following these steps:

1. **Click Start⇨Settings⇨Control Panel, and then double-click the Mail or Mail and Fax icon.**

2. **Select Microsoft Fax from the list box and click Properties.**

3. **Click the Modem tab and click Properties.**

4. **Select either Answer After ... Rings or Manual from the Answer Mode area.**

5. **Click OK.**

Setting up Microsoft Fax

You probably installed Microsoft Fax when you installed Windows. But if you didn't, see Chapter 11 for information on installing Windows Accessories.

After you have installed the Microsoft Fax software, you need to add Microsoft Fax to your *profile* (the settings that describe you and the services that you use) so that you can use it to send faxes from Windows programs. To add Microsoft Fax to your profile, do the following:

1. **Double-click the Mail icon in the Control Panel window.**

2. **Click the Services tab.**

3. **If Microsoft Fax is not listed, click the Add button and then select Microsoft Fax from the Add Service to Profile dialog box and click OK twice.**

The first time you use Microsoft Fax, it asks you to provide it with some information, such as your name, the modem you use for faxing, what phone number your modem uses, and the like. After you provide this information, you are ready to begin using Microsoft Fax.

Special Section
A Preview of Windows 98

In this part . . .

As I write this, Microsoft is planning a new version of its popular Windows operating system called Windows 98. Windows 98 may even be available by the time you read this book.

This section talks about Windows 98 a bit — specifically, what's different about Windows 98 and whether you'll want to upgrade.

Chapter I

Appearances and the World Wide Web

*E*ssentially, Windows 98 really represents a grab bag of new features. You won't find any one really powerful, totally wild, or unique feature that differentiates Windows 98 from Windows 95. Instead, Windows 98 supplies a bunch of whistles and bells — and some intriguing new tools.

Web integration represents the most noteworthy feature of Windows 98. Windows 98 lets you tightly integrate the Internet Explorer Web browser and the Windows operating system. The combination of Windows 98 and Internet Explorer 4.0, for example, lets you use channels and subscriptions, which are new tools designed to address limited bandwidth, a real weakness of the Internet. The combination of Windows 98 and Internet Explorer 4.0 also lets you create an *active desktop* (which is just a desktop that works like a Web page). Figure I-1 shows what an example active desktop looks like. Figure I-2 shows a standard Windows 95 desktop.

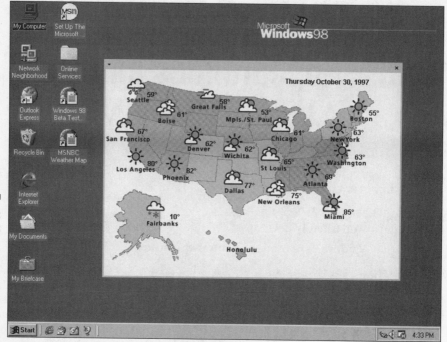

Figure I-1:
Windows 98
may let you
use Web
page
elements on
your
desktop.

Figure I-2:
A standard
Windows 95
desktop.

A big caveat

In this section, I'm been pretty explicit and precise in my descriptions of what Windows 98 will do. I say, with authority, things like, "And Windows 98 will do this!" But I need to tell you something. Although I've tried to be diligent in my research and accurate in my descriptions, the ultimate Windows 98 product will probably differ from the description provided here. Partly, this is because operating system software changes over its development. And if the boys and girls at Microsoft get some clever new ideas or conclude that some old idea maybe isn't so clever, well, then they're going to make changes to the prerelease version of the Windows 98 software (which is what I'm working with).

I need to mention another wildcard, too: the current United States Department of Justice investigation into Microsoft business practices. As I write this, the argument basically boils down to the question of whether Microsoft has pressured people (like computer manufacturers) to include Internet Explorer as part of the Windows 95 operating system. This may seem irrelevant to Windows 98. Essentially, Windows 98 combines Windows 95 and Internet Explorer 4.0. So some people are saying, "Hey, if the Department of Justice has a problem with the current business practices of Microsoft, they are going to totally freak out about Windows 98."

I don't know what's going to happen here. Maybe nothing. But you should probably also be aware of the possibility that Windows 98 may not ever happen. Or it may happen at some point far, far in the future.

Subscribing to Channels and Other Web Sites

Channels and subscriptions sound terribly complicated, but they're actually not. Here's the deal. Typically, you manually initiate the process of moving Web pages from some distant Web server to your PC so your Web client can view the Web page. As you may know (or can read in Chapter 5), you do so by clicking a hyperlink or by providing a URL. The main thing to notice is that in either of these cases, you make the request manually. Channels and subscriptions automate these requests.

> ✔ *Channels,* which are special Web sites, automatically send you updates to the Web site on a regular basis. Subscribing to a channel is called *adding an active channel.* People often subscribe to news channels such as MSNBC.

✔ *Subscriptions* are just any Web pages you tell your Web browser to automatically grab. Unlike channels, subscriptions are often personal Web pages or other less-frequently visited sites. For example, you may subscribe to a vendor's product list Web page so that you can see when the vendor has added new products. When you subscribe to a favorite Web page, you can choose if and how you want to be notified when the page has new content, and you can set a schedule if you want to download new content.

Note: For more information about the World Wide Web and Internet Explorer 4.0, refer to Chapter 5.

Working with channels

Web sites that automatically deliver their content are called *channel sites*. You can tell a channel site that it should regularly deliver content to your PC.

Adding an Active Channel

To subscribe to a channel so that it appears on your Channel bar, follow these steps:

1. **Start Internet Explorer.**

   Windows 98 includes a new batch of buttons next to the Start button. This button set, called Quick Launch buttons, lets you start Internet Explorer or Outlook Express, redisplay your desktop, and display the Microsoft Active Channel Guide.

2. **Click the Channels button to display the Channel Bar — a list of clickable buttons and categories of hyperlinks that you can use to view channel site Web pages.**

3. **Click the Microsoft Channel Guide button.**

   To subscribe to one of the default channels already on the Channel bar, you don't need to display the Microsoft Active Channel Guide. Instead, just select the channel's button on the Channel bar and click the Add Active Channel button when Internet Explorer displays the channel's Web page.

   A complete list of available channels, organized by category, is displayed as shown in Figure I-3.

   Which channels you have available depend on the country you told Windows 98 you live in when you installed Windows 98. The order of the channels changes each time you redisplay the category (to give equal exposure to different companies).

More about bandwidth

With all of the talk about bandwidth, you may have become a little confused due to the overload of information. Let me quickly set the story straight about the Internet's big bandwidth problem. *Bandwidth* refers to the amount of data a computer can pump through a cable in a given time. Typically, bandwidth is mentioned in bits-per-second or the derivative terms, Kilobits-per-second or Megabits-per-second. (A bit is just a 1 or 0 that computers use to represent data. A Kilobit is roughly 1,000 of these 1s and 0s. And a Megabit is roughly 1,000 Kilobits.) Okay, so far, so good.

Now here's the bandwidth problem: Even though people keep buying faster and faster modems and even though the big cables that make up the Internet's connections are always being upgraded and added to, you often have to wait a longer-than-you-expect time for Web pages to download. For example, even though you have a modem that moves data at the rate of 28.8 Kilobits-per-second or 56.6 Kilobits-per-second, you may not actually get, send, or receive data at this speed. You may actually send and receive data at 14.4 Kilobits-per-second — or even slower. The reason for this bandwidth problem is that the data transmission capacity of the Internet isn't growing as fast as the amount of data people are transmitting. The situation, then, is akin to the traffic problem that a fast-growing town (like Seattle, where I live) often has: The number of people and therefore the number of cars on the road grows faster than you can build new roads.

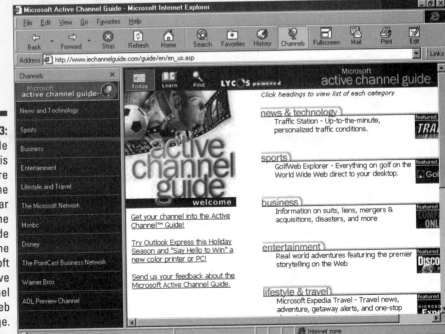

Figure I-3: The left side of this figure shows the Channel bar and the right side shows the Microsoft Active Channel Guide Web page.

4. **Select a category from the Microsoft Active Channel Guide.**

   Doing so displays the first seven channels in that category, as shown in Figure I-4.

5. **Click a channel logo button to preview a channel or click the Next 7 button to see a list of the next seven channels available in the category.**

6. **After you display the channel you want to add, click the channel's Add Active Channel button (see Figure I-5).**

   The Add Active Channel Content dialog box, shown in Figure I-6, is displayed.

   • Click an option to describe if you want to receive notification of content changes to the channel or download the channel for offline viewing.

   • Click the Just Add to Channel Bar radio button to add a button for the channel to your channel bar.

   • Click the Notify Me When Updates Occur button to add the channel to your Channel bar and receive notification when the channel includes new content.

   • Click the Notify Me When Updates Occur and Download for Offline Viewing button to also automatically download the channel according to the channel author's schedule.

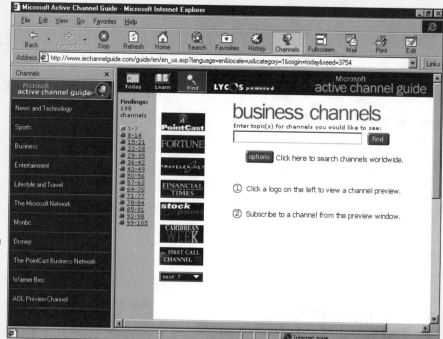

Figure I-4:
The business category of channels.

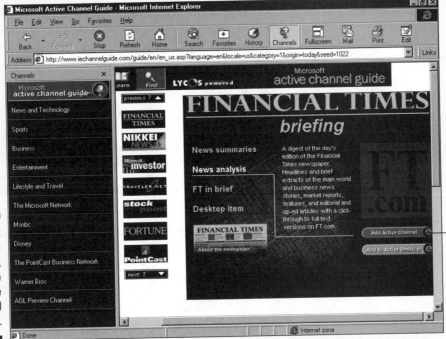

Figure I-5:
To add a channel, click the Add Active Channel button.

Add Active Channel button

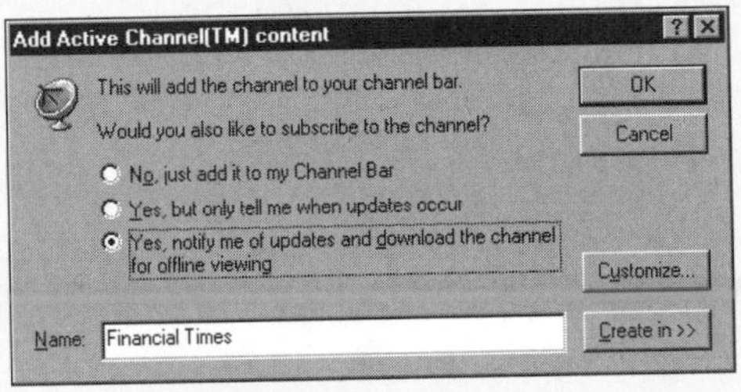

Figure I-6:
The Add Active Channel content dialog box lets you select and customize how you want to stay informed of changes to the channel.

After you add the active channel, you can view a preview of it, as shown in Figure I-7.

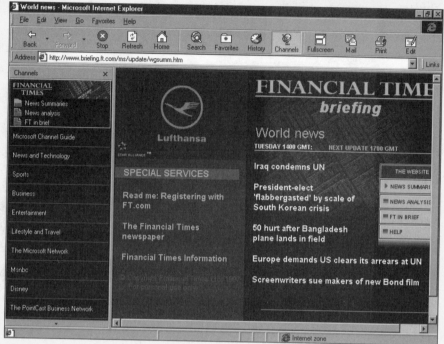

Figure I-7:
The
Financial
Times
channel
site page.

Adding a Channel Screen Saver

If the channel creators designed the channel for use as a screen saver, when you click the Add Active Channel button, the dialog box in Figure I-8 appears.

Figure I-8:
Adding an
active
channel
screen
saver.

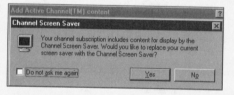

Click Yes to add the channel to your list of available screen savers. To select the channel screen saver, follow these steps:

1. **Right-click a blank area of your desktop.**

2. **Choose the shortcut menu's Properties command.**

3. **Click the Screen Saver tab.**

4. **Select Channel Screen Saver from the list of available screen savers, as shown in Figure I-9.**

5. **Click OK.**

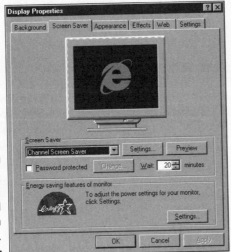

Figure I-9:
Selecting a
channel
screen
saver.

 Moving the mouse doesn't close a channel screen saver. To close a channel screen saver, you need to click the close button in the upper-right corner of your screen.

Adding active desktop elements

Often channel Web sites include another easy way for you to download Web content to your PC. On some channel Web sites you may see a second button called Add to Active Desktop. By clicking this button, you can add some piece of information that the channel author thinks you may find handy. Figure I-10 shows the Add to Active Desktop button.

Figure I-10:
Adding
Web
content to
the Active
Desktop.

By adding content to your desktop in this way, you don't often know what you're getting. With news channels, you frequently get a ticker, but other channels have different elements available for you to add to your active desktop. For instance, when you click the Add to Active Desktop button on the National Geographic channel shown here, you receive the cartoon figure shown in Figure I-11. By clicking the Play Game button, you can play a geographic game.

Working with subscriptions

With a subscription, you tell the Internet Explorer Web browser that it should regularly grab content for your PC. Unlike with channels, you can subscribe to any Web site, not just to special channel Web sites. As with channels, though, subscribing to a Web site is free.

Subscribing to a Web page

To add a subscription for a Web page, follow these steps:

1. **Start Internet Explorer.**

2. **Display the Web page to which you want to subscribe.**

Figure I-11:
A desktop
with an
active Web
element.

3. Choose Favorites➪Add to Favorites.

Internet Explorer displays the Add Favorite dialog box (see Figure I-12).

Figure I-12:
You use
the Add
Favorite
dialog
box to
subscribe
to a Web
page.

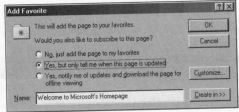

4. Mark the "Yes, notify me of updates and download the page for offline viewing" button to subscribe to the Web page.

You can also mark the "Yes, but only tell me when this page is updated" button if you just want to know when a subscribed-to Web page changes so that you can manually download the Web page. If you do this, Internet Explorer alerts you to a changed Web page by adding a red gleam, or star, to the Web page's icon on your list of subscribed to Web pages.

5. Click OK.

If you indicate that you want to subscribe to a Web page, Internet Explorer automatically downloads a copy of the Web page (assuming the page has changed) every day at midnight.

After you subscribe to a Web page, the Web page gets added to your Favorites bar, as shown in Figure I-13. To access the Web page, follow these simple steps:

1. Click the Favorites button to display the Favorites bar.

2. Click the Web page's button on the Favorites bar.

If you want to specify when Internet Explorer should retrieve a subscribed-to Web page, or to enter your e-mail address to receive notification of changes to the Web page, click the Customize button on the Add Favorite dialog box.

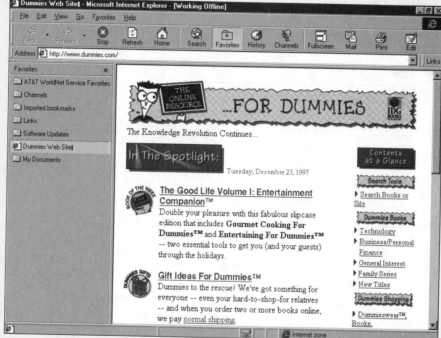

Figure I-13:
Web pages
to which
you
subscribe
appear
on the
Favorites
bar for easy
access.

Managing subscriptions and channels

In order to manually update a subscription or to view the properties of a subscription, you need to display the list of Web pages and channels to which you subscribe. To do so, follow these steps:

1. **Start Internet Explorer.**

2. **Choose Favorites⇨Manage Subscriptions.**

   The Subscriptions window is displayed (see Figure I-14).

   - To update a subscription, select the subscription and click the Update button.

   - To update all of your subscriptions, click the Update All button.

   - To check out the update schedule for a subscription, select the subscription and click the Properties button.

Figure I-14:
The
Subscriptions
window
lists the
Web pages
and
channels
you
subscribe to.

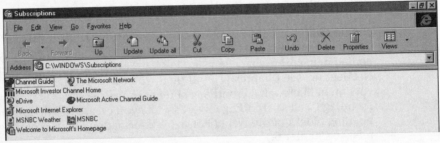

Other Internet Features

I should mention that Windows 98 also provides a handful of other, Internet-
related features. Windows 98 comes with a cool, new e-mail client called
Outlook Express (see Figure I-15). Outlook Express not only lets you read
and send e-mail messages, but it also lets you noodle around with
newsgroups. (For more information about how Outlook Express works, you
can refer to Chapter 7.)

Figure I-15:
Windows 98
comes with
the Outlook
Express 98
e-mail
client and
newsgroup
reader.

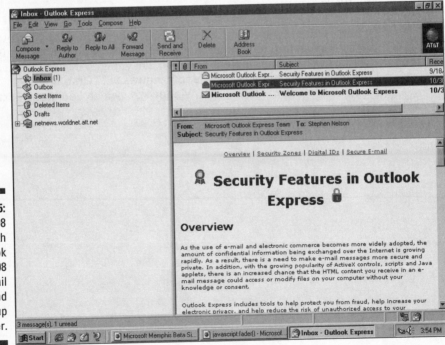

Windows 98 supplies an Internet Connection wizard that makes setting up a Dial-Up Networking connection for some Internet service provider a really easy task. (You have to use a Dial-Up Networking connection in order to connect to the Internet via a modem.) For information on using the Internet Connection wizard, see Chapter 5. Windows 98 also supplies an audio conferencing program called NetMeeting. For information on using NetMeeting, see Chapter 11. And then Windows 98 comes with a "lite" version of Microsoft's FrontPage suite of programs. The "lite" version of FrontPage, called FrontPage Express, lets you create HTML documents, the building blocks of the Web. (For more information about FrontPage Express, refer to Chapter 6.)

Now I should tell you something else. Did you notice how, in the preceding paragraphs, I say stuff like, "For more information about this new feature in Windows 98, refer to this other chapter . . ." That's kind of weird, right? How can this book (which is about Windows 95) contain descriptions of Windows 98 features? The answer is pretty simple. Some of the features that are "new" to Windows 98 are already part and parcel of Internet Explorer 4.0. That means that if you use Internet Explorer (and I made this assumption for Chapters 5, 6, and 7), Windows 98 doesn't really provide additional Web functionality. You already get the extra Web bells and whistles in Internet Explorer 4.0. For example, you can work with active desktops, channels, and subscriptions in Internet Explorer 4.0. You can use Outlook Express in Internet Explorer 4.0; you also get a bunch of other handy programs in Internet Explorer 4.0, including NetMeeting, the Connection wizard, and FrontPage Express.

So now you're saying, "Well, gee, Steve . . . Why upgrade to Windows 98 if I can get its functionality from other places like Internet Explorer 4.0?" My friend, you're asking the right question. I'm going to discuss this later in Chapter III, "Should You Upgrade to Windows 98?" First, however, I need to describe what else is new about Windows 98, which I do in the next chapter.

Chapter II

Other New Doodads

In This Chapter

▶ Exploring Windows 98's new hardware functionality

▶ Taking advantage of easier accessibility customization

▶ Updating your copy of Windows 98

▶ Keeping your computer in shape with ScanDisk and the Registry Checker

▶ Improving performance with the Tune-Up Wizard, a new-and-improved Disk Defragmenter, and FAT32

▶ Having fun and playing games

*W*indows 98 is smarter about the way it works with your computer hardware. (Hardware, as you may know, just refers to things like the circuitry inside your computer box, the monitor, your keyboard, and that old printer you use.) Windows 98 also includes a handful of other features, options, and accessories.

New Hardware Options

Okay, here's the first thing I'll mention: Windows 98 lets you use more than one monitor. This feature may not sound so useful, except remember that Windows 98 (just like its predecessors) lets you run more than one program at the same time. With multiple monitors, you can use one monitor to show one program's program window and another monitor to show another program's program window.

Windows 98 provides a new feature called OnNow that lets Windows start your computer in a few seconds. Earlier versions of Windows, as you may know from painful experience, start up about as quickly as a teenager waking up for high school. Windows 98 also includes some new power management features that reduce your computer's energy consumption. (To make use of these power management features, your computer needs to have the Advanced Power Management (APM) feature or Advanced Configuration and Power Interface (ACPI). These features are most common on laptops, and your computer manufacturer builds these functions right into your computer so that you don't have to do anything with them or worry about them.)

Finally, Windows 98 also provides additional plug-and-play capabilities including support for something called a Universal Serial Bus, or USB. The USB should allow you to more easily connect new hardware devices to your computer.

Note: Plug-and-play means that you don't have to do anything special to get some new hardware device installed and working on your computer. You are supposed to be able to "plug" some new device in and then begin "playing" with it. Plug-and-play existed in Windows 95, but it will work better in Windows 98 (or so Microsoft promises).

Help with Windows Accessibility Settings

If you've been reading elsewhere in this book, you may already know that Windows 95 lets you change the way it works and looks to make things easier for people with specific disabilities. Windows 98 makes these changes easier by including an Accessibility wizard that helps you figure out which changes you want to make and then makes the changes for you.

To use the Accessibility Settings wizard (shown in Figure II-1), follow these steps:

1. **Click Start⇨Programs⇨Accessories⇨Accessibility⇨Accessibility Wizard.**

   Windows 98 starts the Accessibility Settings wizard, which begins by asking about the typesize you find easily readable.

2. **Select the smallest text size you can comfortably read and click Next.**

3. **Select a text option in the next dialog box and click Next.**

4. **Use the check boxes shown in Figure II-2 to describe whether you have special vision, hearing, or mobility needs.**

5. **Click Next to describe these needs in detail and to set up your computer to accommodate your needs.**

   The wizard displays dialog boxes that you can use to answer the information it needs. These dialog boxes differ depending on the accessibility option you selected. Just continue to answer questions and click Next to move through the remainder of the interview.

Figure II-1:
The Windows 98 Accessibility Wizard lets you fine-tune Windows Accessibility options so that Windows works in the best possible way for someone who is disabled.

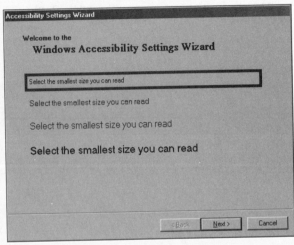

Figure II-2:
The Windows 98 Accessibility Wizard allows you to set several options for different special needs.

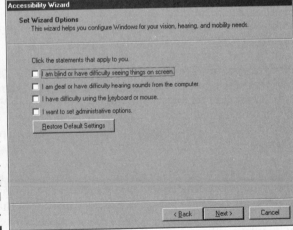

Windows 98 also includes a new accessibility accessory called Microsoft Magnifier. The magnifier shortens open windows and adds a magnified view pane at the top of your screen. When you move your mouse over an area of your screen, the magnifier displays this area in the magnified pane, as shown in Figure II-3. To use Microsoft Magnifier, you must first install the

Enhanced Accessibility options (you install this accessory, and all other Windows 98 accessories, the same way you install Windows 95 accessories, as described in Chapter 11). To start Microsoft Magnifier, click Start⇨Programs⇨Accessories⇨Accessibility⇨Microsoft Magnifier.

Figure II-3:
Using
Microsoft
Magnifier to
magnify a
part of the
screen.

A Kinder, Gentler Help

In Windows 98, Microsoft also beefed up the Help program. While the Windows 98 Help program works in much the same way as the Windows 95 program, Microsoft has made Help prettier (see Figure II-4). The new Help program also lets you rather easily access information from the Microsoft support Web site. (This feature is handy when you can't get an answer from Help but think you may be able to get more or different information from Microsoft's Web site.)

The Windows 98 Help window, like the Help window in Windows 95, provides Contents, Index, and Search tabs. And these work in the same way that the Contents, Index, and Find tabs work in Windows 95. Windows 98 differs from Windows 95 in that it provides the panel of help information on the right side of the window. The Help program uses this panel to display its help information.

By the way, to retrieve Help information by using the World Wide Web, click the Web Help button so that Help displays the Windows Update Product Assistance information in the Help panel. Then click the button that shows in the panel. When you do, Windows 98 starts Internet Explorer, connects to the Internet, and displays a Web page with Windows 98 help information (see Figure II-5).

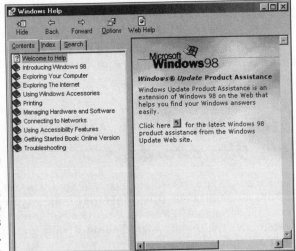

Figure II-4:
In Windows 98, the Help program is prettier.

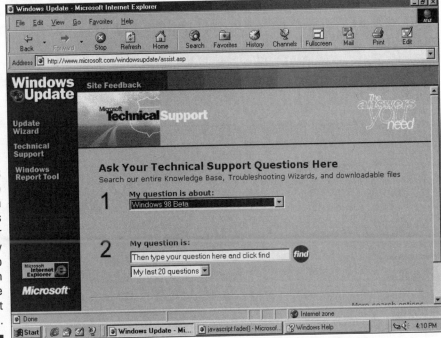

Figure II-5:
The Windows 98 Help program also lets you rather easily grab help information from the Microsoft Web site.

Reliability Is Good

Windows 98 includes some tools to make it more reliable, including an Update wizard, a new-and-improved ScanDisk program, and a Registry Checker.

The Update wizard keeps your copy of Windows 98 up-to-date

Windows 98 supplies an Update wizard, for example, that lets you grab updated versions of system files and other operating system junk from the Microsoft Web site. (For example, if Microsoft posts a Windows bug fix on its Web site, you can have the Update wizard automatically grab the fix.) To use the Update wizard, follow these steps:

1. **Click Start⇨Windows Update.**

   Windows launches Internet Explorer and prompts you to log on to your Internet service provider if you're not currently connected to the Internet.

   If you want a little up-front information, you can start the Help program and use the Index tab to look up the Update wizard topic. Then, when Help displays this information in its panel (see Figure II-6), you can click the Update wizard button.

2. **Click the Update Wizard hyperlink shown in Figure II-7.**

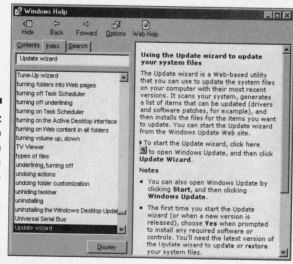

Figure II-6: One way to get to the Update wizard is to use the Windows 98 Help program.

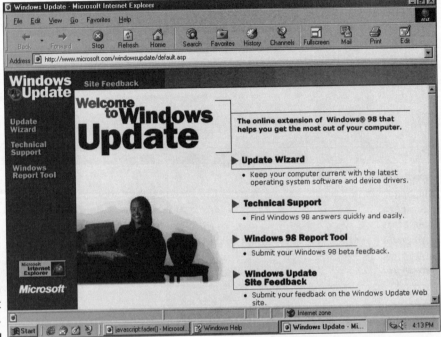

Figure II-7:
The Update wizard opens the Windows Update home page in Internet Explorer.

3. **Click the Update hyperlink to add updated software and patches to your version of Windows 98.**

   The Update wizard scans your computer to see what software versions and updates you already have installed and then lists the updates available to you.

   If you previously updated Windows 98 and want to go back to your old settings, click Restore to remove the update.

4. **Select an update from the list to read a description of the update, as shown in Figure II-8.**

5. **Click install to install the update.**

ScanDisk is now more persistent

With Windows 98, the ScanDisk program (described in Chapter 13) runs automatically whenever something or someone shuts down your computer the wrong way. ScanDisk checks your computer for errors and attempts to fix any errors it finds. In Windows 95, you need to run ScanDisk manually. You can still do so in Windows 98, but ScanDisk also runs automatically whenever Windows has reason to believe that your computer may have errors.

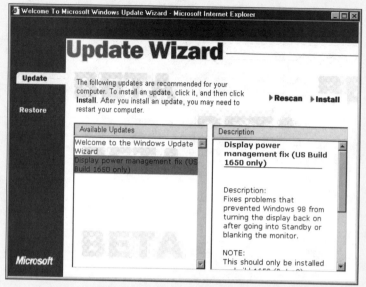

System file and register checking is obsessive but useful

Windows 98 has some other little reliability features that you don't care about but that I still need to mention on account of my compulsive personality. A *system file checker* monitors *critical system files* and fixes them if they get misplaced or corrupted. (A critical system file is just a file that your computer needs to run safely or smoothly.) A *registry checker* monitors the Windows registry and fixes problems as they occur. (The Windows registry holds all sorts of important information about applications, users, and hardware that Windows references as it performs different operations.) And I should mention, too, that Windows 98 supplies a new backup and restore program.

Even though Windows 98 includes a new backup and restore program, I still think that in a small business environment, just copying files to a removable storage device is easiest.

The Speed Angle

Windows 98 includes three new performance features: a Tune-Up wizard, FAT32, and a better Disk Defragmenter. If you've read this far, you're probably really interested in this stuff, so, let me tell you about how these three, new features work.

The Tune-Up wizard works like a good car mechanic

The Tune-Up wizard, in a nutshell, simply schedules times to run the ScanDisk and Disk Defragmenter system management tools (which are described in Chapter 13), and it cleans up your hard disk by removing unnecessary files from your disk. To use the Tune-Up wizard, follow these steps:

1. **Click Start⇨Programs⇨Accessories⇨System Tools⇨Windows Tune-Up.**

   Windows starts the Windows Tune-Up wizard (see Figure II-9).

2. **Choose the Express or Custom installation and click Next.**

   If you choose a custom installation, you can decide which services you want the Tune-Up wizard to perform during the tune-up.

3. **Choose the time of day you want the tune-up to take place (see Figure II-10) and click Next.**

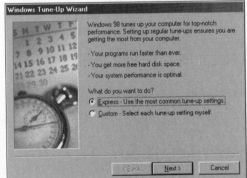

Figure II-9:
The Tune-Up wizard.

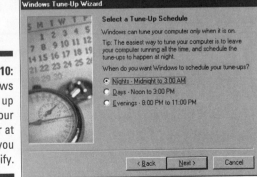

Figure II-10:
Windows tunes up your computer at the time you specify.

You're better off to perform the tune-up when you are not working at your computer. That way, the tune-up does not slow or cause problems with your work.

4. Review the services the Tune-Up wizard will perform and click Finish.

Disk Defragmenter works better than before

While the predecessors to Windows 98 supplied a version of the Disk Defragmenter utility, Windows 98 supplies a new, smarter version of Disk Defragmenter (see Figure II-11). This new and improved version can make your programs start faster because it's smarter about the way it arranges program files on your hard disk. (For more information about Disk Defragmenter, you can refer to Chapter 13.)

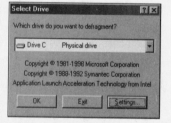

Figure II-11: Windows 98 comes with a new and improved Disk Defragmenter utility.

FAT32 is not an industrial rock music group

Windows 98 uses a new file allocation table, or FAT. This new FAT, called FAT32, lets you work with bigger hard disks (so that's good, of course) and it wastes less space (for reasons I don't need to go into).

To convert your disk to the FAT file system you run the Drive Converter wizard. To do so, follow these steps:

1. Click Start⇨Programs⇨Accessories⇨Drive Converter.

The first dialog box of the Drive Converter wizard, as shown in Figure II-12, is displayed.

2. Click Next to continue.

3. Select the drive you want to convert to the FAT file system, as shown in Figure II-13, and click Next.

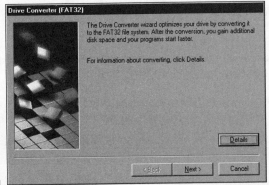

Figure II-12:
The Drive
Converter.

Figure II-13:
Converting
a hard drive
to FAT.

4. **Click Create Backup to use Microsoft Backup to create backups of
   your files before converting your disk.**

   If you don't use Microsoft Backup, that's fine. Just click Cancel, back up
   your files to another disk, and then restart the Drive Converter.

5. **Click Next twice to begin converting your disk.**

Trivia, anyone?

Here are two bits of interesting technology trivia. First, the FAT is a linked-list table used by the operating system. The FAT is used, along with the file directory, to determine what files you've stored on your hard disk as well as their physical locations. (Now you know what a FAT is.) Second, Bill Gates was the one who, reportedly, did the programming for the original FAT that was part of MS-DOS, the predecessor to Windows 95. Kind of neat, huh?

Esoteric hardware support improvements

In addition to all the stuff I talk about elsewhere in this section, Windows 98 also includes support for a bunch of recent hardware improvements. I'm just going to quickly list this stuff in laundry-list fashion:

- ✓ IEEE 1394 (also known as "Firewire") represents a new hardware standard that lets you add high speed serial devices to your computer.

- ✓ Accelerated Graphics Port (also known as "AGP") lets people work with three-dimensional animation.

- ✓ DVD Player lets you connect a DVD drive to your computer and then play DVD disks. (DVD stands for digital video disc, a new type of storage medium that looks like a CD-ROM but can hold much more data and is very high-quality.)

- ✓ TV Viewer lets you install a TV tuner card in your computer so you can receive and display television transmissions. Your coworkers will love this one.

- ✓ NetShow lets you receive streaming content from the Internet or an intranet. (Note, however, that NetShow also comes with Internet Explorer 4.0.)

Fun stuff on the CD

The Windows 98 CD includes a bunch of extras, including video clips you can play to preview software and a handful of trial programs you can install and test out before you decide to purchase. When you insert the Windows 98 CD, the Windows 98 CD-ROM window appears, as shown in Figure II-14.

To install trial versions of software, follow these steps:

1. **Click the Interactive CD Sampler Icon.**

   When you do this, Windows asks if you want to install some files. They don't take up much room, so unless you're really crunched for space, go ahead and install them. After you install them, Windows plays the welcome video.

2. **Click a category icon to preview Microsoft software in that category or click the Install Software button to install trial versions of software programs included on the CD.**

   When you click the Install Software button, Windows displays the dialog box shown in Figure II-15.

Click to play preview videos of software products ⌐

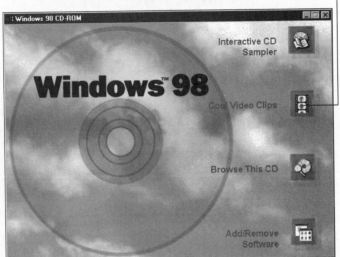

Figure II-14:
The
Windows 98
CD-ROM
window.

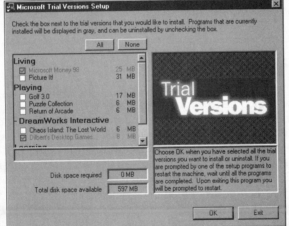

Figure II-15:
Installing
trial
versions of
software.

3. Check the program you want to install.

4. Click OK.

After you have the programs you want installed, play away! Just don't let
your coworkers catch you!

Chapter III

Should You Upgrade to Windows 98?

• •

In This Chapter

▶ Upgrading to Windows 98: A cost-benefit analysis

▶ Looking to the future

• •

1f you're currently using Windows 95 and (ignoring all the hand-wringing in the previous chapter) you get the chance to upgrade to Windows 98, I'm not exactly sure what you should do.

My Gut Feeling

I always encourage people to upgrade just to stay current. Besides, the Web integration stuff in Windows 98 is good, and the grab bag of technical improvements that Windows 98 provides seems pretty reasonable. The upgrade probably won't cost all that much either — around $75 bucks a machine, I'm guessing — so I'll upgrade the half a dozen computers that we use in my small business. (I view upgrading my operating system as essentially equivalent to getting my car's oil changed.)

To be really honest, however, I question my objectivity in this matter. I mean, I'm a computer book writer who makes his living writing books about new software. So maybe I'm just a little too accepting of the Microsoft party line. Is the Web integration and better system management stuff really worth $75 a machine? It's a fair question.

I'll tell you what I heard one well-known industry observer say over lunch a few weeks ago. This guy, whose columns you've probably read, said that Windows 98 is a total joke. His point was that if you already had Internet Explorer 4.0, you don't get anything of real additional value by upgrading to Windows 98. This unnamed observer also, as I remember it, pointed out that buying a new operating system is ridiculous because it supports hardware that doesn't yet exist. (I may be wrong about this last part, however, inasmuch as I got into some trouble with a curry dish midpoint through the lunch.)

You May Want to Wait for Windows NT 5.0

Windows NT 5.0 represents the next version of the NT operating system, the big brother to Windows 95 and Windows 98. Because the drums in the distance are already banging out rumors, another question related to upgrading to Windows 98 is this: Why not just wait for Windows NT 5.0? So let me talk about this briefly.

NT works really well, and it bears a striking resemblance to Windows 95 and 98, as shown in Figure III-1, which makes moving over to NT a comfortable switch. Working with programs in NT is also just as easy as it is Windows 95 and 98, as you can see in Figure III-2.

Figure III-1:
The
Windows
NT 4.0
desktop
with the
Start menu
showing.
Do you
see a
difference?

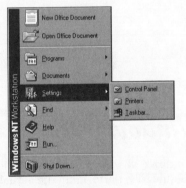

But that much said, I should add that NT isn't really a better version of Windows. NT is for people concerned about security and safety. Although these are good things — who can argue against security and safety — NT complicates your computing environment. All of the big, strong, powerful features that let NT closely watch over your computer and its information also make your computing more complex.

For these reasons, I don't think that you should view NT 5.0 or NT 4.0 (which is available right now) as the better choice. That would be like saying that a big truck is better than a sports car. Sometimes NT (which rather resembles a big truck) works best. And sometimes a leaner operating system like Windows 95 or Windows 98 (which work more like a sports car) works best.

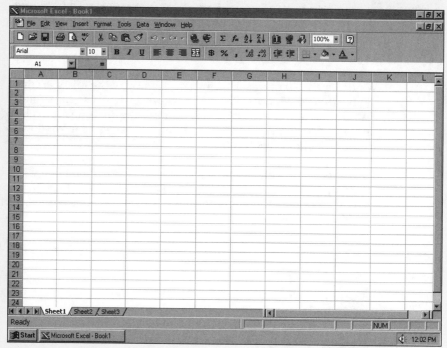

Figure III-2:
Working
with
Excel in
Windows NT.

How to Upgrade to Windows 98

If you do choose to upgrade to Windows 98, you may have questions about how you upgrade the software. Fortunately, performing the actual upgrade is really easy. You stick the CD into the your computer's CD drive — when you do, Windows starts up the Upgrade program — and then you follow the on-screen instructions (see Figure III-3).

Note: The Windows 98 installation, or set up, program is smart. For this reason, you actually don't need to make any decisions as you install the new operating system software. You can just accept Windows' suggestions.

Figure III-3:
If you can
click a
mouse and
read, you'll
have no
problem
upgrading to
Windows 98.

Chapter 9

Small Networks for Small Businesses

The first thing you need to know about this network stuff is that it ain't rocket science. No way. Setting up a small Windows network — despite those horror stories fellow Rotarians may share — doesn't have to hurt like a root canal. With the information that this chapter provides, you can network your office's Windows computers in about two hours. You need to read this chapter (I figure that'll take a leisurely half-hour). You need to call a mail-order computer supplies store and order some gear (I figure that'll take, like, five minutes). Then you need to install the gear (an hour tops) and tell Windows about the gear (five minutes a computer).

The point is, networks don't have to be super-complicated. Some are, but others (the ones this chapter talks about setting up) are actually quite simple. You can make setting up a network nice and easy and, well, maybe even fun.

But let me tell you one last thing — just so you realize the general tone of the following discussion. I am not some sort of super-mechanical handyman (much to my wife's disappointment). I barely know how to use a screwdriver. So when you hear me say this stuff is easy as long as you take your time, you can be assured, it really is easy. I don't mean that it's easy for me because I'm smart and like to show off. (I bet you know someone like that, though, don't you?) I don't mean that it's easy if you have an electrical engineering degree from a major university (I don't). And I don't mean that it's easy as long as you spend forty hours on preparation (that would stink). I just mean that it's easy. Like making a pot of coffee.

Exploring Networking: A One-Minute Lesson

Before you roll up your sleeves, I want to give you a birds-eye view of the whole networking thing. You should understand four things:

- ✔ What a network is
- ✔ Why people network
- ✔ What types, or flavors, of networks you can set up
- ✔ What sort of network I'm suggesting and describing you set up

First things first

Okay, so what's a network? A network is just a group of computers that are connected. So, for example, if you have six computers in your office and they aren't connected, you don't own a network. If they are connected — somebody's cabled them together so they can communicate with other — you do own a network.

I just want to know why

This "networked just means connected" business rather naturally leads to the question, Why do people (and businesses, in particular) network? People network for two basic reasons: so they can more easily share information and so they can share gear like printers and disk drives.

Neither of these reasons is tricky. But just so you're sure to understand, the information-sharing bit just means that if the computers in your office are networked, Julie can easily send information to Joe. All she has to do is move a document from her computer's disk to Joe's computer's disk. Or, she can tell Joe to move the document himself.

Note: Once you have a network set up, you move documents over the network in the same way you move documents around on a computer. I talk about how this works on a standalone computer in Chapter 2. I talk about how this works on a network in Chapter 10.

The gear-sharing part is even easier. If you have a network set up, you and anybody else in the office can share things like printers and disk drives. So, Julie can print a document (from her computer) by using the printer that's actually plugged into Joe's computer and vice versa.

I want to stop here for a minute and make a clarification. Obviously, you can still share printers and share documents even if you don't have a network. For example, if you want to give some document to a coworker like Julie, you can save the document to a floppy disk and then give Julie the floppy. If somebody wants to print some document on your computer (assuming you have the right program), he can put the document on a floppy disk, come into your office, and borrow both your computer and printer (perhaps while you're off at lunch). But this kind of information and gear sharing is a hassle. When you share information and gear in these ways, you use your most expensive resource (people) and a rinky-dink media (floppy disks) in a really disruptive fashion.

You know how this story goes, right? Akmed comes into your office, right as you're getting ready to do some moderately important thing and says, "Hey Bob? I gotta print a big report on your machine. Sorry, but I really need to do it right now. It's for Mr. Big."

Network flavors

If you understand the first preceding two points — what networks are and why people network — you now know the important, big picture stuff. You should also be able to figure out whether you need a network by asking the business question, "Do we, for business reasons, need to share information and gear?"

If you answer this question affirmatively — and I'm assuming that you will — you next need to know that networks come in two basic flavors: peer-to-peer networks and client-server networks. Usually, people's eyes glaze over when they hear these terms, but they really aren't complicated, so let me explain.

In a *peer-to-peer network,* you take everybody's computer and cable them all together. That's it. In this situation, then, the network simply makes it easier to do all the same things you've already been doing. You don't gain any new functionality with the network. All you really get is new plumbing that you can use to pump information from one computer to another. (The individual computers in a peer-to-peer network all do the same work, which is why they're peers.)

In a *client-server network,* you also take everybody's computer and cable them all together. But — and here's the difference — you also typically stick some new, bigger computers into the network and then have these new computers do special network stuff. You may, for example, add a new computer, get the new computer a really big, super-fast printer, and then have everybody print to this new computer's really big, super-fast printer. And you may get a new computer with a monstrously large and awesomely fast hard disk and then let people share disk space on this computer.

In a client-server network, then, you have two types of computers: worker-bee computers, which people like you and me and our coworkers sit in front and do stuff with, and network-workhorse computers, which everybody uses to pawn off work to. The worker-bee computers are called clients and the network-workhorse computers are called servers. (The name client-server comes from the fact that the worker-bee computers — the clients — request the network-workhorse computers — the servers — to do stuff like print documents and save or open files.)

As they're presented here, both peer-to-peer networks and client-server networks are *LANs,* or *local area networks.* That just means that the computers you're networking are all in the same office. With the help of a good network consultant, you can also create networks that stretch beyond the walls of your office, shop, or factory. You'll hear people use other acronyms to describe these larger networks such as WAN for wide area network and MAN for metropolitan area network.

So where does that leave you?

You hear most about client-server networks, but if you haven't yet set up a network, you don't want to jump into the client-server thing as your first network experience. Oh sure, computer consultants love client-server networks because their customers always need help setting up and maintaining them. Software companies love client-server networks because in a client-server network, they frequently can sell you additional (and often expensive) software and support services. But their enthusiasm should give you a clue: You don't want to set up a client-server network as your first network. No way. What you want to do is set up a peer-to-peer network. So that's what this chapter describes how to do.

Getting the Gear You Need

Now for the exciting part of setting up a network. This is the part where you call some mail-order, computer-supplies company, order the gear you need, and thereby earn frequent-flier miles because you have an airlines credit card.

Before you do this, however, you need to make a quick decision. You need to choose what's called a *network medium.* (This term just means that you have to pick the method you're going to use to cable the computers together.) You have two choices:

> ✔ **You can use coaxial cable and barrel-nut, or BNC, connectors.** I use this method partly because I like coaxial cable's durability, but also because the first time I networked, I only networked two computers and I liked the simplicity of coaxial cable.

Going the client-server route

You can very easily turn a peer-to-peer network into a small client-server network. For example, to add a print server (so that people can share a high-powered but very-expensive printer), you can set everything up exactly as described in the next part of this chapter just by pretending the print server is another peer. Then, you can direct everybody to use the new peer for printing. In this case, the network views the new computer and its printer as just a regular old peer and printer. But you use the peer like it's a server.

If you want to go hog wild and use special client-server software (such as Microsoft's BackOffice), you can do that, too. But in this case, what you first need to do is acquire a new, Windows NT computer, set it up as a server (you'll need the NT Server version of the NT operating system), and then set up a simple NT network. You can try doing this yourself by following Microsoft's instructions. And then, if that doesn't work or you get discouraged (and you probably will) you can just pay $200 or whatever to some network consultant.

Note: Microsoft sells a special version of its BackOffice products especially for small business. This special version of BackOffice is called, cleverly, Small Business BackOffice; Small Business BackOffice includes a "lite" version of the Windows NT server software, Internet Information Server (so you can set up a Web server), Exchange Server (so you can set up an internal e-mail system), SQL Server (so you can set up a client-server database system), and a bunch of other, really complicated stuff as well.

✔ **You can use untwisted pair, or UTP, cable and a network hub, or star.** Most consultants probably tell you to use this method because UTP cable (which is like the cable that your office telephone uses) is cheaper than coaxial cable and because a hub reduces the chance that your network will break. (In a coaxial cable network, if one link of the coaxial cabling breaks, the computers on either side of the break can't communicate. In a UTP cable network, if one of the UTP cables breaks, only that computer goes incommunicado.)

Just so you understand the difference between these two network media, take a peek at Figure 9-1. In the coaxial cable with BNC connectors network, you just connect the computers to each other. In the UTP cable with hub network, you connect the computers to the hub. You need to pick one of these media. (If you can't choose with the information I've already provided, just go with coaxial cable.) Once you select a network medium, call your favorite mail-order place and order your gear.

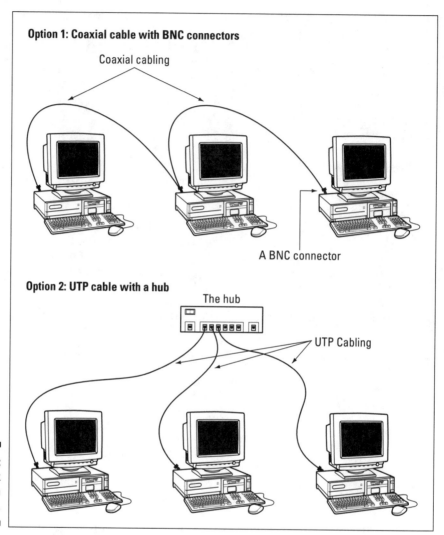

Option 1: Coaxial cable with BNC connectors

Coaxial cabling

A BNC connector

Option 2: UTP cable with a hub

The hub

UTP Cabling

Figure 9-1:
Network
medium on
a napkin.

No matter which medium you choose, you need network cards for each of your computers. The most popular cards are 10 Mbps 16-bit Ethernet adapters. But if you just say, "I need network cards for my Windows 95 PCs," the salesperson at the computer store will know what you're asking for. I don't think it particularly matters which brand you pick. I'd probably go with somebody you've heard of before: Intel, 3Com, or somebody like that. You're not paying all that much anyway (probably less than $100 each). The only really important thing you want to do is make sure that you get network cards that are Windows 95 or Windows 98 plug-and-play compatible. (You want plug-and-play gear because then all you have to do is plop them into your PC.)

Because you're buying multiple network cards, you should ask about a quantity discount. You may just receive a price break for buying five or ten units at a time.

You also need a handful of additional items, depending on the medium you select. If you've selected coaxial cable, you need the following the things:

- ✔ A piece of appropriate-length network coaxial cabling to connect your computers to each other. If you have six computers, for example, you need five pieces of cabling. (The cables need to be long enough to reach from one computer to the next computer.) You can purchase this ready-to-go at a computer or network supply shop.
- ✔ 1 "T"-shaped barrel connector for each network card.
- ✔ 2 BNC terminators.

If you've selected UTP cable, you need the following two items:

- ✔ A hub with an appropriate number of connection sockets.
- ✔ One piece of appropriate-length UTP cabling for each computer so you connect the computer to the hub. (The cable needs to be long enough to reach from the computer to the hub.)

You can go ahead and order this stuff when you order your network cards. Or, if you really want to save some money you may be able to shave a little off the price of the cabling by running down to some electrical or networking supply store.

You can actually buy your network cards at some local computer supplies store, too. The only reason I'm suggesting that you order something through the mail is that the mail-order method means you only have to make a five-minute telephone call. And that's important to me because I'm trying to get you networked with less than a couple of hours of your time. Sure, you can decide instead to drive across town to the local discount computer supplies place. But then you'll spend time in traffic, have to wait around for help from some sales clerk who really wants to be in a blues band, and stop for coffee on the way back. All totaled, you're going to spend an hour or more on the trip (at least you will if you live in Seattle like I do), and then you're going to feel that I lied to you because I promised the whole process would only take two hours. You see my dilemma.

Making the Hardware Connection

After you get all the gear you need, you need to install the network cards and then connect the cabling. I know you're expecting this part — I mean, hey, it's a major chapter section — to be really big, but this stuff is pretty easy.

You need to follow the manufacturer instructions for installing the network card. The lawyers say I have to tell you this. Don't, for example, do what I do. Don't just disconnect the power, pull the cover off your computer, and then plug the networking card into a slot on your motherboard. By the way, I figure the first network card that you install will take you, hmmm, maybe forty-five minutes. (Sorry.) But if you have an electric screwdriver, the next ones will all take about five minutes a piece. No kidding.

Once you get the network cards installed, the hard part is done. All that's left is the cabling.

If you choose coaxial cabling, you need to connect your "T" connectors to the sockets on the backs of the network cards. (You'll see how this works — they kind of twist on and then click.) Then you need to begin connecting the computers with the cable. First you connect computer 1 to computer 2. Then you connect computer 2 to computer 3, and so on. (The cabling you use will have the BNC connectors that connect to the "T" connectors.) When you use up all your cabling, you're left with two open, or unused "T" connector sockets: one on your first computer in the line and one on your last computer in the line. So the last step is to plug these "holes" by connecting your terminators to the open "T" connector sockets. This all sounds really complicated, but take a look at Figure 9-2 once you get your gear. I really think that you'll have no difficulty figuring how this the stuff plugs together.

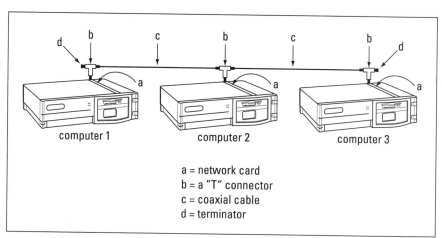

Figure 9-2: Notice how I've deftly avoided the always awkward discussion of female and male connectors.

a = network card
b = a "T" connector
c = coaxial cable
d = terminator

If you choose the UTP cabling, you set up the hub (following any special instructions provided by the manufacturer) and then you start plugging in cables. Take the first UTP cable and plug one end into Computer 1's network card and then the other end into the hub. Then you take another piece of UTP cable and do the same thing for Computer 2. And then you move on to Computer 3.

After you get the cabling done, you're almost there. All that's left is to tell Windows that you want people to be able to work together as a network, which I describe next.

Note: You can add new computers to the network. To add a new computer, you just need to connect it to the other computers by using the same cabling. For example, if you have three computers connected with coaxial cable and you want to add a fourth, just remove the terminator from Computer 3's "T" connector, and then cable in Computer 4. (Remember to put the terminator on the empty "T" socket you now have on Computer 4.) If you want to add a new computer to a network you've built with UTP cable and a hub, you just get a new piece of UTP wire and then use it to cable in the new computer.

Telling Windows About the New Network

After you get the network cabling work done, you're ready to tell Windows about the new network. And shortly after that, well, it'll be Miller time. But don't start thinking about that yet — you still need to get the network up and running.

You want to do just three things to get the network up and running:

- ✔ Verify that Windows sees that new network card you installed.
- ✔ Name the network, or what Windows calls a *workgroup,* and each computer in the network.
- ✔ Choose a protocol for the network.

Verify that the whole plug-n-play thing worked

To verify that Windows sees the network card you just installed — in particular, to verify that Windows *correctly* sees the network card you just installed — click Start⇨Programs⇨Settings⇨Control Panel. When Windows displays the Control Panel window, double-click its System tool. When Windows displays the System Properties dialog box (see Figure 9-3), here's what you do:

1. **Click the Device Manager tab.**

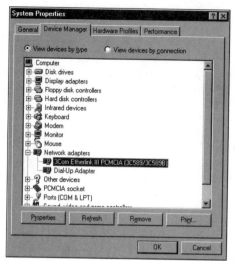

Figure 9-3:
The System
Properties
dialog box.

2. **Expand the Network adapters branch of the device diagram.**

3. **Confirm that one of the network adapters shown is the network card you just added.**

   As long as you see your network card listed here correctly, you know that everything is working correctly. (*Note:* You'll also see a Dial-Up Adapter listed as a Network adapter. That's okay. When you tell Windows you want to connect to the Internet, it starts treating your modem as just another network connection device.) If everything is okay at this point, you're done verifying the network card. And you don't need to do anything further, so just skip Steps 4 and 5.

4. **Optionally, if you don't see your network adapter but you see another network adapter — the wrong one listed — click it and then the Remove button. Or, if you see your network card but a bold, red exclamation point is placed over the top of the network card name, click it and then the Remove button.**

   Then cross your fingers and restart your machine. What's happened in either of these cases, by the way, is that Windows, either today or sometime in the past, has broken the promise of plug-and-play. And now it's all confused and befuddled. Your only hope in this case is to start over from scratch with a clean slate. After Windows restarts, repeat Steps 1 through 3. If everything seems okay after you complete Step 3, you're done. If you have the same problem, proceed to Step 5.

5. Call the network card's technical support number.

I should warn you that if you get to this step, you may not finish this little project in two hours unless the technical support specialist answers the phone quickly and knows what he's doing. Tell the technical support specialist what you've done so far and ask where you went wrong. The only tip I have for you if you get to this step is that you not let the technical specialist off the phone until you have your answer. For example, if he wants you to pull the network card out and then replug it in (he'll probably ask you to do this first, in fact), tell him it'll only a take a second (not a minute, a second) and then do it while he's still on the telephone.

Setting Windows straight

If you know your network cards are working right, you next need to tell Windows it's supposed to network. To do so, you need to set up a client (this is just the computer), choose a protocol, name the client, and then activate file and print sharing. To do all of this, follow these steps:

1. **Click Start⇨Programs⇨Settings⇨Control Panel.**

2. **When Windows displays the Control Panel folder, double-click the Network tool.**

   Windows displays the rather scary looking dialog box shown in Figure 9-4.

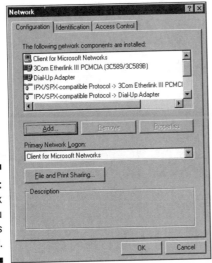

Figure 9-4:
Don't freak when you see this dialog box.

3. Click the Add button.

Windows redisplays the Select Network Component Type dialog box (see Figure 9-5).

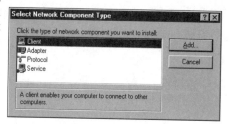

Figure 9-5:
You use the Select Network Component Type dialog box to tell Windows what piece of the networking puzzle you want to add next.

4. Click Client and then Add.

Windows displays the Select Network Client dialog box (see Figure 9-6).

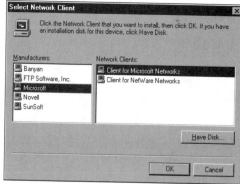

Figure 9-6:
The Select Network Client dialog box is easy to use. You just click a couple of times.

5. Click Microsoft in the Manufacturers list box; click Client for Microsoft Networks in the Network Clients list box; and then click OK.

6. Click the Add button.

Windows displays the Select Network Component Type dialog box (see Figure 9-5).

7. Click Protocol and then Add.

Windows displays the Select Network Protocol dialog box (see Figure 9-7).

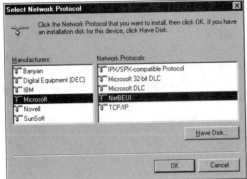

Figure 9-7:
The Select
Network
Protocol
dialog box.

8. Click Microsoft in the Manufacturers list box; click NetBEUI in the Network Protocols list box; and then click OK.

Congratulations, you're done with the hardest part.

9. Click the Network Properties dialog box's Identification tab.

Windows displays the not-so-scary looking dialog box shown in Figure 9-8.

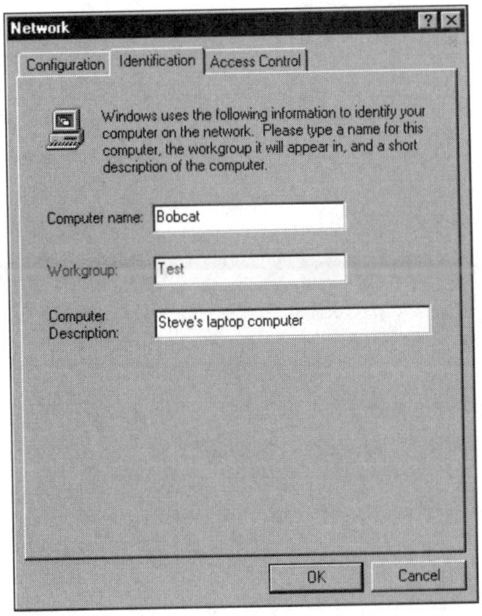

Figure 9-8:
The
Identification
tab lets you
name the
computer
and identify
the
workgroup.

10. Give the computer a name by entering something clever into the Computer name box.

Use something short but memorable. (My editor, who perhaps is a bit of a worrier, wants me to suggest that you don't get too esoteric here. And that's probably a good idea.)

11. Give the network a name by entering something clever into the Workgroup box.

By the way, whatever you enter as the first computer's workgroup name needs to be the same thing you use for the subsequent workgroup names.

12. Click the Configuration tab and then its File and Print Sharing button.

When Windows displays the File and Print Sharing dialog box (see Figure 9-9), check both boxes, and then click OK.

Figure 9-9:
The File and Print Sharing dialog box lets you tell Windows that you're networking so you can share information and gear.

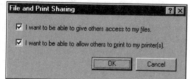

13. Click OK to close the Network Properties dialog box.

When Windows asks whether you want to restart the machine, click the Yes button.

And that's it. You just repeat these steps for each of your computers. If you're running short on time or you want to test your understanding of these steps, go ahead and set up the first two or three computers and then verify that the network's working by following the steps in the preceding section.

Protocol is easy

I've always been fascinated with protocol (which has nothing to do with my secret desire to someday be an ambassador to some small, exotic country). Although, let me digress a bit and tell you about my ambassadorship idea. You may yourself be interested. Here's my idea. You make a major contribution to the political party that's going to win the presidential election. (It shouldn't matter which party because I think they both work this way.) When you give the money, you let them know that you want the ambassadorship to, oh, say, Sweden or Uruguay or some other small, interesting country. (Neither you or I have a snowball's chance of getting a really big country like Japan or England or Germany. Those positions go to the heavy hitters.) But anyway, you make this big contribution — maybe $100,000 or even more (I'm still working on where to get the money). When this party wins the election, you get to live someplace cool for four or maybe eight years and learn all sorts of diplomatic protocol. You get a house with domestic staff. You meet real secret agents. And here's the kicker: My guess is that by the time you figure in the pension benefits that you'll probably get, you actually make money if you do this just before you retire.

This ambassadorship thing doesn't have much to do with networking protocol. But, then again, maybe it does. If you do get a diplomatic post, you are going to have to follow all sorts of rules and conventions. You'll need to learn how to address royalty, for example. And you'll probably also need to learn the right way to mingle at a diplomatic party. It works the same way with networked computers. For the computers in your network to be able to work together happily, they need to all use the same protocol — the same set of rules and conventions for sharing information and working together. While you have a variety of protocols you can use — and each has its own pros and cons — in the preceding section I suggest that you use NetBEUI because it's the one that works best for small networks. (Small in this sense means something less than, say, 200 computers.)

Testing, 1, 2, 3, testing, 1, 2, 3

Once you tell Windows about your new network, you need to test the network to make sure that it's ready to go. To do so, double-click the Network Neighborhood icon that appears on the Windows desktop. When the Network Neighborhood window appears, it should show each of the computers you've added to the network (see Figure 9-10).

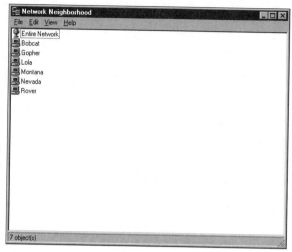

Figure 9-10:
The
Network
Neighborhood
window.

If you double-click the Entire Network icon (which appears in the Network Neighborhood window), Windows opens another window that shows the workgroups you've set up. You can double-click a workgroup to open a window that shows its computers.

Note: In my instructions, I tell you to set up only a single workgroup, but you actually can set up more than one and then use workgroups to sort of segregate computers. (I don't think this practice makes all that much sense, however, so I wouldn't go to the work of doing this.)

If the network isn't set up correctly and you followed the instructions I provided and Windows sees your network cards, your problem almost surely boils down to one of two things:

- ✔ Your cabling is goofed up (particularly common with coaxial cabling because you have all those terminators and "T" connectors to deal with).

- ✔ You didn't restart all your computers after telling Windows about your network.

Now I know that you think the cabling is fine because that's what I always think, too. And I know that you did restart your computers when Windows told you to because that's also what I always think. But even though you're as sure of these two points as you are that the sun rises in the east, what you really should do is physically check all of your cabling again. (Please check every connection even the one you just made two minutes ago.) Then turn off all the computers in the network (so they're all off at the same time) and then turn them all back again.

I know the techniques just described sound crazy. But that low-technology, double-checking approach will probably solve your problems. If it doesn't, your next step should to be use the Help program's Network Trouble-shooter. (To find this aid, start the Help program as described in Chapter 3 and then use the Index or Find tab to search on the terms "Network" or "Troubleshooter.")

As part of writing this chapter and the next one, I set up and then tore down a little network about a dozen times. But the last time I did so, I had terrible trouble and just could not get the network to work. I knew the cabling was okay because I could see the cabling lying on the table in front of me. And I'd tried the "turn everything off" gambit. But, still, I just couldn't get the network up and running. I actually started thinking, "Well, yeah, I've done this a million times before, because maybe that was all just dumb luck. Maybe I'm really just a knucklehead." Anyway, at this point, I'm pretty bummed out and I figure that I better check the cabling again if only because I've been nagging on you to check the cabling and, well, you guess what happened. One of the cables wasn't fully plugged in.

Upgrading to a Client-Server Network

Earlier in the chapter, I suggested that a peer-to-peer network usually works great for a small business. But I pointed out that you can use the precise instructions here for creating simple client-server networks, too. All you have to do is consider all your computers "peers" of the realm. In other words, you treat both clients and servers the same way. What I said was true. But just in case you've done this, let me tell you one other quick thing that I'd like you do to do. Windows fine-tunes the way it operates for machines that principally work as servers if you tell it to. (What it does is way beyond the scope of this book and totally boring but nonetheless still worthwhile.) To make Windows fine-tune a machine's deepest, darkest operations, follow these steps:

1. **Click the Start button and then choose Programs⇨Settings⇨Control Panel.**

   When Windows displays the Control Panel window, double-click its System tool. Windows displays the System Properties dialog box.

2. **Click the Performance tab.**

3. **Click the File System button (which appears on the Performance tab).**

4. **When Windows displays the File System Properties dialog box, activate the drop-down list box that's labeled, "Typical role of this machine," and then select the network server entry.**

5. **Click OK to make your changes and close the File System Properties dialog box.**

6. **Click OK again to close the System Properties dialog box.**

Exploring Remote Access and Virtual Private Networks

The local area network that this chapter describes is pretty simple. A bit of cabling. Some network cards. *Voilà,* you're there.

You should know, however, that you can network with computers that aren't in the same office, shop, or factory. Windows lets you use its Dial-Up Networking feature (that same one that you use to connect to the Internet) to remotely access your network. For example, you can, while sitting at home, connect your laptop to the network at work by using the Dial-Up Networking feature. And by doing so, you can move files back and forth between the lap and the office network.

To remotely access a network, one of the computers in the network either needs to be a Windows NT Server with NT's Remove Access Service feature turned on and working or one of the computers in the network needs to have the Windows 95 Plus Pak Remove Access Service turned on and working. I'm not going to describe how you do this here. But if you have questions — and you already have your local area network working — you can almost certainly figure out how things work by perusing the documentation, getting a bit of help from a network consultant, or by getting one of those big, fat books on Windows networks.

While I'm on the subject of remote network access, let me also just mention that you can also create a virtual private network for a Windows network. In essence, a *virtual private network* lets you use the Internet (rather than a telephone line) to connect some remote computer and your local area network. For example, if you're traveling in Europe, you can connect to the Internet (perhaps through a Parisian Internet service provider) and then use the Internet to connect to your LAN back in the home office. The thing that makes a virtual private network neat (and the reason it's private) is that even though you use the Internet to make the connection, all of the transmissions that occur over the Internet are *encrypted.* That means that people can't intercept and read your transmissions.

I actually don't think you should worry or think about remote access or virtual private networks — at least not for a while. So I'm not going to say more about them here. Do remember, however, that they're possibilities. Sometime in the future (probably after you've made the move to a client-server network) you'll want to also consider adding this feature to your network, because then, my friend, you'll be in the big leagues.

For more on building and maintaining more complicated networks, check out *Small Business Networking For Dummies,* by Glenn Weadock (IDG Books Worldwide, Inc.).

Chapter 10

Working with a Small Network

*R*oughly 95 percent of small businesses aren't networked. And you? Well, if you've networked your computers, or read through the instructions on how to do so in Chapter 9, you're part of the 5 percent that's realized sharing information and gear by using a network is good business. But I suppose that's enough self-congratulation. You're ready to move on to the real work of networking.

A peer-to-peer network, after you get it set up (see Chapter 9 for more information), is really easy to use. But just so everything starts out smoothly and you don't let some unanswered question get in the way of things, this chapter explains what you need to know about working on a network.

Getting Started

To start up your network (after you do everything described in Chapter 9), you just turn all the computers back on. If you have printers that you want to use, turn them on, too. At this point, people can begin using the network.

If you want to use the network, log on. Logging on just means that you identify yourself to Windows by giving your name and password. Okay. Now here's the weird part: You can use any name you want. And, the first time you use a name, you can specify any password you want. Windows just memorizes the name-and-password combination and then, in the future, to use the name you must supply the password associated with the name. You, therefore, also need to memorize the name and password you enter. Pay close attention, because you must enter your name and password exactly the same way each time, and little things matter. For example, if you use all uppercase letters the very first time you enter your name and password, you must use all uppercase letters each subsequent time.

Unfortunately, I can't show you the logon dialog box — the one that asks for your name and password — because Windows doesn't let people take pictures of this dialog box. But what the dialog box does is simple. It supplies a Name text box (into which you enter your name) and a Password text box (into which you enter your password).

I need to make one final comment about this logging on business. Someone doesn't actually have to log on. She turns on the computer and then, when she sees the logon dialog box, clicks its Cancel button. At this point, someone can use the computer (although sometimes not the network) even though she hasn't logged on. So this logging on business isn't really a security thing. It's more like those guest books you sign when you visit a local museum.

Seeing Who is Who and What is What

You can see which computers are part of the network by double-clicking the Network Neighborhood icon. When you do, Windows displays a window that looks something like the one shown in Figure 10-1. In Figure 10-1, for example, you see two computers: Bobcat and Felix.

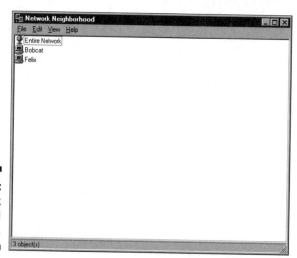

Figure 10-1:
The Network
Neighborhood
window.

Technically, the Network Neighborhood window doesn't show all the computers in a network, only those in a workgroup. If you set up multiple workgroups — and I talk about this a tiny bit in Chapter 9 — you can double-click the Entire Network icon (which appears in the Network Neighborhood window) to see a list of the network workgroups. Then, when this new list appears, you can double-click the workgroup icon to see a list of its computers.

You Gotta Give to Receive

In order for someone to use your computer's printer or to grab documents from your computer's disks, you first need to say that sharing these things is okay. The same thing is true for you: In order for you to use someone else's printer or to grab documents from someone else's disks, he first needs to say that sharing these items is okay. Fortunately, sharing is really easy.

Sharing a printer

To share a local printer, click Start⇨Settings⇨Printers. When Windows displays the Printers folder, right-click the local printer's icon and choose the Sharing command from the shortcuts menu. When Windows displays the Properties dialog box (see Figure 10-2), follow these steps:

1. **Mark the Shared As button.**

2. **Use the Name text box to give the printer a short name that network users can use to refer to the printer.**

   If the printer is a Hewlett Packard Inkjet printer, for example, you may want to call it "HPinkjet."

3. **Use the Password text box if you want to require people who use the printer to know a secret password.**

   If you do enter a password in this text box, Windows prompts you to enter the password a second time just to make sure that you know what you entered the first time.

Remember: Before you can share a printer, you need to add it as a local printer to the Printers folder of the computer to which the printer is connected. After you share a printer, you and others can add the printer as a network printer to the Printers folders of the other computers on the network. As described in Chapter 4, you add local printers and network printers by using the Add Printer wizard, which appears in the Printers folder.

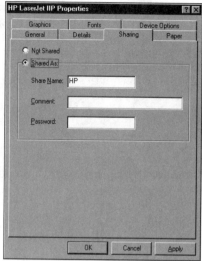

Figure 10-2:
The
Properties
dialog box
you use to
say that
sharing a
printer is
okay.

After you share a printer and other people who want to use the printer add it to their respective Printers folders as a network printer, everybody on the network uses the printer in the usual way. For more information about any of this stuff, refer to Chapter 4.

Sharing a disk or folder

To share a local folder or disk — a hard disk, a floppy disk, or some other more exotic storage device connected to your computer — start Windows Explorer. When Windows Explorer displays the diagram of your computer including all of its storage devices, right-click the folder or disk storage device you want to share and choose Sharing from the shortcut menu. When Windows displays the Sharing tab of the disk or folder's Properties dialog box (as shown in Figure 10-3), follow these steps:

1. **Mark the Shared As button.**

2. **Use the Share Name text box to supply a Share Name that network users can use to refer to the disk or folder.**

    One convention, by the way, suggests that you use the disk's letter. So if you're sharing disk "C," you enter the share name as C. If you're sharing a folder, you can just use the folder's name.

3. **Use the Access Type buttons to specify what people can do with the disk or folder:**

If you want network users to be able to grab documents from the disk or folder so they can read what's in the document but cannot change the original document, mark the Read-Only button.

If you want to let network users do anything, mark the Full button. (With Full access, someone can grab documents, change them, and even delete them.)

If you want to segregate network users into two groups — Read-only users and Full access users — mark the Depends on Password button.

4. **Use the Password text boxes if you want to require people who use the disk or folder to know a secret password.**

You can supply different passwords for Read-only users and Full access users. (If you do enter a password in either of these text boxes, Windows prompts you to enter the password a second time just to make sure that you know what you entered the first time.)

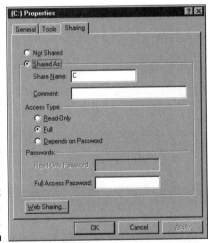

Figure 10-3: The Properties dialog box you use to say that sharing a disk is okay.

This point is probably obvious, but you need to share each of the disks or folders you want people to be able to get to. That means that if you have ten computers and they each have two hard disks that you want to share, you or one of your coworkers needs to go around and share 20 different disks, following the step-by-step instructions I've just provided.

If you share a complete disk, all of the folders, subfolders, and files on that disk are automatically shared. To limit sharing to only certain folders on a disk (which is necessary if you want to keep some files inaccessible to others on the network), you must designate sharing for each of the individual folders you want to share.

Mapping Network Drives

After a disk is shared, you (and anybody else on the network) can connect, or *map,* to the disk drive over the network. Mapping to a network drive is important. Why? Because after you connect, or map, you can use a network drive the same way that you use a local drive. (A local drive is a disk drive that's inside your local computer — the one on your desk or the floor beside your desk.)

To map to a network drive, start Windows Explorer. When Windows Explorer displays the diagram of your computer including all of its storage devices, follow these steps:

1. **Choose Tools⇨Map Network Drive.**

   Windows displays the Map Network Drive dialog box (see Figure 10-4).

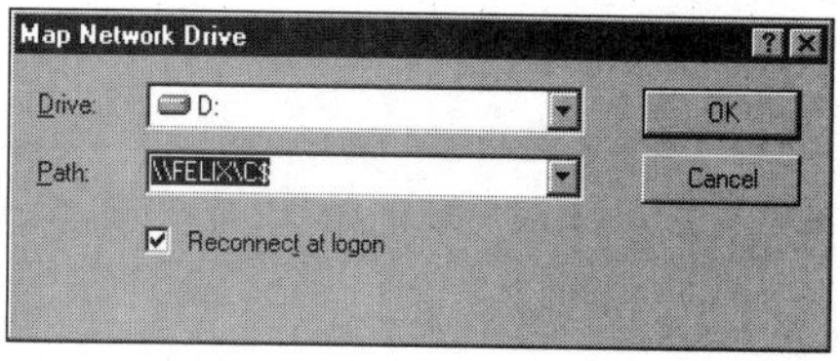

Figure 10-4:
The Map
Network
Drive dialog
box looks
more
complicated
than it is.

2. **You can just accept whatever the Drive drop-down list box shows as the new letter that Windows will use to refer to the network drive, or you can activate the list box and select some other letter.**

   What Windows does, by the way, is just the next letter in the alphabet. If your computer has a "C" drive, it suggests "D" for the next drive's letter. If your computer has a "C" local drive and you've already mapped to a "D" network drive, Windows suggests "E" for the next drive's letter.

3. **Enter the path of the network drive into the Path box by using the form \\COMPUTERNAME\DISKSHARENAME.**

   For example, if the name of the computer that has the disk is felix and that disk's share name is c$, you enter the path \\FELIX\C$

4. **Optionally, if you want Windows to automatically map to this network drive every time it starts, check the Reconnect at logon box.**

   If you don't check this box, by the way, you'll need to map the network drive each time you want to use it.

5. Click OK.

If the person who shared the disk said that you should provide a password, you may be asked to supply this — which you do by typing the password — and then Windows connects your computer to the network drive using the network.

Congratulations. You're now ready to use the network.

You can now work with any mapped drive in the same way that you work with a local drive. In other words, after you map to a network drive, it's as if the network drive is just another disk in your local computer. You can see the disk in the Windows Explorer window. You can browse its folders and subfolders. You can work with program and document files stored on the network disk in the same way that you work with program and document files stored on a local disk. The real difference is that with a network disk, rather than connecting to the disk with cabling inside your computer, you're connected with the coaxial or UTP cabling that makes up the network. (For more on cabling, see Chapter 9.)

You Say You Can't Map

Oh, wait a minute. What's that? You say the network isn't working correctly and you can't map to a network drive. Hmmm. Okay, here's the deal. If you can't get the drive to map correctly, your problem can be only one of three things:

- ✔ Your network isn't really up and running.
- ✔ You haven't used the right names for the computer or the share name.
- ✔ You used slashes (/) instead of backslashes (\) or your used the wrong number of backslashes.

Checking the network

You can get your network up and running by following the instructions provided in Chapter 9. (You want to pay particular attention to the section entitled, "Testing, 1, 2, 3, testing, 1, 2, 3.")

Double-checking names

You can rather easily verify that you've used the correct computer and disk share name. Go sit down in front of the computer to which you're trying to map. To verify that you have the right computer name, follow these steps:

1. **Click Start⇨Settings⇨Control Panel.**

2. **When Windows displays the Control Panel folder, double-click the Network tool.**

3. **When Windows displays the Network dialog box, click its Identification tab (see Figure 10-5).**

   Verify that the name you see in the Computer name box is what you expect. You may even want to write the name down.

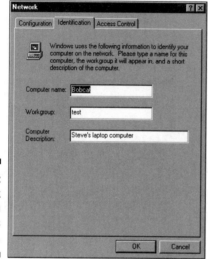

Figure 10-5: Don't freak when you see this dialog box.

To verify that you know the right share name, follow these steps:

1. **Start Windows Explorer.**

2. **Right-click the disk you want to map to; when Windows displays the shortcuts menu, choose its Sharing command.**

3. **When Windows displays the Sharing tab of the Properties dialog box, verify that the name you see in the Share Name is what you expect.**

   Again, you may want to write the name down.

The slashes versus backslashes thing

You don't need my help with this, right? All you need to do is make sure that you're entering path names with backslashes. In other words, your pathname should look something like this:

```
\\FELIX\C$
```

You don't want to use slashes.

Unmapping a Network Drive

You can unmap a network drive, too. You may want to do this, for instance, if the computer to which you're mapped is no longer on the network. Here's what you do:

1. **Start Windows Explorer.**
2. **Right-click the mapped drive.**
3. **Choose the shortcut menu's Disconnect command.**

Some Network Management Stuff

With a peer-to-peer network, you really don't need to worry about much. You won't have the same problems as you do with large client-server networks. Nevertheless, you probably still want to think about some stuff.

Information confidentiality

First, let me say that unless you get real obsessive about using passwords to control access to disks, you're not going to have much data confidentiality in a peer-to-peer network. But, as a small business, I'm not sure that's all that big a problem. Sure, everyone has secrets, but especially in a small business where people are wearing a bunch of different hats, keeping secrets doesn't work very well. If you want to truly keep some things secret, your best bet may be to set up separate networks. You may use one network in accounting or the business office, for example, and you may use another network for everybody else. You're not going to be able to share information or gear between the two networks, but you'll have more security.

Backing up

I'm not sure what you should do about backing up people's documents. Oh, I know what the text books say. They tell you that everybody should stick the stuff they really want to protect on some central file server. And then somebody (maybe you) is supposed to regularly backup the documents stored on this central file server.

Note: Remember that even in a peer-to-peer network, you can just start using one of the peers as a place to store all your files. And in this case, that peer becomes a de facto file server.

You can employ a conventional backup system like this, and it's great for your coworkers. But what I always see in small offices is that it doesn't work as well as people like to think. Some people forget to stick their stuff on the server. Other people — because it's no skin off their nose — just load up stuff on the server and never clean house. And then you or some other poor slob has to remember to regularly back up the server.

If you use a formal system like this, you'll probably want to get a tape drive and just call one of the computers in the network a server. (Nobody with half a brain is going to want to use this computer for real work because it's going to be busy handling people's documents.) Then you can start backing stuff up every other day or whatever.

You know what I do, though? I just tell people to back up their own stuff, and then I make sure that we have a number of high-speed, high-capacity removable disk storage devices scattered around the network. We have a couple of Iomega Zip drives, for example (these store around a 100 Mbps of stuff), and we have a recordable CD drive (a CD stores around 600 Mbps of stuff).

Playing Big Brother

Windows comes with a little accessory called Net Watcher. Net Watcher lets you see who has connected to your computer and what they're doing. To use Net Watcher, click Start⇨Programs⇨Accessories⇨System Tools⇨Net Watcher. When Windows starts the Net Watcher program, you see a Window that shows who's connected to your computer and what document files they've opened (see Figure 10-6).

You don't need to know much to use Net Watcher, but let me just quickly tell you a few things:

  ✔ The information shown in the Net Watcher is current as of the time the program starts. If you want Net Watcher to update its information, you need to choose View⇨Refresh.

  ✔ The right-most three buttons on the toolbar — Show Users, Show Folders, and Show Files — change the information shown in the Net Watcher window. If you're going to use this accessory much, go ahead and experiment with these buttons to see the different information that Net Watcher provides.

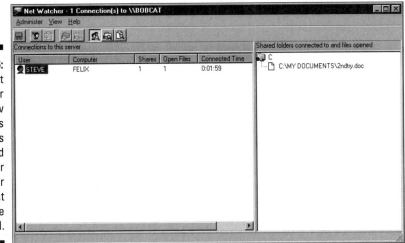

Figure 10-6:
The Net
Watcher
window
shows
who's
connected
to your
computer
and what
files they've
opened.

✔ If you want to disconnect some network user from your machine, you can do so. Just click the Disconnect User button. (Recognize that the person may lose changes he's made when you do this.)

✔ If you want to close a file that some network user has opened, you can do this, too. All you need to do is click the Close File button. (Again recognize, however, that when you do, the person may lose changes he's made to a document.)

Some Final Words About Viruses

People always worry about viruses. Much of the time, the fear is overblown. I've been using personal computers since the very beginning, for example, and I've only caught one virus. (I caught it from a friend who brought over a laptop that his games-crazy son often brought to school. We casually shared a single floppy disk and, whamo, I had the bug.)

Nevertheless, in spite of the fact that viruses often aren't that huge a risk, you really should get some virus protection — the protection programs are called *antiviruses* — and install this protection on each of the PCs in your network. If you want to get information about how antivirus programs work, two good sources are the www.mcafee.com and www.thunderbyte.com Web sites.

Part IV
Business Accessories and Tools

The 5th Wave   By Rich Tennant

"THE PHONE COMPANY BLAMES THE MANUFACTURER, WHO SAYS IT'S THE SOFTWARE COMPANY'S FAULT, WHO BLAMES IT ON OUR MOON BEING IN VENUS WITH SCORPIO RISING."

In this part . . .

Windows comes with a bunch of gizmos and gadgets that you can use to work on business problems, change the way your computer works, and perform do-it-yourself repair and maintenance. This part talks about these gizmos and gadgets.

Chapter 11

Tools of the Trade

In This Chapter

▶ Making calculations with the Windows Calculator

▶ Speed Dialing numbers on your computer

▶ Traveling with files using the Briefcase

▶ Connecting two computers

▶ Conducting Internet meetings

▶ Playing movies, audio files, and CDs

▶ Recording audio files

▶ Adjusting your computer's volume

▶ Installing Windows accessories

*W*indows 95 comes with a bunch of little programs, called accessories. Many of these programs aren't all that useful to small business users like you and me. But some of them are pretty useful in a small or home office setting. So, in this chapter, I'm going to quickly describe those accessories that are most useful to small businesses. (At the end of the chapter, I'll also provide a table that summarizes the accessories I haven't described here.)

Note: The companion CD that comes with this book also includes two other special accessories especially for use in a small business or home-based business: BizCalculator, which is an easy-to-use financial calculator, and PVCAnalyzer, which performs break-even and profit-volume analysis. If you're interested in using either of these accessories (which are only available to readers of this book!), refer to Appendix B and C.

Using Calculator

If you just want to make a quick calculation, you don't need to take the time to search for your calculator under the stacks of paper on your desk — you can use the Windows Calculator instead. This calculator (shown in Figure 11-1) looks and works just like your basic everyday calculator. To start the Calculator, click Start➪Programs➪Accessories➪Calculator. Windows displays the Calculator on top of any application window you currently have open. To use the calculator, you can either enter numbers and operators by using your keyboard, or you can click the calculator's buttons by using the mouse.

To use your keyboard's numeric keypad, click the Num Lock key, located in the upper-left corner of your numeric keypad.

Figure 11-1:
The
Calculator.

You're probably familiar with most of the buttons you see on the Windows Calculator, but the purpose of some of them may not be so obvious to you. Table 11-1 gives a list of the buttons that you may not be familiar with and a description of what these buttons do.

Table 11-1	The Calculator Buttons
Button	**What It Does**
Back	Deletes the last digit of the number you are typing.
CE	Clears only the displayed number but keeps the rest of the numbers and operators in the calculation.
C	Clears the entire calculation.
MC	Clears a number stored in memory.
MR	Recalls a number stored in memory.
MS	Stores the displayed number in memory.

Button	What It Does
M+	Adds the number you have displayed to the number stored in memory.
/	Divides one number by another.
sqrt	Displays the square root of a number. To use this button, enter the number and then click the button.
*	Multiplies one number by another.
%	Converts the answer you get after multiplying two numbers into a percentage. For example, if you enter 4*2 and then click the % button, the calculator returns .08 instead of the usual 8.
1/x	Calculates the reciprocal of the displayed number. If you enter the number 4 and click the 1/x button, the calculator displays .25, or $^{1}/_{4}$.
+/-	Changes the sign of the number displayed. To enter a negative number, enter the number and then click the button.

Using Phone Dialer

The Phone Dialer is a handy accessory for quickly dialing telephone numbers (especially long international numbers) of suppliers, clients, manufacturers, and so on. This tool is also practical for on-the-go laptop business-people to store frequently-dialed numbers. To start the Phone Dialer, click Start➪Programs➪Accessories➪Phone Dialer.

To have the Phone Dialer store a list of frequently-dialed numbers so that you don't need to enter them each and every time, click one of the Empty Speed Dial buttons to display the Edit Speed Dial dialog box shown in Figure 11-2.

Figure 11-2:
Entering
speed dial
numbers.

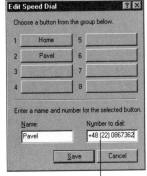

A telephone number

Enter the name of the person or business that you're calling in the Name box. Or if you'd rather, you can enter a nickname or note about the person instead. But just to let you know, the Phone Dialer can only display 15 digits on the Speed Dial buttons, so you probably don't want to enter "The most difficult people to deal with." After you name or describe the person or business you want to call, enter the number you want to dial in the Number to dial box. But you probably guessed that.

What you may not have guessed, however, is that entering a telephone number is not as simple as it sounds. You have to be exact when you do so. You can enter a telephone number in two ways. If you always dial from the same location (say from the desktop computer in your office), you can just enter the number exactly as you would dial it. (If you need to dial a certain number to access an outside line, however, don't enter this number here. You do that later.) If you frequently dial from several different locations using your laptop, you can enter the number in international format. This way, when you're computing away from the office, you only need to specify where you're calling from. The Phone Dialer determines whether or not the call you're making is long distance from where you are and dials the number accordingly. To enter a phone number in international format, use the following formula:

```
+CC (AC) number
```

Replace CC with the country code (the United States is 1, France is 33, Tanzania is 255, and so on. If you don't know the country code, you can probably find it in the phone book). Replace AC with the area or city code and replace number with the number you want to dial (but don't add any hyphens). When you finish, click Save.

To dial a speed dial number, just click its button in the Phone Dialer window (see Figure 11-3). If somebody answers, pick up the phone and click Talk. If nobody answers, click Hang Up.

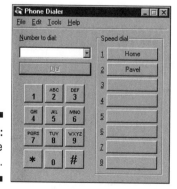

Figure 11-3:
The Phone
Dialer.

To make a calling card call, specify where you're calling from, disable call waiting, or specify a number you need to dial to access an outside line, choose Tools⇨Dialing Properties command. Doing so displays the Dialing Properties dialog box. For help with this dialog box, see Chapter 5 about making Dial-Up Networking connections.

Using Briefcase

When you go on business trips, you probably take any necessary paper documents with you in your briefcase. When you want to take computer files or documents with you, you can also pack them in a special kind of briefcase. Windows Briefcase lets you take several files with you, work on them, and then update the files all at once when you return to the office. To use the Briefcase, follow these steps:

1. **Before you leave, pack your Briefcase with the files you want to work on.**

   If you're taking your laptop computer with you, hook it up to your desktop computer (this is described later in the section called "Making a Direct Cable Connection"). Then drag the files you want to take with you to the Briefcase icon on your laptop computer.

    If you want to take your files with you on a floppy disk, drag them to the Briefcase icon on your desktop computer and then drag the Briefcase to the floppy disk. When you do, the Briefcase icon disappears from your desktop (because you're taking it with you, after all).

   For help on using Windows Explorer to drag files from one location to another, see Chapter 2.

2. **Work with the files in the Briefcase while you are away and save your work like you always do.**

3. **When you return, unpack your Briefcase.**

   If you took a laptop with you, reconnect your laptop to your desktop and open the Briefcase. The Briefcase window lists the files that need to be updated, as shown in Figure 11-4. Click Update All in the Briefcase to replace all of the files on your desktop computer with the revised versions you took with you.

   If you took your files on a floppy disk, reinsert the floppy and double-click My Briefcase. Click the Update All button to update the files with the latest versions. Then drag your Briefcase back to your desktop so that you can take it with you on another trip.

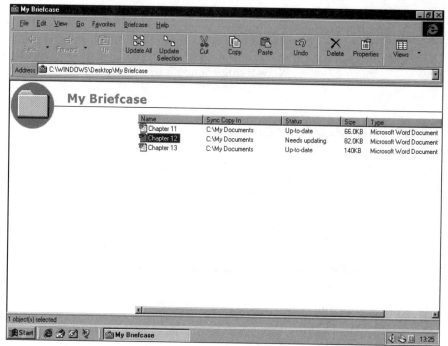

Figure 11-4:
Updating
your files
with the
Briefcase
copies.

If you only want to update certain files with their Briefcase copies, select the files you want to update in the Briefcase and click the Update Selection button.

To empty the Briefcase before your next trip, select its contents and press the Delete key. Files you delete in the Briefcase will not be deleted from their original locations on your computer.

Making a Direct Cable Connection

Making a direct cable connection is another useful Windows accessory for laptop users. The Direct Cable Connection wizard allows you to connect a laptop computer to your desktop computer by using either parallel or serial cables. Once you have connected the two, you can share files between them.

Before you can begin sharing files by using a direct cable connection, you have to do a bunch of other things to set up the connection. All of these things are pretty complicated, but luckily you only have to do most of this stuff once. After you get the connection working the first time, connecting a second time is a snap.

You first need to permit sharing of the folders containing the files. To do so, follow these steps:

1. **Open Windows Explorer and select the folder you want to share.**

2. **Choose File⇨Properties and click the Sharing tab in the folder's Properties dialog box (see Figure 11-5).**

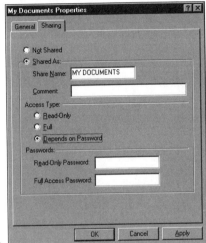

Figure 11-5:
Granting
sharing
permissions.

3. **Click the Shared As option button and specify the permission level by clicking the Read Only, Full, or Depends on Password option button.**

   If you select Read Only, you can read the folder's files from the other computer, but you can not add, edit, or delete files from the folder. If you select Full, you can read, edit, save, and delete files in the folder. If you select Depends on Password, the person at the other computer must enter the correct password in order to save changes to a file in the folder or delete or add files to the folder.

   Optionally, enter a password. If you enter a password in the Read-Only Password text box, a person must enter this password in order to read the files in the folder. If you enter a Full-Access password, a person must enter this password in order to change or delete the files in the folder.

If you are the only person who is going to share files, click the Full option button and don't enter a password. You don't need to worry about all of this security stuff.

After you designate folders for sharing, they show up in Windows Explorer with a little hand icon holding them up. Now you're ready to take the next step in preparing to make a direct cable connection: making sure that both computers use the same protocol, or speak the same language. To do so, follow these steps:

1. **Click Start⇨Settings⇨Control Panel.**

2. **Double-click the Network icon to display the Configuration tab of the Network dialog box.**

3. **Check to make sure that the IPX/SPX-compatible Protocol is listed on both computers (see Figure 11-6).**

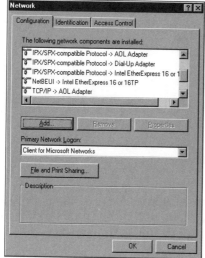

Figure 11-6:
Adding an
IPX/SPX-
compatible
protocol.

If the protocol is listed, click OK and you're set. You can skip the rest of these steps. If the protocol is not listed, click the Add button to display the Add protocol dialog box.

4. **Select Protocol from the list and click Add again.**

5. **Select Microsoft from the Manufacturers list and IPX/SPX-compatible Protocol from the Network Protocol list and click OK.**

Windows may ask you to insert the Windows 95 CD so that it can copy some files. Windows also tells you that you need to restart your computer. Go ahead and do so. When your computer is up and running again, you're ready to make the direct cable connection.

Now you're ready to set up the actual cable connection. Click Start⇨ Programs⇨Accessories⇨Direct Cable Connection. Doing so starts a wizard that guides you through the process of connecting the two computers. You need to run this wizard on both your laptop and desktop computer.

In the first wizard dialog box, specify whether the computer you're currently at is a guest or a host. You need to designate one computer as a host and one as a guest. The host computer has the information you want to share and the guest computer accesses the information.

In the second wizard dialog box, specify the port you want to use to connect the two computers. If you're making a parallel cable connection, select a parallel port on both computers. If you're making a serial cable connection, select a serial port on both computers. After you select a port for each computer (see Figure 11-7), plug the cable into the computers and click Next to have the wizard attempt to establish a connection.

Figure 11-7:
Selecting a port to use for the connection.

After the wizard has established a connection, it displays a window that you can use to move files just like in Windows Explorer.

A word about cables and ports

Figuring out which type of cable you have and which port you've plugged it in to can be the trickiest part of making a direct cable connection. So let me give you a few pointers. Take a look at the plugs on the cable you have. If it looks like the wide plug you use for your printer and has 25 pins on the inside, it's probably a *parallel cable.* It's called parallel because information can flow both ways at once. If the plug is smaller and has only 9 pins, it's probably a *serial cable.* A serial cable is like a one-lane road. Information at one end has to wait if information from the other end is on its way over.

Figuring out which port to plug the cable into can get more complicated yet. If you have a whole bunch of ports listed, you can figure it out by trial and error by selecting each one and then testing to see if it works. But this method can get a little tedious and time-consuming. Your best option is to just unplug any printers from both computers and use their parallel ports. (This port is probably even marked with a printer icon on your laptop.) You can be pretty certain that these are the LPT 1 ports. You may have to buy a different cable that connects both of these ports, but they should work.

Using NetMeeting

Microsoft NetMeeting is a new program that allows people in distant locations to gather in cyberspace for meetings. Depending on the hardware the meeting participants have installed on their computers, they can actually see and hear the other meeting participants, live and in color. People can also share applications and documents in meetings and write or sketch on a virtual whiteboard.

To use NetMeeting, click Start⇨Programs⇨Internet Explorer⇨Microsoft NetMeeting. The first time you run NetMeeting, it takes you through a wizard that asks you to enter some information about yourself and your modem. NetMeeting also asks you to pick a directory server to log on to. (Choosing a directory server is like picking a conference room for the meeting. As in the real world, all of the meeting participants must show up for the meeting in the same place at roughly the same time.) After you provide all of the information the wizard requests, it asks you to speak into the microphone so that it can automatically tune it and optimize the sound quality. When you complete the wizard, click Finish to log on. NetMeeting lists the people logged on to the directory server you selected, as shown in Figure 11-8.

To begin a meeting, select the person you want to include in the meeting and click the Call button.

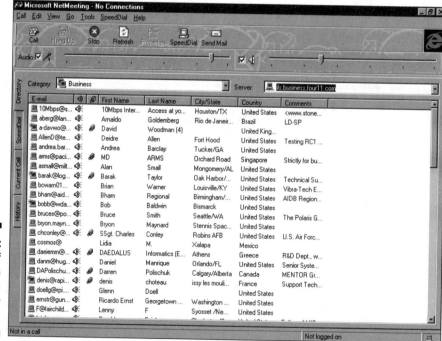

Figure 11-8:
The list of people present on a directory server.

To draw on the whiteboard, choose Tools⇨Whiteboard.

Using NetShow Player

NetShow Player is an accessory that comes with Internet Explorer 4.0. With NetShow Player, you can spool live asf files or play asf files stored on your computer. (*Asf,* or *active streaming files,* are files that spool to your computer as you play them.) To use NetShow Player, click Start⇨Programs⇨Internet Explorer⇨NetShow Player. If you know the location of the asf file you want to play, choose File⇨Open Location and enter the complete pathname or URL of the video file you want to play. (For more information about how URLs work and what pathnames are, refer to Chapter 5.)

If you want to play a file on the NetShow server, don't forget to add the mms protocol mms://. If you want to play a file on the World Wide Web, begin the URL with the HTTP protocol.

If you don't know the location of the asf file you want to play, choose File⇨Open and use the Open dialog box to find the video file.

Playing CDs

If you're working long hours at your computer, playing a CD in the background may help you get through the day. Windows comes with the CD player accessory, so that all you really need to play a CD is a CD-ROM drive and either speakers or headphones.

If you have a sound card on your computer, you can plug your speakers or headphones in to your computer and then adjust the volume either on your computer or by using your speakers' volume controls.

If you don't have a sound card, you can plug your headphones or speakers directly into your CD-ROM drive. You can then adjust the volume on the CD-ROM drive.

To play an audio CD, all you usually have to do is insert the CD. Your computer usually recognizes it as an audio CD and launches the CD Player program. If this doesn't happen, you can launch the CD Player manually by clicking Start⇨Programs⇨Accessories⇨Multimedia⇨CD Player. This opens the CD Player application window shown in Figure 11-9. Then click the play button to begin playing the CD. The CD Player has buttons just like those on a regular stereo. You can click them to rewind, fast forward, or skip to certain songs on your CD. If you want to play the songs (called *tracks*) on your CD in a random order, choose Options⇨Random Order.

Figure 11-9:
The CD
Player
application
window.

You need to keep the CD Player application running as long as you want the CD to keep playing. If you exit the application, the CD stops playing. You can minimize the CD Player so that it only shows up as a button on the Windows Taskbar by clicking the Minimize/Restore button.

Recording sound files

If you have a sound card and a microphone, you can record your own sound files. To do so, you use the Sound Recorder accessory. To start the Sound Recorder, click Start➪Programs➪Accessories➪Multimedia➪Sound Recorder. Make sure that your microphone is hooked up and turned on and then click the Record button to begin a recording. After you create a sound file, you can edit it by mixing it with other sound files or by adding special effects such as an echo (see Figure 11-10).

Even if you don't plan on using Microsoft NetMeeting, going through the NetMeeting wizard is still a good idea. This wizard sets up your microphone for you to optimize the sound quality.

Figure 11-10:
Use the
Sound
Recorder to
create and
edit sound
files.

Click here to record

Adjusting volume

You can precisely control the volume of all of the sound devices on your computer by using the Volume Control accessory. To adjust the volume on your computer (see Figure 11-11), follow these steps:

1. **Double-click the Volume icon (the one that looks like a speaker) on the Windows taskbar.**

   Doing so displays the Volume Control window.

2. **Use the small horizontal slider in the Volume Control area to adjust the balance between the left and right speakers.**

3. **Use the large vertical slider in the Volume Control area to adjust the playback volume.**

4. **Use the Wave, MIDI, CD, and Line-In sliders to adjust these sound features if you have them on your computer.**

5. **To adjust the recording volume, choose Options⇨Properties and click the Recording button.**

6. **Click OK to display the recording volume controls.**

   Check the Mute all box in the Volume Control area to turn off all of the sound on your computer.

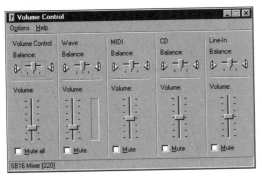

Figure 11-11:
Adjusting
the
computer's
volume
settings.

Installing Windows Accessories

When you installed Windows 95, you almost certainly didn't install all of the accessories that came on the CD. And if you purchased your computer with Windows 95 already installed on it, you probably don't have quite all of the accessories installed either. This is because most people don't need or want them, so Windows doesn't install them automatically. But some people do want them, which is why they're included on the CD for you to install yourself if you need to. To install an accessory, follow these steps:

1. **Click⇨Start button⇨Settings⇨Control Panel.**

2. **Double-click the Add/Remove Programs icon to display the Add/Remove Programs Properties window.**

3. **Click the Windows Setup tab to display a list of the categories of components you can install.**

If you've installed all of the accessories in a category, Windows puts a check mark beside the category. If you've only installed some of the accessories in a category, Windows puts a check mark beside the category but highlights the category in gray. If you have not installed any of the accessories in a category, Windows leaves the check box beside the category empty.

4. **Select a category of components and click the Details button.**

Windows displays a list of the individual components available within the category, as shown in Figure 11-12. To install a component, check the box beside the component.

To remove a component, remove the check box beside the component.

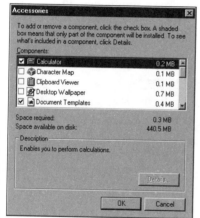

Figure 11-12:
Selecting accessories to install.

5. **Click OK twice to begin installing the component.**

Windows may ask you to insert the Windows 95 CD.

Reviewing the Other Windows Accessories

This book is too short for me to talk about all of the different accessories that come with Windows, so you may have some installed on your computer that I haven't mentioned in this chapter. If you wonder what one of the accessories does, take a brief look at the Table 11-2 or just try it out for yourself.

Table 11-2	Windows Accessories: The Rest of the Story
Accessory	**What It Does**
Fax	Lets you send and receive faxes and create cover sheets. See Chapter 8 for more information on using Microsoft Fax.
Games	Contains a bundle of fun: three card games (Hearts, Solitaire, and FreeCell) and the strategic game Minesweeper.
Internet tools	Contains shortcuts to Internet Explorer and Web Publishing wizard.
ActiveMovie Control	Plays movie and audio files.
MediaPlayer	Plays movie, video, sound, and MIDI sequencer files.
System tools	Contains tools you can use for monitoring and repairing your computer. For more information on using these tools, see Chapter 13.
Dial-Up Networking	Displays your dial-up accounts in a dialog box. You can create a new Dial-Up Networking account to connect to the Internet or to a remote access server.
Dial-up scripting	Automates a Dial-Up Networking connection. First, you must write a script using a text editor like WordPad or Notepad, and then you assign the script to the Dial-Up Networking connection by using the Dial-up scripting tool.
HyperTerminal	Allows you to make a basic connection to the Internet if you have a shell account. With HyperTerminal, you can browse text and navigate by entering commands.
Paint	Lets you create and edit bitmap images and paint-brush files.
Online Registration	Guides you through the process of registering your copy of Windows 95 online, if you haven't already registered it.
WordPad/Notepad	Allows you to view and edit text files. These accessories work like rudimentary word processors.

Chapter 12

Customizing Windows

. . . .

In This Chapter

▶ Adjusting monitor display properties

▶ Customizing the Windows desktop

▶ Using accessibility options

▶ Customizing the Windows Taskbar and the Start menu

▶ Installing software

▶ Installing hardware

. . . .

*Y*ou can change the way that Windows looks and works so that it more closely meets the requirements of your office. You can adjust the quality of the display, for example, and choose what colors Windows uses for items such as its windows and dialog boxes. If you or a coworker has a disability or impairment, you may be able to more easily work with Windows by taking advantage of its accessibility options. You can add new programs or hardware devices to your computer. And you can make a bunch of other changes as well. This chapter describes how you do all of this stuff.

Adjusting Display Properties

One of the best ways to avoid unnecessary eye strain and save yourself a couple of headaches from working on the computer is by optimizing the display capabilities of your monitor. To do so, follow these steps:

1. **Right-click a blank area on your desktop and choose the shortcut menu's Properties command.**

   The Display Properties dialog box is displayed.

2. **Click the Settings tab (see Figure 12-1).**

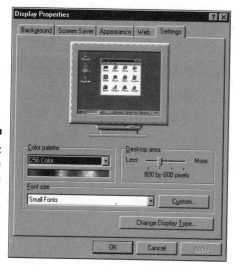

Figure 12-1:
The Settings tab of the Display Properties dialog box.

3. **In the Color Palette drop-down list box, choose either 256 color, High Color, or True Color.**

   A greater number of colors improves image quality, but images take up more memory. Stay away from 16 color if you can. With 16 color, graphic images look grainy and are difficult to make out.

4. **Move the Desktop Area slider to adjust your monitor resolution.**

   A small number, such as 640 by 480 pixels, makes everything on your screen bigger so that you can see it more easily. The only problem with this is that because everything takes up more space on your screen, you always have to scroll back and forth because all of the information won't fit on your screen at once. A really large number, such as 1280 by 1024 pixels, allows you to display several things on your screen at once, but you can hardly see or read anything because it's all so small. Personally, I like working at 800 by 600 pixels because it's faster (I can fit a good amount of information on my screen at once and so don't have to constantly scroll) and yet I can still easily see and read everything.

5. **In the Font Size drop-down list box, choose large fonts if you have difficulty reading the default small fonts.**

6. **Click Apply.**

   If you chose in Step 3 to change your color palette, Windows may tell you that you need to restart your computer in order for the changes to take effect. Save all of your work and then go ahead and do this. If Windows does not need to restart, it makes the changes and then asks you if you want to keep them. Click Yes to keep them or No to go back to your old settings.

The monitor display settings that you have available depend on your monitor and your graphic adapter. You may not be able to adjust all of the settings described here.

Customizing the Windows Desktop

In addition to changing the way your monitor displays information, you can also change the look of your computing environment by customizing the Windows Desktop. You can do just about the same things to your computer screen as you can to a wall in your house. You can wallpaper it, hang a picture on it, paint it a different color, or paint the trim different colors.

Applying a color scheme

As any interior decorator can tell you, the first step in decorating a wall is painting it. Before you hang wallpaper or pictures, you need to come up with a color scheme and paint the wall and the trim. Windows has two options for painting your desktop and all of the other elements on your computer screen. You can go with one of its designer color schemes, which have complementary colors for the desktop background and the other screen elements picked for you. Or you can let the artist in you shine and create your own color combinations by selecting a color for each element.

To use a predefined Windows color scheme, follow these steps:

1. **Right-click a blank area on your desktop and choose the shortcut menu's Properties command.**

   The Display Properties dialog box is displayed.

2. **In the Display Properties dialog box, click the Appearance tab, shown in Figure 12-2.**

3. **Select a scheme from the Scheme drop-down list box.**

   For example, if you have difficulty reading small fonts, choose a scheme that has the word large after it.

4. **Click Apply to apply the scheme to your desktop.**

   If you don't like the new scheme, you can preview a different one by selecting it from the Scheme drop-down list box and clicking the Apply button.

5. **When you find a scheme you like, click OK to keep it and close the Display Properties dialog box.**

Figure 12-2:
The
Appearance
tab of the
Display
Properties
dialog box.

If you choose to later add wallpaper or a picture to your desktop, the wallpaper or picture covers up the paint color underneath.

If you're the creative type, you can design your own color scheme by picking colors yourself for each of the different screen elements. To do so, call up the Display Properties dialog box and then follow these steps:

1. **Click the Appearance tab in the Display Properties dialog box.**

2. **In the Item drop-down list box, select the item you want to paint.**

   You may want to begin by selecting Desktop, for instance, to specify a desktop background color.

3. **In the Color drop-down list box, select the color that you want to use for the element you chose.**

   The preview area at the top of the dialog box shows what the new color will look like.

4. **Repeat Steps 2 and 3 for each element whose color you want to change.**

5. **When you finish creating your masterpiece, click Apply to apply your changes and click OK to accept the changes.**

If you find that you like working with the color scheme you created, you can save it by redisplaying the Display Properties dialog box, clicking the Appearance tab, and clicking the Save As button. Enter a name for the color scheme in the Save Scheme dialog box.

Adding wallpaper patterns

If you want to liven up your computer screen by adding a pattern or picture to it, here's what you need to do:

1. **Right-click a blank area of the desktop and choose the Properties command.**

   Doing so displays the Background tab of the Display Properties dialog box.

2. **Select a wallpaper from the list box.**

   The preview monitor on this tab shows you what the wallpaper will look like on your screen. If you select a very small picture, you can select Tile from the Display drop-down list box to have the picture fill the entire screen. Or you can click the Pattern button to choose a wallpaper pattern to put around the picture (like a picture frame).

3. **Click OK.**

   Windows closes the Display Properties dialog box and adds the wallpaper to your desktop, as shown in Figure 12-3.

Figure 12-3:
The Desktop with a wallpaper pattern.

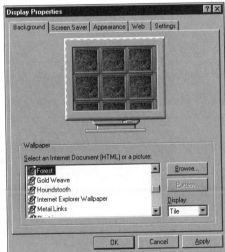

You can choose your own picture (such as your company logo) to use as wallpaper for your desktop by clicking the Browse button and selecting the image file you want to use.

Creating a Weblike Desktop

Internet Explorer 4.0, which is included on the companion CD, lets you customize your desktop even more by adding parts of Web pages to your desktop. You can add these Web page elements to your desktop by clicking the Add to Active Desktop button when you view a channel in Internet Explorer. When you add an active element to your desktop, you can schedule it to automatically update for offline viewing. To specify which active elements you want to display on the desktop, click the Web tab in the Display Properties dialog box.

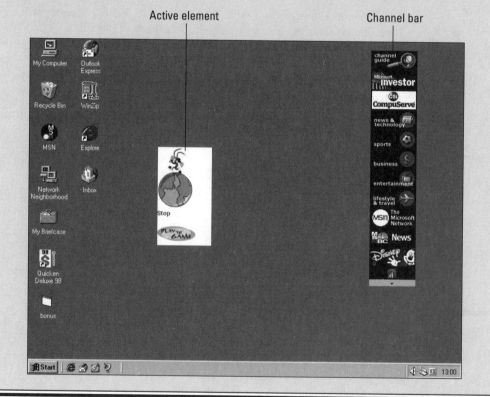

Using Screen Savers

If you usually keep your computer running for hours at a time, you probably want to use either a screen saver or a shut-off feature. You use a screen saver for three possible reasons: first, for style, because screen savers look pretty; second, for security reasons, so that someone must log on if you've left your desk and the screen saver has come on; and third, if you have an older monitor, you use a screen saver so that static elements on your screen don't create permanent burn marks on your monitor. To use a screen saver, right-click a blank area on your desktop and choose the shortcut menu's Properties command to summon the Display Properties dialog box, and then follow these steps:

1. **Click the Screen Savers tab in the Display Properties dialog box.**

2. **Select the screen saver you want to use from the Screen Saver drop-down list box.**

3. **In the Wait box, specify how long the computer should wait before it starts the screen saver.**

4. **If you have a monitor with energy-saving features, check the Low-Power Standby or the Shut-Off Monitor box to switch the monitor to low power or to turn it off after long periods of inactivity.**

5. **Click OK to close the Display Properties dialog box and apply the screen saver.**

If you get tired of the standard Windows screen savers, you can download a ton of different interesting screen savers from the World Wide Web. You'll find something there to appeal to just about every delight. You can also download programs for creating your own custom screen savers. Conduct a search on the words "screen saver" with a search engine to see a list of different shareware and freeware screen savers.

Working with Windows Accessibility Options

If you or any of your workers have disabilities, you can use Windows' Accessibility Options to customize your computing environment so that it fits your special needs. You can install the accessibility options in the same way that you install the other Windows accessories (see Chapter 11). To activate an accessibility option once you have the accessibility feature installed, click Start➪Settings➪Control Panel. Doing so opens the Control Panel window. Double-click on the Accessibility Options icon to display the Accessibility Properties dialog box.

The Keyboard tab of this dialog box (see Figure 12-4) has three options you can set for people who have difficulty typing on the keyboard:

- StickyKeys holds down the Shift, Alt, or Ctrl key until the next key is pressed so that people who can't press two keys simultaneously don't need to.

- FilterKeys ignores quick or repeated keystrokes for people whose hands tremble.

✔ ToggleKeys plays a tone when you turn the Caps Lock, Scroll Lock, or Num Lock functions on or off in case you accidentally press those keys.

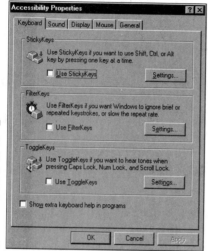

Figure 12-4:
Adjusting
the
keyboard
settings for
people with
disabilities.

The Sound tab has options you can set to accommodate your computer for people with hearing-impairments:

✔ The SoundSentry option tells your computer to flash a part of the screen when the system plays a sound (such as a warning).

✔ The ShowSounds option tells programs to display captions or icons instead of sounds.

The Display tab allows you to customize your computer for visually impaired people. If you check the High Contrast box, software programs use the high-contrast color scheme you specify.

The MouseKeys option on the Mouse tab allows people who have difficulty controlling the mouse to use keyboard keys to move and click the mouse.

The General tab allows you to specify when you want accessibility options turned on and off, and how you want to signal to users that accessibility options are running. The General tab also has an option for installing an input device other than a keyboard or a mouse. These kinds of input devices allow mobility-impaired people to give commands to the computer by nodding their head, or by tapping only one finger, and so forth.

Customizing the Windows Taskbar

One of the best features of Windows 95 is the ease with which you can switch between programs. The Windows Taskbar plays a vital role in your ability to do so. By customizing the Taskbar, you can make it an even more efficient tool. To do this, right-click a blank area of the Taskbar and choose the shortcut menu's Properties command. Doing so displays the Taskbar Options tab of the Taskbar Properties dialog box (see Figure 12-5).

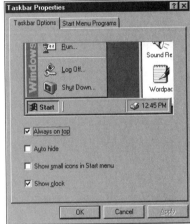

Figure 12-5:
The Taskbar Options tab of the Taskbar Properties dialog box.

✔ Check the Always On Top box if you want to keep the Taskbar visible at all times — even when you're running a program in full-screen format.

✔ Check the Auto Hide box if you want the Taskbar to pop up only on command — when you run the mouse over the bottom part of your screen.

✔ Click the Show Small icons in Start Menu box if you want the Start menu to take up less room on your screen by using smaller icons.

✔ Check the Show Clock box if you want Windows to display the clock in the right corner of the Taskbar.

✔ To move the Windows Taskbar to another side of your screen, click any blank area of the Taskbar and drag it to the top or to one of the sides of your screen.

Customizing the Start Menu

The Start menu is another tool that helps make the time you spend at the computer more efficient by allowing you to quickly start applications and open documents. To make the Start menu even more helpful, you can customize it so that it includes the programs and documents you use the most — nothing more and nothing less.

Adding programs

Most of the time, when you install a program, the installation program automatically adds the program shortcut to the Start menu. But sometimes you may need to add programs to the Start menu yourself. To do so, follow these steps:

1. **Right-click a blank area on the Windows Taskbar and choose the shortcut menu's Properties command.**

2. **Click the Start Menu Programs tab (see Figure 12-6).**

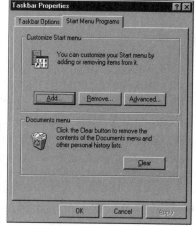

Figure 12-6:
The Start
Menu
Programs
tab.

3. **Click the Add button to display the Create Shortcut dialog box, as shown in Figure 12-7.**

4. **Click the Browse button to search for the program file.**

   When you find the file, select it, click Open, and then click Next.

5. **Select a Start Menu folder to which you want add the program shortcut or click the New Folder button to create a new Start Menu folder.**

6. **Enter a name for the program shortcut and click Finish.**

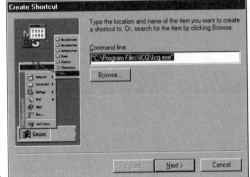

Figure 12-7:
Customizing
the Start
menu.

Deleting programs

There's no sense in keeping programs on the Start menu that you never use. They just take up space and slow you down in getting to the programs you do use. To delete programs you don't use from the Start menu, follow these steps:

1. **Click the Remove button on the Start Menu Programs tab.**

2. **Select the program you want to delete from the menu and click Remove.**

3. **If Windows asks you to confirm the delete, do so, and then click Close.**

If you have a program on your computer that you don't use, you probably want to delete the entire program and not just its shortcut on the Start menu. This way, you can free up space on your computer for other things. See the section "Adding and Removing Programs" later in this chapter for more information on how to do this.

Clearing the Documents Menu

Windows keeps a list of all of the documents you last used on the Documents menu. You can use this menu to quickly open a document you recently worked on. When your Documents menu gets filled up with old documents you no longer need to access, however, you may want to empty it. To clear the list of documents on the Start menu, click the Clear button on the Start Menu Programs tab.

Adding and Removing Programs

To add or remove programs in Windows 95, follow these steps:

1. **Insert the disk or CD-ROM containing the program you want to install.**

   If the program is on a CD-ROM, the setup window may open automatically when you insert the CD, so you can skip the rest of these steps. If the setup program doesn't run, continue to Step 2.

2. **Click Start⇨Settings⇨Control Panel.**

3. **Double-click the Add/Remove Programs icon to display the Add/Remove Programs Properties dialog box, as shown in Figure 12-8.**

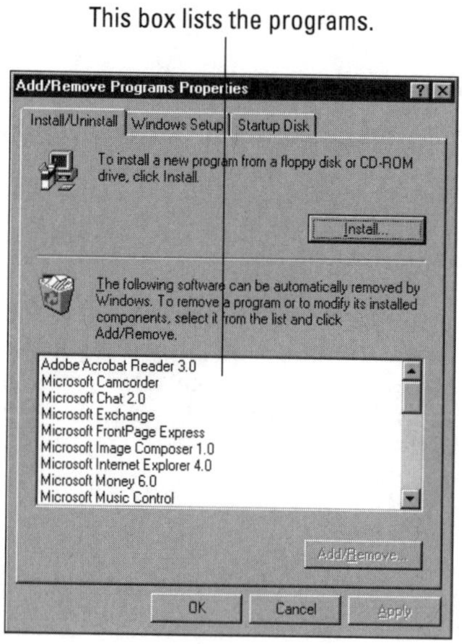

This box lists the programs.

Figure 12-8:
Installing
programs.

4. **Click the Install button.**

Windows looks for the new software's setup program. First, it looks on your floppy disk drive. If Windows can't find a setup program there, it looks on your CD-ROM drive. If Windows still can't find one, it displays the Browse dialog box, which you can use to locate the setup program. (Sometimes the setup program is in a folder so that Windows can't see it.)

5. **When you find the setup program, click Next.**

Windows starts the Setup wizard, which takes you through the process of installing software on your computer. The wizard may ask you what folder you want to store the program in or which components of the program you want to install. Just answer the questions the wizard asks and follow the instructions to install the program. You may have to restart your computer when the installation is complete, and then you are ready to begin working with the program.

Adding Hardware

With Windows 95, you add all types of hardware — disk drives, video adapters, sound cards, scanners, and so on — in the same way. And the best part yet is that Windows usually does almost all of the work for you. All you have to do is plug the hardware in.

To install new hardware, save all unsaved work in any programs and shut down your computer. Then unplug your computer and any of its attached peripherals (such as your printer or monitor) from the power source. I don't want you electrocuting yourself. Install the hardware following the manufacturer's instructions. When you plug your computer back in and turn it on, with any luck it will recognize that you've added something new. Your computer will probably give you a message box telling you, "Hey! I have some new piece here that I've never met before — do you want me to set this thing up for you?" and you tell it, "Yeah, that's exactly what I want you to do." And your obedient computer does it for you and everybody is happy.

Sometimes, though, your computer doesn't recognize right away that you've installed new hardware, so you have to make the computer look for it. To do so, follow these steps:

1. **Click Start⇨Settings⇨Control Panel.**

2. **In the Control Panel window, double-click the Add New Hardware icon.**

This action starts the Add New Hardware Wizard shown in Figure 12-9.

3. **Click Next to begin the wizard.**

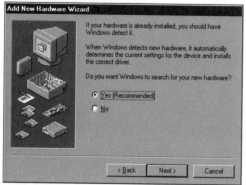

4. **Click the Yes option button and click Next to tell Windows that you want it to look for the new hardware.**

5. **Click Next to begin detecting added hardware.**

When the wizard finds the added hardware, it tells you so and all you have to do is follow the instructions on screen to set up the hardware. If, however, the wizard doesn't find any new hardware, click Next to begin installing it manually.

Whenever possible, you want to avoid installing hardware manually. Installing hardware can be a virtual nightmare. You have to make sure that you pick all of the right drivers for the hardware and you have to configure the hardware so that its interrupts and input/output ranges don't conflict with other hardware you already have installed. (Yikes.) If you're not careful, you can mess up other hardware devices on your computer so that they won't work. (Double Yikes.) To make the hardware installation process as worry free as possible, buy plug-and-play hardware devices. These devices install themselves as described earlier so that you don't have to.

Setting interrupts and input/output ranges is beyond the scope of this book, but just in case you were wondering what these terms mean, I thought I'd describe them a little so that you know what they're about. When a piece of hardware needs attention from the brain of your computer, it sends an interrupt request. Your computer's brain (called the processor) recognizes exactly what piece of hardware sent the request. The input/output range is like the phone line that passes information back and forth between your processor and the hardware on your computer. If more than one device has the same input/output range, you get interference, and your hardware doesn't work properly.

Using Other Control Panel Tools

You can customize Windows 95 to fit your needs or preferences in several ways. Table 12-1 describes how you can use the other Control Panel tools to customize Windows.

Table 12-1	Other Common Control Panel Tools
Tool	*What It Does*
32-bit ODBC	Displays the ODBC Data Source Administration dialog box. If you have a database program installed on your computer, you can use this dialog box to set up Open Database Connectivity (ODBC) drivers so that database programs can communicate with each other and share information.
Date/Time	Displays the Date/Time Properties dialog box, where you can set the current date, time, and time zone.
Find Fast	Displays the Find Fast program window. If you have Microsoft Office installed on your computer, this program builds an index of Office files that you can use to quickly locate Office files.
Fonts	Displays the Fonts window, which lists the fonts you have installed on your computer. If you want to install a new font, choose File⇨Install New Font.
Internet	Displays the Internet Properties dialog box (the same one you can get to by choosing View⇨Internet Options in Internet Explorer). You can use this dialog box to specify a start page, security and content ratings settings, and which programs you want to use for Internet mail and news. You can also use it to launch the Connection wizard.
Joystick	Displays the Joystick Properties dialog box. If you have a joystick installed on your computer, you can use this dialog box to specify the joystick's settings.
Keyboard	Displays the Keyboard Properties dialog box where you can set the speed of repeat keys and of the cursor blink. You can also use this dialog box if you need to set up a different keyboard, such as one with a different alphabet.

(continued)

Table 12-1 *(continued)*

Tool	What It Does
Mail or Mail and Fax	Displays a dialog box that allows you to change your mailbox settings, profiles, services, address lists, and where you want your mail delivered.
Modems	Displays the Modems Properties dialog box, where you can add or remove a modem, access your dialing properties, and view your modem's port connection information.
Mouse	Displays the Mouse Properties dialog box. Use this dialog box to specify whether you want a right-handed or left-handed mouse, to set the double-clicking and movement speed, and to describe what you want the mouse pointer to look like in different situations.
Multimedia	Displays the Multimedia Properties dialog box. This dialog box allows you to adjust the volume and sound quality of multimedia devices. You can also use this dialog box to select devices for playback and recording and view the properties of your multimedia devices.
Network	Displays the Network dialog box, which lists your installed network components. Use this dialog box to specify file and printer sharing with other computers on a local area network, and to give your computer a network name. The Network dialog box also allows you to control access to shared folders on your computer. (See Chapter 9 for more information.)
Passwords	Displays the Passwords Properties dialog box, where you can specify Windows and network passwords, enable remote administration, and specify the use of customized preferences for different users. (When a user logs on, Windows switches the settings for the user).
Power	Displays the Power Properties dialog box, which tells you whether your laptop is plugged in or running on battery power. It also tells you how much juice you have left in the battery.
Printers	Displays the Printers window, where you can add and remove printers and set which printer you want to use as a default if you have more than one printer. You can also use this window to check the status of a printer and of documents in a printer queue. (See Chapter 4 for more information.)

Tool	*What It Does*
Regional Settings	Displays the Regional Settings Properties dialog box, which allows you to specify in which format you want Windows to display the time and the date. You can also specify which currency symbol and measurement system (U.S. or metric) you want to use.
Sounds	Displays the Sounds Properties dialog box, which lets you specify the sounds that the computer plays to signal certain events.
System	Displays the System Properties dialog box, where you can verify that your hardware connections are working properly and see how your system is functioning.
Users	Launches the Enable Multiple User Settings wizard, which you can use to save different Windows settings for each person if more than one person works at your computer.

Chapter 13

Do-It-Yourself Repair and Maintenance

• •

In This Chapter

▶ What to try first when your computer freezes up

▶ Using the Windows System tools to monitor, maintain, and repair your computer

▶ The last troubleshooting straws

• •

Computer woes can not only cause you major headaches, but they can also quickly turn into a costly hassle for your business. When your computers aren't working up to speed, your productivity drops. When your computers are down completely, your work may come to a halt. Add to this the cost of getting technical support from a professional and a computer problem rapidly becomes a rather hefty expense. This chapter talks about how you can avoid computer problems (as much as possible) and how you can fix several common problems yourself when they arise.

The First Tactics

If your computer hangs up or stops working as you're used to, you can take a few easy steps to see if you can't get things running back to normal again.

Your first line of defense is always the two-part tactic of frequently saving your work and backing up, or copying, your files to a removable medium (such as a floppy disk). If you're working on something really important, you may want to save your work every 15 minutes or so. This way, you never lose more than about 15 minutes of work when a program crashes. You should probably back up your work at least once a week. However, if you've been working a great deal at the computer, you may want to back up at the end of each day, just in case your hard drive crashes.

Exiting stalled programs

Often your computer freezes up because a program stalls. So whenever your computer starts acting funny, you should first save what you're working on and restart the program you're running. You can exit a program by clicking its Close button or by choosing File⇨Exit. If neither of these methods work, you can press the Ctrl, Alt, and Delete keys on your keyboard all at once. This action should bring up a dialog box listing all open programs and identifying any programs that have stopped responding. Select the stalled program from the list box and click the End Task button.

If you repeatedly encounter the same problem when you run a certain software program, the problem almost certainly lies with the software. Try reinstalling the program.

Restarting Windows

An old computer joke goes something like this: Three engineers are riding in a car when the car suddenly stalls. The mechanical engineer says he thinks the problem with the car is mechanical and that they should verify that the fuel pump works. The electrical engineer says she thinks the problem is electrical and that they should test the battery. The computer engineer says he has no clue what is wrong with the car but suggests that everyone step out of the car and then hop back in to see if the car will start.

However strange it may sound, simply restarting your computer solves many computer problems. Restarting frequently works because one or more of the Windows components that run in the background has stalled. By exiting and restarting Windows, you get this program up and running again.

To restart Windows, first try clicking Start⇨Shut Down. You should see the Shut Down Windows dialog box. If you do, click the Restart button and then click OK. If that doesn't work, press the Ctrl, Alt, and Delete keys on your keyboard all at once. Doing so should bring up a dialog box that lists any programs that aren't responding. Click the Shut Down button to shut down your computer. After your computer has rested for a couple of minutes, turn it back on. If neither of the two ways I just described work, click your computer's Reset button to restart your computer.

Checking your connections

If shutting down and restarting your computer doesn't help, check your computer's cabling. This step is especially important if you work on a network. If your computer doesn't respond to your keyboard commands or to your mouse, the keyboard or mouse cable may have come loose. Make sure that all cables are firmly plugged in to the back of your computer. If your computer connects to a network, make sure that the network cable is firmly plugged in to the back of your computer and to all of the other computers in the office. Also make sure that the ends of the cable have caps, called terminators, firmly attached to them. (See Chapters 9 and 10 for more information on setting up and troubleshooting a network.)

Troubleshooting error messages and recurrent glitches

Every now and again you'll probably receive a Windows error message. They're usually nothing to panic about. Most of the time, they go away when you restart your computer. But if Windows repeatedly displays error messages, or if your computer frequently seems to get stuck in the same place, you have a problem. Unfortunately, error messages only tell you what the problem is, not how to fix it. To find a solution for the problem, follow these steps:

1. **If you receive an error message, write it down.**

   If a Details button is available, click it to get more information about the error, and then jot down the first couple of lines of the error details as well. If something frequently crashes when you attempt to perform a certain task, try to remember and write down as much as you can about the circumstances of the situation.

2. **Visit the Microsoft Support Web site at** `http://support.microsoft.com/support/` **and perform a search of the Microsoft Knowledge Base and Troubleshooting wizards databases.**

   You may need to do this on a different computer if the problem you're having prevents you from running your Web browser.

The Windows Repair and Maintenance Tools

Windows also comes with a few tools that you can use to locate and repair problems on your computer. You can use these tools if the methods described earlier in this chapter don't fix a problem you're having. You also can and should use these tools as a part of regularly maintaining your computer.

Scanning your disk for errors

Sometimes the problems you have with your computer are not software related, but hardware related. You can find out if your hard disk has errors and sometimes fix these errors by using ScanDisk, a Windows accessory. Even if you can't fix the errors on your hard disk, by running ScanDisk you can at least mark bad areas on your hard drive so that your computer won't store data there.

To use ScanDisk, follow these steps:

1. **Click Start⇨Programs⇨Accessories⇨System Tools⇨ScanDisk.**

2. **Select your hard drive from the list box.**

   If your computer has only one hard drive (which is probably the case), select the C: drive.

3. **Click the Thorough option button to have ScanDisk scan your entire disk, and then click the Options button to specify which areas of the disk you want to scan.**

   Click the System and Data Areas option button to have ScanDisk scan the entire drive, or click the System Area Only button to find if your hard drive has system errors. If your computer has a system error, the drive will probably need to be replaced.

4. **Leave the Do Not Perform Write Testing box unchecked.**

5. **Check the Do Not Repair Bad Sectors in Hidden and System Files box if you don't want ScanDisk to move data from hidden or system files.**

   If ScanDisk finds bad sectors on your disk, it moves the data in the bad sector to a good sector. The only problem with this is that when you move program data, your programs may no longer run because they often verify the physical location of data to make sure that the program hasn't been illegally copied.

It's a throw away

Although you can use all of the Windows System tools (including ScanDisk) to work with and repair floppy disks, doing so is never worth your time. If you've been having problems with a certain floppy disk, throw it away and use a different disk. If you recycle disks by reformatting them, always display the formatting results. If the Format results show that a disk has bad sectors, throw away the disk and use a new one.

6. **Click OK to return to the ScanDisk window shown in Figure 13-1.**

7. **Check the Automatically Fix Errors box if you want to have ScanDisk go ahead and repair all errors according to the settings you specify or leave the box unchecked if you want ScanDisk to ask you what it should do with individual errors as it finds them.**

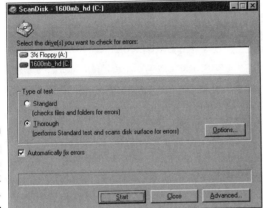

Figure 13-1:
The
ScanDisk
window.

8. **Click the Advanced button to specify what ScanDisk should do with the errors it detects.**

9. **In the Display Summary box, click the Always option button.**

   You always want to see what kinds of errors ScanDisk finds.

10. **In the Log File box, click the Replace Log option button.**

    A log just keeps track of ScanDisk's results. You don't need to hold on to old log files for any reason.

11. **In the Cross-Linked Files box, click the Make Copies option button.**

    Cross-linked files occur when two or more files use the same area of the disk at the same time. Although you probably don't need the data in either of these files (because it's corrupted), you may as well make copies of both files so that you can check them out if you need to.

12. **In the Lost File Fragments box, click the Free option button.**

    If you click the Convert to Files option button, ScanDisk converts the fragments to files, but you usually can't read or restore the files anyhow.

13. **In the Check Files For box, check the Invalid File Names box and the Invalid Dates and Times box.**

    Invalid file names may prevent a program from opening a file. Invalid dates and times affect the chronological sorting of files and the way some programs back up the last copy of a file.

14. **Check the Check Host Drive First box.**

   If you have compressed your disk by using DriveSpace (see "Compressing drives" later in this chapter for more information on doing this), checking this box tells ScanDisk to check the uncompressed part of your disk first. Errors on the uncompressed part are often the cause of errors on the compressed part.

15. **Click OK to return to the ScanDisk window and click Start to begin scanning your disk for errors.**

   While ScanDisk is running, you probably don't want to work at your computer; this allows ScanDisk to work faster. When ScanDisk is finished, it displays a summary of what it has found, as shown in Figure 13-2.

Figure 13-2:
The
ScanDisk
summary.

Defragmenting your disk

After you run ScanDisk to repair physical errors on your computer, you can use the Disk Defragmenter to organize the data stored on your computer. Defragmenting your disk allows Windows to work with files more quickly and easily. The Disk Defragmenter basically just searches your disk for the bits and pieces of data that belong together in a single file. Then it puts all of these fragments together in one spot on your hard drive. Storing all of a file's data in one place not only makes it quicker for Windows to find and load files, but it also creates larger chunks of free space for new files.

To use the Disk Defragmenter, follow these steps:

1. **Click Start⇨Programs⇨Accessories⇨System Tools⇨Disk Defragmenter.**

2. **Select your hard drive (probably the C: drive) from the drop-down list box and click OK.**

The Disk Defragmenter quickly scans your hard drive and tells you how fragmented it is. If only a small percentage of the disk is fragmented, the Disk Defragmenter will tell you that you don't need to defragment your disk. Click Exit to exit the Disk Defragmenter. If, on the other hand, your disk is significantly fragmented, click the Start button to start defragmenting.

3. **Click the Show Details button to view how the Disk Defragmenter groups data to make more space, as shown in Figure 13-3.**

4. **Click the Legend button to see what the colors of the boxes represent.**

5. **When the Disk Defragmenter is complete, click OK to exit.**

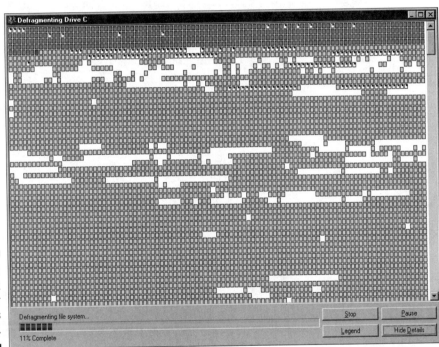

Figure 13-3:
The Disk
Defragmenter
Details
window.

Compressing drives

Windows comes with the DriveSpace accessory that you can use to compress your hard drive and to work with compressed drives. But you probably won't need or want to use DriveSpace.

Long, long ago, when new computers came with only a couple hundred megabytes of storage space, people rapidly filled up all of the space on their disks. They really only had one practical option for adding storage space: using a compression tool like DriveSpace. Nowadays, however, new computers come with more space than most people can ever dream of filling up. You also have much better ways of adding to your storage capacity. You can easily and confidently zip up and archive old files so that they take up less space. You can use removable storage devices, which are commonplace, reasonably priced, and capable of storing hundreds of megabytes of data. You can even buy a second hard drive for your computer if you need more space (and it shouldn't cost you an arm and a leg). These options are all much safer for storing data than compressing your hard drive.

When you compress your hard drive with DriveSpace, you create a single file in which you store all of the data on your hard drive. If this one file becomes corrupted or if someone deletes it, you lose your entire drive's worth of data.

 To see how full your hard drive is, right-click the My Computer icon on your desktop and choose Properties from the shortcut menu. Click the Performance tab and see what percentage of your hard drive is full by reading what the System Resources line says.

Repairing your Inbox

If you've been having problems with e-mail, the source of the problem may be a corrupted Inbox. To repair your Inbox, follow these steps:

1. **Click Start⇨Programs⇨Accessories⇨System Tools⇨Inbox Repair Tool.**

2. **Click the Browse button to locate your Inbox file.**

   Your Inbox is a pst file and is probably located in the Windows folder but may also be located in the Exchange folder. If you can't find a pst file, use the Windows Find utility to search for one. (I describe how to find files in Chapter 2.)

3. **Select your Inbox and click the Start button.**

4. **If the Inbox Repair Tool finds errors in your Inbox, check the Make Backup of Scanned File Before Repairing box and click Repair (see Figure 13-4).**

   If the Inbox Repair tool does not find any errors, click OK.

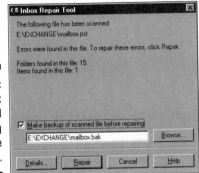

Figure 13-4:
The Inbox
Repair Tool
reporting
errors in the
Inbox.

You may have more or fewer system tools installed on your computer than I
have described in this chapter, depending on how you installed Windows on
your computer and on how long ago you purchased your copy of Windows.

If All Else Fails

If the repair methods described in this chapter don't solve your problem,
you have two last resources. First, you can try reinstalling Windows. Just
click Start⇨Settings⇨Control Panel. Then double-click the Add/Remove
Programs icon. In the Add/Remove Programs Properties dialog box, click the
Install button. Windows locates the Windows 95 setup program on the CD.
The setup program guides you through the process of installing Windows.

If nothing else works, you need to get technical support. The best way to do
so is to unplug your computer and take it in to a repair shop. They can tell
you if the problem is software or hardware related and can usually fix
everything for you.

Part V
The Part of Tens

The 5th Wave — By Rich Tennant

"A STORY ABOUT A SOFTWARE COMPANY THAT SHIPS BUG-FREE PROGRAMS ON TIME, WITH TOLL-FREE SUPPORT, AND FREE UPGRADES? NAAAH — TOO WEIRD."

In this part . . .

I doubt that my high-school English teacher would approve, but this part simply provides you with ten-item lists of information about using Windows in a small business: ten things home office users should know about Windows, ten things prospective Web publishers should consider, ten business software programs you'll want to use (or at least consider), and so on.

Chapter 14

Ten Quick-and-Dirty Lessons on Using Popular Business Software Programs

. . . .

In This Chapter

▶ Word-processing programs

▶ Spreadsheet programs

▶ Small business accounting programs

▶ Tax preparation programs

▶ Database programs

▶ Presentation programs

▶ Project management programs

▶ Integrated programs

▶ Other programs

. . . .

*T*his book talks mostly about Windows, as well it should. But you're not only going to using Windows when you work at your computer. You're also going to be using application programs to get your work done. Accordingly, this chapter provides quick-and-dirty crash courses on the ten application programs that you are most likely to use in a small business.

Now I want to be up front. This chapter doesn't provide exhaustive descriptions of each of these programs. I just don't have space. But, this chapter probably can get you started with most of these programs, and that may be all you need.

Note: This chapter's information can help you decide whether you need a particular program, even if it doesn't show you how to use it.

Word Processing Applications

A word-processing program is probably the most valuable type of software your business can own. With your word processor, you can create all sorts of business documents, such as letters, memos, and fax cover sheets, to name a few. You can also use your word processor to print sheets of mailing labels or addresses on envelopes.

To create a business document by using Microsoft Word (one of the most popular word processors), follow these steps:

1. **Start Word by clicking Start⇨Programs⇨Microsoft Word.**

2. **Choose File⇨New.**

   A list of templates is displayed that you can use for creating several common business documents.

3. **Use the tabs in the New dialog box to locate the word-processing document template you want to use.**

   Select the template (or select Blank Document if you want to start with a fresh piece of blank paper) and click OK.

If you have a business form that you commonly use, you can create a template for it and then save the template so that you can use it over and over again. To do so, create the document and then choose File⇨Save As command. From the Save As Type drop-down list box, select Document Template and then click Save. The next time you want to create a document based on this template, you can select your hand-made template from the New dialog box discussed in Step 3 above.

Type the text you want and then click the Save toolbar button to save the document or click the Print toolbar button to print the document. (See Chapter 2 for more information on opening and saving documents.)

WordPerfect is another popular word-processing program. It actually works much like Microsoft Word. Your screen will look a little different than the one shown in Figure 14-1, but you can do the same things with WordPerfect that you can with Word.

Spreadsheet Applications

Spreadsheets are pretty neat. They make business calculations easy. You can use them to create visual pictures — graphs and charts, in other words — of your data. (This feature is often handy if you're not really a numbers person.) They also let you quickly organize data by using tables or grids.

You can format text by using the Formatting toolbar.

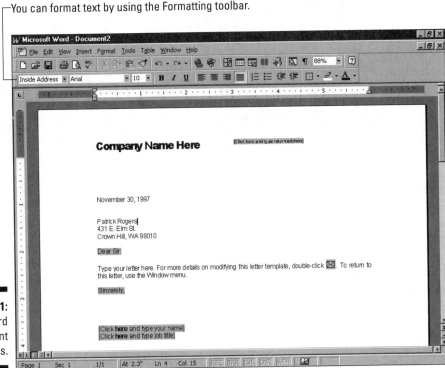

Figure 14-1:
A Word
document
in progress.

Let me take a step back now and describe exactly what a spreadsheet is, in case you're not familiar with the term. A spreadsheet is just a grid. The grids are divided into rows (running horizontally) and columns (running vertically). The little boxes in the grid are called *cells*. In each cell you can enter one of three different types of content: labels, values, or formulas (see Figure 14-2). *Labels* are usually words that describe what your data means. They describe whether the 1998 you enter is a year, a dollar amount, or the number of widgets you sold. *Values* are the actual numbers that you want to work with. And *formulas* are instructions you give to the spreadsheet program to tell it to make a certain calculation by using the numbers you select.

To create a business calculation worksheet by using Microsoft Excel (a popular spreadsheet program), follow these steps:

1. Start Excel by clicking Start⇔Programs⇔Microsoft Excel.

2. Enter the labels you want to use for describing the data you have.

You can choose whether you want your labels to run horizontally or vertically.

3. Enter your data.

Data is just all of the numbers you want to work with.

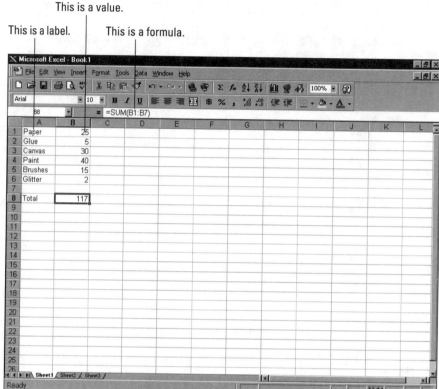

This is a value.

This is a label. This is a formula.

Figure 14-2
A simple
spreadsheet
in Microsoft
Excel.

4. **Enter formulas by clicking the Paste Function button and using the Paste Function dialog box to select the function you want to use (as shown in Figure 14-3).**

   Excel displays a dialog box that you can use to describe which cells it should use for the various parts of the calculation.

After you enter your data in the spreadsheet, you can plot it in a chart. To do so, follow these steps:

1. **Select the data and labels you want to use in the chart.**

   Excel plots the data and uses the labels to label the chart axes.

2. **Click the Chart Wizard button.**

3. **Go through the Chart Wizards steps to describe what kind of chart you want to use and how you want it to look — including what you want plotted where and where you want the finished chart to go. (See Figure 14-4.)**

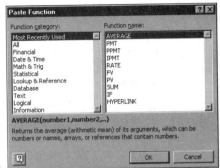

Figure 14-3:
Selecting a
function
to use.

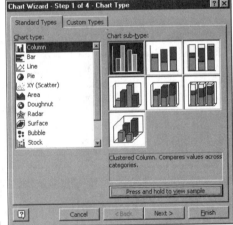

Figure 14-4:
Using the
Chart
Wizard to
describe
the chart
you want
to create.

I used Microsoft Excel to describe how you can use a spreadsheet program
to perform business calculations and to graph data, but I should let you
know that Lotus 1-2-3 and Quattro Pro work in the same basic manner.

Small Business Accounting Applications

If you don't have an accounting software program for your business, you
probably want to invest in one. Small business accounting programs perform basically three things.

 ✔ They help you create business forms such as checks and invoices.

 ✔ They show you whether you are making or losing money by calculating
   and illustrating your profits and your cash flow.

✔ They help you keep track of your assets and liabilities by keeping detailed lists of your inventory and your accounts payables and receivables, and by monitoring the balances and activities in your bank accounts.

My favorite accounting program for small businesses is QuickBooks. When you first start using QuickBooks, it takes you through an interview where you give it all sorts of prerequisite information about your business: what type of work you're in, what kind of income and expenses you have, who your employees are, what your inventory consists of, how much money you currently have in your bank accounts, and so forth. Entering all of this initial information takes quite a while, but once you've done so, you're ready to begin using QuickBooks.

Using QuickBooks is really easy. It displays forms on-screen and you just fill them out. The nice part about these forms is that they're very familiar to you. For example, when you want to enter transactions in a bank account register, you use an on-screen register that looks just like a paper checkbook register. When you want to create an invoice, you just fill in the fields of QuickBooks' ready-made invoice form and then click the Print button to print the invoice. And when you want to cut a check to pay a bill (as shown in Figure 14-5), you just fill in the on-screen check form. QuickBooks helps you out by doing all of the math for you. It keeps track of things like your account balances and how much you owe in payroll liabilities so you don't have to.

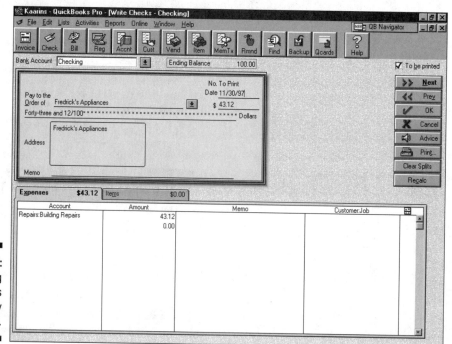

Figure 14-5:
Using QuickBooks to pay your bills.

Just to let you know, other small business accounting programs (like those from Peachtree) work in the same basic manner. For more information about using Quicken for very small businesses, see Chapter 18.

Tax Preparation Applications

I know you don't like to do your taxes. Me neither. But if you do your own taxes, you definitely want to consider using a tax preparation program. These programs save you great gobs of time when April 15th rolls around, and they aren't difficult to use. In a nutshell, all you have to do is fill in an on-screen version of the tax form. (Often you fill in these on-screen forms by answering questions the tax program asks during the initial interview.) The program then makes all the calculations for you (which saves you time and makes mistakes less likely).

Let me see if I need to tell you anything else . . . Oh yes. Most of the programs audit your return for funny or suspicious entries. And most of the programs also provide tax saving tips that you may be able to use to save way more than you spend on the program itself. (In case you're interested, I use TurboTax for Business — shown in Figure 14-6 — and I'm always really happy with it.)

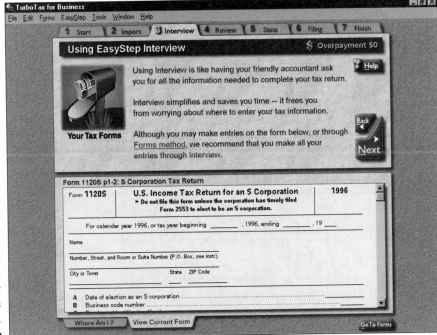

Figure 14-6:
Using
TurboTax
for
Businesses
to enter
business
deductions.

Database Applications

If your business needs to keep track of an expansive list of inventory, contacts, or projects, you can use a database program to help you keep these lists under control. Databases work just like card files except they let you easily organize, sort, and filter information so that you can find exactly what it is you're looking for and display it the way you want.

To manage databases by using Access (a popular database program from Microsoft), you use forms to enter bits of information about something. Say, for example, that you use Access to store information about your customers. You may enter the customer's name, address, telephone number, and ID number on a form (see Figure 14-7). All of the information you enter about this customer put together is called a *record*. You store records in *tables*. So you may have a table for your customers, a table for your projects, and a table for your inventory if you use Access to manage these things. When you want to gather information that fits certain criteria, you perform a *query*. A query lets you filter information so that you can see, for instance, all customers who live in a certain city, or all the projects that used certain pieces of your inventory. To format or summarize the information so that it looks the way you want, you can create a report.

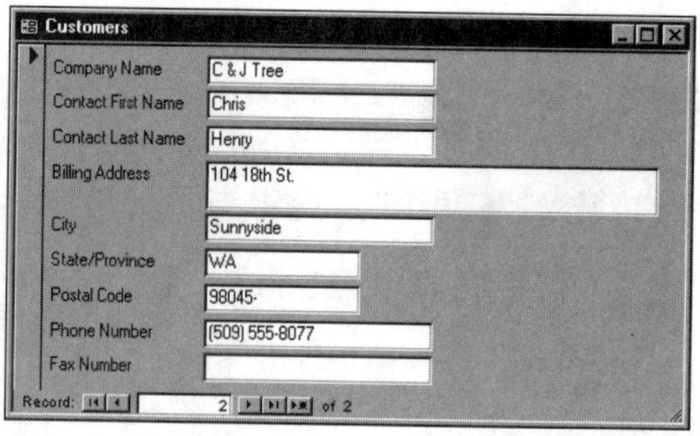

Figure 14-7:
Entering a record with a form.

Just to let you know, other database programs like dBASE, Lotus Notes, Approach, and Paradox all work in the same manner.

Presentation Applications

If you need to make sales presentations, a quick and easy way of whipping up an impressive, professional-looking presentation is by using presentation software. Presentation software is usually simple to use and doesn't take long to learn. It allows you to create a single slide or a series of slides to flip through as you present. You can also decide whether you want to display your presentation on-screen, print it off and hand it out on paper, or create overhead transparencies from it.

To create a presentation by using PowerPoint (a popular presentation software program), follow these steps:

1. **Start PowerPoint by clicking Start⇨Programs⇨Microsoft PowerPoint.**

2. **Click the AutoContent Wizard button and click OK.**

   The AutoContent Wizard organizes the presentation for you and lays it out by using one of the design templates that come with PowerPoint.

3. **Go through the AutoContent Wizard and select the type of presentation you want to create, what medium you plan to use to display the presentation, and what information you want included in the presentation.**

4. **Add the content to each individual slide by clicking on the placeholders and entering text and graphics.**

After you create a presentation (Figure 14-8 shows an example), you can spice it up in several ways to make it more lively, colorful, and interesting. You can change the presentation's color scheme, you can add animation to text, and you can specify transitions to use between slides.

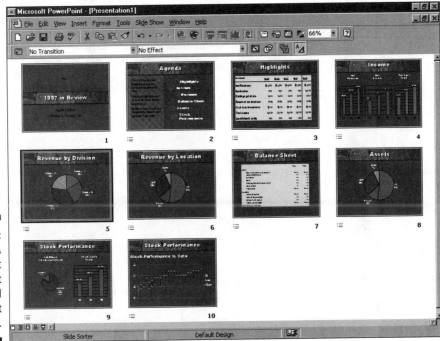

Figure 14-8:
A PowerPoint view that shows all slides at once.

Project Management Applications

If meeting deadlines is important in your business, you need project management software. With a project management software program, you can define the steps necessary to complete a project. You then describe how long each of the steps takes and which steps you need to complete first before you can begin other steps. You can also use project management software to manage your resources and make sure that some employees aren't overscheduled at some times and underscheduled at others.

With a project management program, you can easily see when tasks must be completed in order for a project to stay on track. You can also see who is responsible for each task. To create a schedule by using Microsoft Project, follow these steps:

1. **Start Microsoft Project by clicking Start⇨Programs⇨Microsoft Project.**

   The Microsoft Project window, shown in Figure 14-9, is displayed.

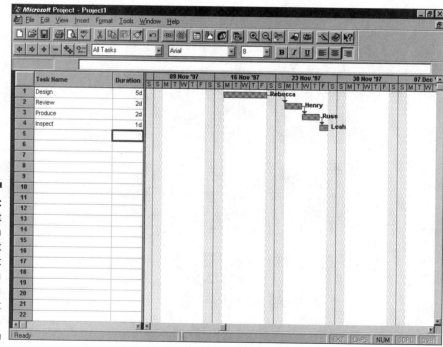

Figure 14-9: A Gantt chart in Microsoft Project lets you visualize a project schedule.

2. **Enter a name for the task in the first Task Name box.**

3. **Enter how much time you want to allot for the task in the Duration box.**

   If a task takes two hours, type **2h.** If it takes two days, type **2d.** If it takes two weeks, type **2w.**

4. **In the Resources box, enter the name of the person responsible for completing the task.**

5. **To make one task dependent upon the completion of a previous task, drag the mouse from the end of the predecessor task's blue bar to the beginning of the dependent task's blue bar.**

   Microsoft Project draws a line connecting the two tasks and schedules the last task to begin only after the first task has ended.

6. **To schedule backwards from a deadline, choose File⇨Project Info.**

7. **In the Project Info dialog box, select Project Finish Date from the Schedule From drop-down list box.**

8. **Enter the deadline for the project in the Finish Date box and click OK.**

If you only need to schedule your own tasks, you may consider planning software such as Schedule+ (which comes with Microsoft Exchange) or the full version of Outlook (which comes with Microsoft Office).

Integrated Applications

Another option for word processing, creating spreadsheets, and organizing databases all within one application is an *integrated program*. Integrated programs amount to "lite" versions of full-fledged word processing, spreadsheet, and database programs all rolled into one. If you don't use the computer very much in your business, and you don't think you'll need to exploit the power of the individual programs, an integrated program is an efficient and economical possibility. While you sacrifice the advanced features you get if you buy the programs separately, you can get an integrated program for a fraction of the cost of a suite of full-fledged programs (such as Lotus Suite or Microsoft Office Suite). When you start a program like Microsoft Works, it usually asks you what kind of a file you want to create. Figure 14-10 shows the window Works displays when you tell it you want to create a letter using a letter template.

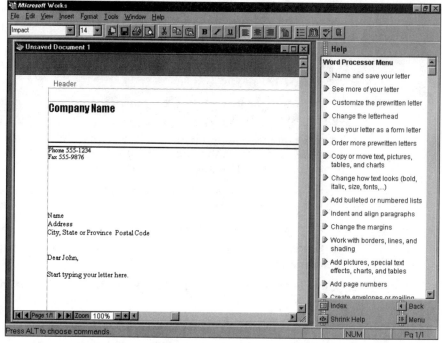

Figure 14-10:
Creating
a word-
processing
document
with
Microsoft
Works.

The Confession

Okay, if you've been keeping count here, you caught me. I only introduced eight types of useful small business software, and I said I would introduce ten. However, the other two types of software I wanted to include here have already been discussed in this book, and I didn't want to sound like a broken record. The other types of software that I think are most useful to businesses are e-mailing software, such as Outlook Express, which I discuss in Chapter 7, and Web browsing software, such as Internet Explorer, which I discuss throughout this book, but especially in Chapter 5.

Even with these ten types of business software, this list is far from exhaustive. All sorts of other business software may be vital to your business. Your business may not be able to live without desktop publishing software, for example, if you publish complex newsletters or flyers. Or you may use graphic software if you need to create and edit graphics. And you almost surely use software that is specialized for your business. If you're running an architectural firm, you probably have a 3D-modeling program. If you keep genealogical records, you probably have a family-tree-making program, and so on.

Chapter 15

Ten Random Thoughts from a Fellow Small Business Guy

I wish that you and I, as fellow small business people, could talk just in general terms about using personal computers in a small business. Over a cup of coffee, say. We could trade war stories, maybe share some ideas, and just generally pick each other's brains. We can't do that, of course. A book like this only allows for one-way communication. Even so, I'd like to share some random thoughts with you. This is the stuff I'd say to you if we could have a heart-to-heart talk.

Standardization Makes Sense and Saves Cents

Okay, here's my first thought. While I appreciate diversity in just about everything, I think you ought to standardize your hardware and your software. In other words, just be totally boring and buy all your personal computers from one manufacturer and then get all your software from one software vendor.

I don't think that which manufacturer or software vendor you pick matters all that much. You can buy your personal computers through the mail or at the place down the street from your office. You can get all your software from Microsoft or Corel or Lotus or somebody else.

The point of standardization is to simplify your life, business, and computing. You have a million things to do, and many of them are critical to the success of your business: servicing an important customer, hiring the right workers, and thinking about where you should go strategically. For these reasons, you absolutely don't want to multiply the work of using PCs by having to learn more than one word processor, spreadsheet program, or Web browser. You don't want to get entangled in the idiosyncrasies of different manufacturer's machines. And you don't want to have to learn how to fix those little glitches that occur with painful but predictable regularity on every computer.

This makes sense, right? As it is, you or some other coworker will spend a few hours every week or maybe every month (if you're lucky) playing "Joe Answerboy" or "Jane Answergirl." You can minimize the time you spend answering questions and trying to solve problems by limiting the number of different pieces of hardware and software in your office.

Let me say one final thing about this whole standardization business. I can guess that you won't be the one saying, "Hey, let's buy different word processors for everybody and different PCs, too!" That's not the way it works. What really happens is that you hire a new secretary and he doesn't want to learn your word processor. He wants to use the one he already knows. (He'll probably say something like, "Oh, this other word processor is much better than the one you guys are using.") But the problem with this idea — another word processor for Jerry — is that the Answerboy or Answergirl then needs to learn a new word processor.

Or here's another example — only this time using hardware. Your graphic designer used a Mac at her last place of employment and she really, really wants to use a Mac in your office — thereby forcing you to learn a whole new hardware platform. At first blush, you can easily let yourself get sucked into decisions that lead you away from standardization. But I warn you, in the end, it's never worth it.

The Leading Edge is Often the Bleeding Edge

A while back I used to get this popular PC magazine. I swear that every month for two years straight, they had this big cover headline that basically said something like, "Why you MUST have the new [fill in blank] PC!" I finally let my subscription lapse. Partly, I confess, because I got tired of always hearing the message, "Hey, if you were a real man, you'd get this new piece of gear."

But I stopped reading this particular rag for another reason, too. This notion that you should always go out and buy the newest, greatest piece of computer gear often isn't very good business. Much of the newest technology hasn't been adequately tested. (This, in my experience, is true of both hardware and software.) Most of time, you pay a premium to get leading edge technology (which is ironic because the stuff often hasn't been tested adequately). And then a surprising percentage of the time, new, leading edge technology never becomes popular enough, so the manufacturer or maker just drops it. (I'm sure that this has nothing to do with the inadequate testing thing I just mentioned, right?)

Anyway, for all of these reasons, I recommend that you stay off the leading edge of technology. Don't buy products that aren't already popular. Don't buy products that you have to pay extra for just because they're new. Don't buy products unless you're sure that they're going to be around in a year or two.

My editors thought I was maybe a little vague with my "don't do this" advice dished out in the preceding paragraphs. They pointed out, in fact, that what I advised was too general to be of much use in some specific situations. So let me throw out two decision rules you can use. First, if you're buying software, wait to make your purchase until after the software publishers releases the first service pack (which will take care of the first set of bugs) or six months, whichever comes first. (By the way, if you're buying software that's revised every year — like Quicken or QuickBooks — I'd go ahead and buy the new software when it comes out because the new software often includes bug fixes.) Second, if you're buying hardware, don't buy the newest, fastest gizmo that's available until it's at least six months old — and consider buying the second newest, second fastest gizmo if you're on a budget.

People Need Training

Okay, an obvious point: People need training. Or, at least, they typically need training if they're going to be truly productive with all the expensive technology you plop onto their desks. Good administrative assistants can produce truly amazing amounts of work with a PC and good suite of office productivity applications such as Microsoft Office or Corel Office: beautiful reports and proposals, huge mass mailings, sophisticated presentations, and other stuff as well. But they can't do this work with just a PC and some software. They need the knowledge to use these tools. And that means that they probably also need training.

PCs are Cheap Compared to People

I sometimes get bummed out by how expensive all this technology is. You can rather easily spend $3,000 on a computer. A printer can cost anywhere from a few hundred bucks to a few thousand. And then the software usually runs you several hundred bucks — and sometimes much more. If you put a PC and a printer on every worker's desk, therefore, you're often talking $4,000 to $5,000 a head. That's a bundle.

And yet, as an accountant at heart and as a small business owner with an almost pathological obsession about profit, I think that PCs are cheap compared to people. I don't have some big quantitative academic study to back this up — only anecdotal evidence. But I will say that in my little business, we don't need an administrative assistant, clerk, or secretary because people, in essence, make their computers do almost all of this work. Our graphic designer creates as many books a year (working maybe half-time) as it used to take whole of team of typographers working full-time only a few years ago. It takes me a few weeks to write a book that used to take better writers than me months and months. And I do all of the accounting for my business myself in about an hour a week.

I'd like to think that our productivity stems from some cleverness on our part, or at least that our productivity reflects hard work and discipline. But, to be really honest, I think it mostly stems from our use of PCs. We've used PCs and PC software to automate routine tasks that small businesses like ours used to pay at least minimum wage for (and often some multiple of minimum wage, in fact).

Another way to say this same thing — and I think this is roughly true — is that we buy $5,000 of computer (which often lasts a couple of years or more) and thereby don't have to pay some employee $10,000 or $20,000 (or more) a year. So we buy $5,000 of technology and save $20,000 or more in labor costs. That's a pretty sweet deal.

Ergonomics is a Word You'll Want to Learn

You know what? My back just aches some days. Partly, this is because I'm getting old. But it's also partly because I've spent almost the last 20 years hunched over a keyboard, peering into a monitor, ignoring the ergonomics of my work environment.

I don't say any of this to make you feel sorry for me, because, to be quite honest, it's my own dumb fault. But, please, don't make the same stupid mistakes that I've made. Sit up straight in a good chair that lets you plant your feet firmly on the ground. Make sure that your monitor is slightly less than eye level and that it's the correct distance from your eyes (probably two to three feet). Make sure that your keyboard is at the right level (your arms should hang loosely from your shoulders and your forearms should be parallel to the ground. When you see an ergonomics article written by someone who seems to have half a clue, read it. You have to take care of yourself.

You can often get good ergonomic information from hardware manufacturers. A keyboard manufacturer may tell you the right way to position your keyboard, for example. And a monitor manufacturer may include with the monitor packaging a diagram that shows how to position your monitor for optimal, ergonomic viewing.

Performance Improvement Doesn't Have to Cost an Arm and a Leg

You maybe already know this, but in case you don't, let me tell you that you can often make your PC run faster without spending a ton of money. Windows and Windows programs run faster with more memory, so an easy way to boost your computer's speed, often times, is just to add memory.

I also think bigger monitors also pay you back with a boost in performance — up to a point. Why? People see more on the screen and spend less time scrolling through large documents. In our office, by the way, we used to use the standard 14-inch monitors in our office and have tried the large 20-inch monitors, but have now settled on 17-inch monitors (which maybe cost twice as much as a 14 inch monitor but half as much as the larger 20-inch or 21-inch monitors).

And then, just training people to really exploit their computer — but, oh yeah, I mention this point earlier in the chapter.

The Trials and Travails of Telecommuting

My first real managerial job was as the controller of a small, fifty-person manufacturing firm. My only full-time accountant was a very nice woman who wanted to work at home. While I was moderately frustrated with that arrangement at the time, it was a great lesson. I learned that telecommuting rarely makes sense except as an exceptional gambit — a technique that's only applied to unusual people or unusual situations and even in these cases only infrequently. If you think about this for a minute, you already know the two basic reasons:

- ✔ Unless a person works exclusively at home, you have two workstations to set up: two computers, two desks, two phones, two fax machines, two printers, and so on. Of course, you can just choose not to set up a second workstation at home. But then you have the challenge of figuring out why if people need things like office equipment at the office to be productive, they don't need them at home. Hmmmm. (I'm not even going to get into the issue of whether someone really has room for all of this stuff in his apartment or house.) This makes sense, right? Setting up a good office is expensive. You know that, and you shouldn't ratchet up your costs just so somebody can work at home. Yeah, the technology supports the telecommuting thing. But economically, it's not really viable.

- ✔ Supporting a person who works at home is very difficult. Earlier in the chapter, I alluded to the fact that somebody needs to be "Joe Answerboy" or "Jane Answergirl" when it comes to your computers. Unfortunately, Joe and Jane aren't going to be able to support Bob Homebody or Jennifer Stayathome, because they're at home. So, now you have a situation where Bob or Jennifer isn't getting the support they need — which negatively impacts their productivity. (If Bob or Jennifer are so smart that they don't need the support, by the way, I don't think they should be home. They should be at work playing the "answerboy" or "answergirl" role.)

A couple of final comments about telecommuting: First, the only situation in which I've seen telecommuting work well is when you have someone who needs to work alone on projects. Take, for example, the case of a writer or editor who, by the very nature of her work, needs to spend hours of time working quietly, alone, and without interruption. These people often telecommute with great success. In fact, you often want them to telecommute at least part-time.

But, one tricky part of successful telecommuting — from the employer's perspective — is monitoring productivity. This is awkward to say, but with telecommuting, how do you know people are working? How do you know they're not just fooling around or, just as bad, spinning their wheels? I don't have a good answer to this question. The only thing I've found that works is quantifying somebody's output. For example, you can measure a writer's production in words per hour. You can measure an editor's production in pages edited an hour. Once you do this, you can get some idea about how productive somebody is. If Akmed is writing 500 words an hour and Jeannine is writing, say, 50 words an hour, you probably want to figure out what's going on.

If you're the person telecommuting, my experience is that you need to think about your employer's perceptions of your productivity. If the boss can't see you sitting at your desk, hard at work, you need to find some other way to frequently remind him or her that you're working hard, producing value, and staying busy.

People Don't Back Up Unless You Make It Easy

A quick point: People (that includes you and me) don't like to back up any more than they like calling the photocopier repair-person, making coffee when the pot is empty, or cleaning out the office refrigerator. So you'll want to make backing up really, really easy. What we do in our office is provide a variety of backup mediums. If someone has few megabytes, she uses a floppy disk while sitting right there at her computer. If she has more stuff, she uses a high-density, removable storage device called an Iomega ZIP drive (which is connected to a network server) because it allows for storage of roughly 100 megabytes on something that looks like an over-sized floppy disk. If someone needs more space than that, she uses a CD (which is also connected to a network server) because it allows for storage of up to just over 600 megabytes.

By the way, we don't use tape backups in our little office. Sure, tapes let you store a ton of data, and that's good. But what we've found with tapes is that they typically require someone to learn a new application (the tape backup and restore utility), and that makes them harder to use.

When you use a disk to back up — even if the disk is an Iomega disk or a CD — you copy documents to it the same way that you copy documents to any other disk. For more information, refer to Chapter 2.

Secrets: Yours, Mine, and Theirs

I have another quick point for you. With computers in an office environment, you don't really have secrets — or at least not secrets about the document files you store on your hard disk. I don't say this to scare you. You just need to know that, in general, the documents you store on your hard disk are equivalent to documents you leave lying about on your desk. While people may not necessarily intend to rifle through the stacks of paper on your desk, they can. You can imagine how this happens. You're out of the office. Some coworker needs to find some document that you had last, so he rifles through the stacks of paper you've stored on your desk or the document files you've left in some folder on your hard disk. And then, before he knows what's happened, he's found a list of people's salaries (if you're the boss) or a resume you've created (if you're an employee looking for a new job).

So, the bottom line is that Windows and computers only give you the illusion of security, not total security. Sure, you can hide stuff on your hard disk (as discussed in Chapter 2), but that's roughly akin to hiding stuff in some unlocked file cabinet. People can still find what you hide if they look hard enough or just because they stumble onto something out of dumb luck.

As a practical matter, you can only secure your data in two ways:

- You can put a PC into a locked room and prevent people from having access to the room. (This technique is how big-company computer departments increase their security.)

- You can store a document on a disk that you can physically remove to some other location. (For example, you can store a file on a floppy disk and then take the floppy disk home with you every night.)

And Let Me Just Mention Windows NT

This book describes one flavor of Windows, called Windows 95. In another few months, you'll hear lots of hoopla concerning Windows 95's successor, Windows 98. (And, in fact, the yellow section of this book describes Windows 98.) But Windows NT, or NT for short, is a whole other flavor of Windows.

NT amounts to an industrial-strength version of Windows. On the surface, Windows NT looks like Windows 95. But beneath the surface, NT provides beefed-up security and safety features that mean NT can work well when Windows 95 and Windows 98 doesn't.

If you're really interested in NT, you can get more information from Microsoft's Web site at www.microsoft.com. You can also read a book like *Windows NT For Dummies*. But I can, in a sentence or two, explain what's essentially different about NT.

NT lets you virtually assure that someone can't view or open or fool around with a program or document file unless you say that it's okay. This tight security is what's unique and different and good about NT.

Predictably, this extra security doesn't come free. NT costs more than Windows 95 and will probably cost more than Windows 98. It's also more complicated to work with (mostly because of all the practical aspects of implementing its super-tight security). And product support for NT is expensive. (After you get NT installed on a desktop computer, you pay around $200 every time you call Microsoft's product line. Ouch.)

Because NT is more expensive and more complicated, people who don't need the extra security probably shouldn't use it. People who do need the security should use it.

I know an attorney, for example, who uses NT because it assures the confidentiality of the legal documents he's stored on his computer and on his office's network. So in his business, the trade-off makes sense: He accepts the extra complexity because he gets tight security.

Many small business users, however, aren't going to want to make this trade-off.

Chapter 16

Things Every Business Should Know about Web Publishing

● ●

In This Chapter

▶ How to create Web pages with regular programs

▶ About Web publishing costs

▶ About the complexity of Web publishing

▶ Why Web publishing can be better than paper publishing

▶ How to make money with Web publishing

▶ Unique risks of Web publishing

▶ Cost of content creation

▶ Alternatives to Web publishing

▶ When Web publishing doesn't make sense

● ●

*I*n Chapter 6, I discuss the mechanics of Web publishing: what HTML is, how you use it to create HTML documents, and how you can use tools that come with Internet Explorer (such as FrontPage Express and the Web Publishing wizard) to rather easily create Web pages and set up Web sites. All that information is good and fine. And if you're even considering becoming a Web publisher, you'll want to start by exploring the stuff in Chapter 6. All that said, I still want to talk about a few other things in this chapter.

Mechanics Are Simple

In terms of mechanics, Web publishing isn't all that complicated. As Chapter 6 shows, you can rather easily set up a simple collection of Web pages by creating from scratch HTML documents (using any word processor or text editor like the Windows Notepad). And, if you use a simple HTML Editor like FrontPage Express (which comes with Internet Explorer 4.0, included on the CD that comes with this book), setting up more sophisticated Web pages is very straightforward.

The next step, of course, is to move your Web pages to a server someplace so people can look at your Web pages. But this step typically isn't very difficult either. All you really have to do is move the files from your PC to the ISP's Web server. You can do so with the Web Publishing wizard that comes with Internet Explorer (which I talk about a little bit in Chapter 7). And you can also do the same with the FTP client that's part of Windows 95, although that approach is a bit more complicated (see the sidebar "Using the Windows FTP client").

Using the Windows FTP client

Using the FTP client to move HTML documents to a Web server isn't that complicated. Here's what you need to do:

1. **Make a Dial-Up Networking connection in the usual way.**

   You may, for example, need to first start your Web browser.

2. **Start the FTP client program.**

   You can do so by starting Windows Explorer, viewing the contents of the Windows folder, and then double-clicking the ftp program file when you find it. The ftp window opens, which is really just a command prompt (like you used to see in MS-DOS).

3. **Connect to your ISP's Web server by typing the command** open **followed by the name of the server to which you're going to move your HTML documents.**

   For example, if the server's name is `ftp.bignet.com` you type the following command: **open ftp.bignet.com**

4. **Tell the ISP's Web server which directory or folder you want to move your HTML**

documents to by typing the command cd followed by the directory pathname.

For example, if the ISP says that you should store your stuff in the yourstuf subdirectory, which is stored in the pages directory (this would mean the directory path is pages/yourstuf), you type the following command: **cd pages/yourstuf**

5. **To move a file — this may be an HTML document or a graphic image — to the Web server, type the command send followed by the complete pathname of the file.**

   For example, to move a document named `intro.htm` and stored at the location `c:\pages\intro.htm`, type the following command: **send c:\pages\intro.htm**

6. **Repeat Step 5 for each file you want to move.**

7. **When you finish moving the files to the Web server, type the following command:** bye

You Can Create Web Pages with Standard Applications

Because the Web is so hot, many standard application programs let you create HTML documents. Most of the programs that make up the Microsoft Office suite of programs let you create HTML documents, for example. And the same thing is true of many other popular office suites, word processors, desktop publishing programs, and illustration programs.

To create an HTML document with a regular old program, you often use either a Save As HTML command (which should appear on the File menu) or you save the document in the regular way but then specify the file format as HTML. (To do so, activate the Save As Type drop-down list box as HTML Document.)

Costs to Begin Web Publishing Are Low

Web publishing costs are surprisingly low. If you're on a shoestring budget, you may be able to publish to the Web for next to nothing. For example, you probably don't need any special tools to create your HTML documents. (In a pinch you can use a text editor like the Windows Notepad accessory.) And many popular application programs, including Microsoft's, let you do HTML editing.

After you create the HTML documents, you have to move them to a Web server. But it's just possible — no, make that likely — that your ISP will let you store a handful of Web pages on one of its Web servers for no extra cost. In the shoestring budget case, for example, you spend time, but maybe no money.

If you aren't as concerned about the costs and want to do things in a fancier way, you actually don't have to pay all that much more. For about $500, you can set up a very nice Web site. If you wanted to do this, you'd spend maybe a couple of hundred bucks on a Web publishing program like the FrontPage suite of programs, which makes creating sophisticated Web pages really easy, including Web pages that use forms and webbots. You can probably register your own domain name for $100 bucks or so. (Doing so lets you use your company name or trade name in your URL.) You may pay another $200 as a fee to an ISP that's set up to provide Web server space to Web publishers and who, therefore, does special, extra stuff for people like you. In this case — the $500 case — you can do a really professional job (excluding your time) for not that much money. Or at least not that much when you compare the cost to things like letterhead stationery, color brochures, and Yellow Pages advertising.

Webbots

Webbots are small programs that work with Web pages. A webbot, for example, can change a Web page's content automatically.

And a webbot can automatically store the information a form collects.

Web Publishing is Sometimes Better than Traditional Paper-Based Publishing

This fact is probably obvious to you, but Web publishing provides at least three unique advantages as compared to traditional, paper-based publishing: lower printing costs, faster publication schedules, and easier corrections. Let me just quickly talk about each of these things.

The most obvious advantage, I guess, is that you don't have any printing costs. With some fancy-schmancy color brochure, you pay a pretty penny to print, say, 1,000 copies. And if you want to print 5,000 or 50,000, you're often talking serious money. But Web publishing, once you get your HTML documents created, usually doesn't have much additional cost. Oh sure, you will pay the ISP something to store your pages (I talked about this earlier). It's also conceivable that if your Web site enjoys just monstrous traffic, your ISP will come to you and say, "Hey, buddy, you need to pay more money because you're getting thousands of hits a day." But in general, no additional cost is accrued to show your Web site's pages to another 500 or another 5,000 people. So your printing costs are really low — especially when you talk about the situation where your publication is viewed by thousands and thousands of people.

Another advantage of Web publishing is that once you have your Web pages ready, you can publish them almost instantaneously. You get them done, you move them to the Web server, and you're finished. In comparison, with paper publishing, you have to send the stuff to printer (which probably takes a day just for transportation). Then the printer has to schedule your print job and actually do your printing (you're probably talking at least a few days here and maybe even weeks). Finally, you have to get the printed material back from the printer (another day) and then send them off to your readers (I have no idea how long this will take).

A third, big advantage of Web publishing is that making changes is easier and quicker. With a book like this one, for example, making easy or quick changes is basically impossible. If I misspell some word and then the publisher goes out and prints 10,000 copies, which then get distributed to 1,000 different book stores, my mistake can't be fixed in a practical way. With a Web page, all you have to do is correct the HTML document (by fixing the misspelling) and then move the corrected copy to the Web server. You make your correction immediately. (This ability may seem like a small point, but mistakes in your business publications can be far more serious than a misspelled word. What if you quote a price that's below cost, for example? Or what if you make some terrible error describing some important product feature?)

Some Small Businesses Make Oodles of Money Off Their Web Sites

I should probably tell you something. Some people are making big money off of their Web sites. This is kinda awkward to talk about, but I think I should, because the topic is germane to small businesses. While some very smart cookies (including Microsoft) have failed, to date, to make a bunch of money off of their Web sites, one category of business has done very well financially: the adult entertainment sites. Now don't freak out. I'll be real careful here about how I talk about this stuff. And I'm not suggesting that you consider this business opportunity. Instead, I think that you should understand and reflect on their success. You may want to apply some of their techniques.

So here's the deal. What an adult Web site does is heavily advertise their, er, product (typically pictures and videos) by posting samples in appropriate newsgroups. They also create (some people say they also sometimes steal) lots of fresh content so customers have a reason to continually revisit their Web sites. These Web publishers create Web sites that enjoy heavy traffic, and that appears to be the first step toward success.

To actually produce revenue — and here I'm relying on information reported in my local newspaper and in the *Wall Street Journal,* not personal experience — these Web sites make incremental sales. If you visit one of these Web sites, for example, they may ask you (or may require you) to subscribe in order to get access to special pictures or videos. This may cost, I don't know, $3 a month. They may also advertise and sell special deals — like a video that you can buy only from them for $15 or a CD that'll save you from having to download pictures for $8 a pop. You get the picture, right? They have all these little, almost impulse purchase items that they sell. What happens, and this is probably predictable, is that with a heavy-traffic site, a certain percentage of the Web site visitors do spend some money. They subscribe for $3, and then they buy that one thing for $8. Maybe they do or maybe they don't buy that other thing for $15. Not every visitor does, but enough do that reportedly many of these sites are making $4,000 to $6,000 a day.

One other feature of the adult entertainment Web sites is noteworthy: They've basically reengineered the process by which people acquire adult literature or products. Rather than having to stand in line at some book-store, for example, you just anonymously visit a Web site and place an order. This reengineering makes sense given the awkwardness of the product they sell. And this reengineering appears to be the another piece to the puzzle.

Now I'm not going into all this detail in order to embarrass you. (In fact, I should tell you that I'm a bit embarrassed myself at this point in the discussion.) And I'm not thinking that you should all rush out and get into the adult entertainment business. But you can learn some lessons from their success. Specifically, I think you have four lessons to learn:

✔ You need to actively advertise a Web site in order to build heavy traffic.

✔ You need to maintain the traffic by regularly providing fresh content.

✔ You make money through incremental sales: $3 to subscribe, $6 for a book, $12 for video, and so on.

✔ You probably need to use the Web as part of reengineering some business process.

The above points are all pretty abstract, so let me give you a concrete example. Say that you run a travel agency. If you didn't know any better, you may just create a Web site that amounts to an advertisement for your agency. And, I guess, that'd be okay, but what if you instead did what the money-making Web sites do?

✔ **Building heavy traffic:** You may be able to build Web site traffic by maintaining a Web page that shows the lowest fairs to Europe or Hawaii and by posting travel tip articles to appropriate newsgroups.

✔ **Fresh new content:** Maybe you could also easily generate lots of fresh new content by letting people post reports of travel scams to your Web site. (You'd probably want to talk with your attorney about this just to make sure that you weren't opening up yourself to some law suit.)

✔ **Incremental sales:** You may be able to get into the incremental sales business by having a special weekly mailing list that reports on the 20 best travel bargains and that costs a mere $3 a year, by selling $8 travel books, and maybe by selling items of interest to travelers like hard-to-find luggage or electronic adapters for international travel.

✔ **Reengineer a process:** Okay, I don't know enough about the travel business to know how this may work. But what if it turns out that your clients all tend to be affluent, retired, international travelers who leave the country for extended trips? (I'm making this stuff up, obviously.) Maybe what you could do is provide a service where you let these people set up their mini-Web sites — just stories and pictures — that show their friends and family what and how they're doing. You may even set up this Web site in a way that lets the travelers as well as their families and friends use this Web site as bulletin board for posting messages. This extra service would not be very expensive so you may just include it as part of the package. Or you may turn it into another profit opportunity by charging minimal fee — maybe $50 — to do this.

Web Publishing Also Presents Unique Risks

In spite of the advantages of Web publishing as compared to paper publishing, it also presents at least a couple of challenges to businesses. For one thing, you can't really control who gets access to your Web site. That means that everybody and her mother — including your competitors, the guy who's trying to sue you, and some government agency that's about to audit your financial affairs — can use your Web site to research you. This maybe sounds like a small point made by someone with paranoia, but I think you need to reflect on it, if only for a moment. If your biggest competitor calls you up and says, "Hey, send us all your brochures," you may decide not to; you don't have this option with your Web site.

Another problem is that your site can easily get lost in the vastness of the Web. Hopefully, you can do things (as described in Chapter 6) that let you publicize your Web site enough that your URL appears in directory-style and index-style search services. And maybe you can advertise your Web site a bit and thereby build up some traffic. But even with these tactics, your Web site may get lost. In comparison, with paper publications, you can hand-deliver them (which means they don't get lost). You can do targeted mailings (which increases the chances that people will read your stuff). And you can even do bulk mass mailings, which maybe means that your publication is one of eight pieces of "junk" mail that someone receives, but at least that's a better presence than the case where your Web site is one of 300 listed in some directory sub-category or on an index.

Big Cost Stems from Content Creation

One of the things that sometimes gets lost in all the excitement about Web publishing is that while Web publishing isn't all that expensive (at least in terms of the money you spend on hardware, software, and ISPs) and while it also isn't very complicated, creating the content you publish on a Web site can be very expensive and very time-consuming.

I've talked a bit about the fact that you probably need to continually update your Web site's information in order to have people revisit your site. But what that means is that you really have to become a publisher, and publishing is a great deal of work. Writing a good article for your Web site can easily take a day. Writing something the length of a book can take months. Photographs and illustrations can easily take an hour a piece. If you start rolling all of this data around in your head, you quickly figure out that setting up a Web site — and doing it right — may take a day or two a week of someone's time, and that gets really expensive.

The bottom line? You need to think about this often overlooked aspect of Web publishing. A while back, for example, my small business looked into setting up a Web site for communicating with people who read the books we write and package. (Most of the stuff we do, by the way, is about using computers for personal or business financial management.) Our basic idea was that I'd write an article a week (to keep the site fresh), and then create a "Dear Abby" sort of column where I answered reader's financial questions. We actually could have provided good content. But in the end, when we looked at the cost of creating that content — probably more than 20 percent of my time a year — we decided that it didn't make any sense.

Other Alternatives Exist

Let me make a quick point here. While the Web is really cool and can be a great business tool, if what you're looking for is a way to communicate with your customers, employees, and vendors, other Internet resources are available that let you do much of what the Web does. For example, you can use e-mail to send people textual messages and, in many cases, document files. And another interesting option is to set up a mailing list that lets you send e-mail messages to a whole bunch of people at one time. (For more information about mailing lists, refer to Chapter 7.) A mailing list, by the way, shouldn't need to cost much more than a few hundred bucks.

Web Publishing Probably Doesn't Make Sense for Most Small Businesses

A final thought to close this chapter: My feeling is that Web publishing probably doesn't make sense for most small businesses. I know that's heresy in some circles. But unless you have the time to produce good content — and you probably don't — I think that a Web site easily turns into way more work than it's worth. Yeah, you'll pick up some customers if you're lucky, and some people will visit your Web site if you do a good job with your content. But I really believe that most of the people who've become Web publishers don't understand the work involved in publishing. I suspect that most of the businesses who are Web publishing aren't making any money off of it when you consider all the costs.

If you decide to become a Web publisher, by the way, I propose that you think about how you turn the Web into something more than just an expensive advertising vehicle. You should, I respectfully suggest, make your Web site into a profit center or, if that's too crass, use it as a tool to smartly reengineer some process in your business.

Chapter 17

Especially for Home-Based Businesses

· ·

In This Chapter

▶ PC security in your home

▶ Your PC and your homeowners policy

▶ Tax laws and your PC (Parts I and II)

▶ Networks in a home office

▶ Sharing a PC with your family

▶ Mobile computing

▶ Multimedia

▶ Quicken

· ·

Most small businesses — as you can probably guess — don't have some fancy-schmancy office, storefront location, or warehouse. They operate out of the owner's home. Small business owners work from home partly because doing so saves money (and therefore increases profits). But more than just that is involved. Some businesses work better and more smoothly when they're operated out of the home. With a home-based business, the owner doesn't have to spend time in traffic or money keeping up out-dated appearances about what a business is supposed to look like. A home-based business also often allows the owner to better balance work with the rest of life. (If you're home, for example, you can deal with your six-year-old's scraped knee.) And with a home-based business, you can often more easily respond to customer needs and deal with business tasks. For example, you can often fit in a bit of work Saturday morning before the rest of the house is up and watching cartoons or CNN.

You may already know all of this information, of course. What you may not know, however, is that you need to think about some special computer and Windows issues if you're running a home-based business. So that's what this chapter does.

Making Your PC Safe and Secure

Let me start out by making a quick point. While in a home-based business you probably don't have computer security risks related to nefarious employees or sneaky shoplifters, you still have to be careful. A well-meaning but computer-illiterate spouse can wreck havoc on your business documents. Your kid can easily bring home virus-laden computer games from grade school — or worse even than that — friends who think computers are just toys to have fun with.

For these reasons, you need to view the PCs that you keep in a home office as security risks. Specifically, you should take several steps:

- **You must back up your data.** You should probably also make sure that you store this data offsite just in case of theft, natural disaster, or fire. (I know this offsite stuff is tough, but it really ought to be done.)

- **You need to get and use anti-virus software if kids are sharing the PC.** Kids not only bring home cold viruses from school, they also bring home computer viruses.

- **You need to take all the same data confidentiality steps that you do with a business office PC.** For example, you may want to use passwords to restrict access to sensitive business documents. You may want to restrict access to a PC (like by saying that the neighborhood kids can't play games on your business computer). You may want to hide business documents in camouflaged or hidden folders. You may even want to store some business documents on removable disks that you can lock up.

All this stuff makes perfect sense, right? You're probably already doing most of it. I guess the main thing I want to say is that you need to be just as careful with a home PC as you do with the one in a regular business office. Sure, by keeping a PC at home, you reduce some of your security risks, but you may also expose yourself to new risks.

Your PC and Your Homeowners Policy

A quick comment: You need to confirm that your homeowners policy covers your computer gear. It probably does, but you want to check by calling your insurance agent. Be sure to mention, too, that you're using the gear in a home-based business.

By the way, you know what's sort of weird? Your homeowner's policy almost surely says that if you're a writer, you can't get coverage for a manuscript you're working on. This specific tidbit may not apply to you because you're probably not a writer. (It did apply to me when I wrote books at home a few years back.) But, still, I think you should file the tidbit away in the back of your mind. Important elements of your business may be part and parcel of your computer system: a mailing list, records of customer receivables, and so forth. If you need or want insurance for these items, your homeowners policy almost certainly doesn't provide coverage. So you want to discuss the possibility and pros and cons of additional coverage with your insurance agent.

U.S. Tax Laws, Part 1 (Section 179 Rules)

As long as you use your computer exclusively for business, you (well, U.S. taxpayers) can use what's called a Section 179 election to depreciate your computer. This law allows you to write off the complete cost of your computer in the year you buy it. If you spend $5,000 on some computer, for example, you don't have to allocate this $5,000 as $1,000-a-year depreciation expense over the next five years. You just write off the whole $5,000 in the year you make the purchase. (By the way, you do need to begin using the computer.)

Section 179 is a great deal for two reasons. First, you can reap the tax savings from the Section 179 deduction in the year that you make your purchase, which helps your cash flow. Second, bookkeeping is easier if you just expense your equipment rather than dealing with the tedious and time-consuming calculations required when you depreciate, or allocate, the cost of some item over several years.

While I'm on the subject of this Section 179 stuff, let me also mention a couple more things. As I'm writing this, you can only write off $17,500 or less in Section 179 elections. This amount should not cause a problem, however, because it's way more than the typical small business spends annually on equipment.

One other item I should mention is that if you're going to use Section 179, you don't want to have your kids fooling around on your PC for non-business stuff. And you don't want to do personal stuff on your PC either. I suggest that you consider buying a second, cheap PC for the family if they need one or that you buy a new PC for your business and then let them use the old, probably-outdated-and-largely-obsolete PC.

U. S. Tax Laws, Part II (Home Usage of a PC)

If you have to share a PC between the business and the family, you can't take the Section 179 election. What you need to do instead is keep a usage log of the time you spend using a PC for business and then the time that family members spend using the computer for personal stuff. At the end of the year, you then allocate a portion of the PC's cost to the business. For example, if you use a PC for business stuff 75 percent of the time, you get to deduct 75 percent of the PC's cost on your business tax return. (The other 25 percent of the cost is a personal expense and, therefore, isn't deductible for tax purposes.)

Keeping a log isn't difficult. But if you have questions about how you do so, you should ask your tax advisor. Er, this is a little difficult to bring up — I absolutely don't believe that you should fudge the figures, but I'd ask your tax advisor about how aggressive you should be in keeping your log. For example, if you tell your PC to download some huge set of business program files from the Microsoft Web site and it takes eleven hours, can you count that time in your log as business usage? Or if you tell your computer and printer to print 50 copies of some 30-page report and it takes all weekend, can you can that time as business usage? I think that in both cases you can. Note, then, that if you're really diligent about counting your business usage, your business usage percentage goes up and, therefore, your tax deduction goes up, too.

Just food for thought.

When Does a Home Network Make Sense?

In Chapters 9 and 10, I talk about how cool networks are because they let you share information and gear. Despite the fact that those chapters assume a network means multiple users, that's not always the case. As crazy as it sounds, you may want to set up a small, two-computer network even for a home office. The situation in which this works well (even when only one person is using a computer) is when you can work both machines and thereby increase your productivity. But that's too abstract, so let me explain.

In some situations, you sit in front of your computer and do some work. And then you wait while the computer does some work. Then you do some more work, and so it goes. A network often helps in a situation like this because you can have one machine that's your machine — the one you sit in front of and work at. Then you can have another machine that does the computer grunt work.

The most common example is printing long or multiple copies of documents. I used to work with a desktop publisher, for example, who had a small, two-computer network he used for his design and desktop publishing work. He sat at one machine and did his work with the desktop publishing program (creating books, newsletters, and so on). Then he used a second machine to print the documents he had already created (a process that often took hours for each document). True, he could have used a single machine for his business. But if he'd done that, he would have had to stop using his machine whenever he printed, because printing required almost all his computer's processing power.

The Kids, the Spouse, and the Dog

I already broached this subject both in Chapter 2 and in this chapter, I guess, but I want to just quickly say something again. If you have business documents that, essentially, describe the very essence of your business, then your computer and information it stores is just super, super critical to your business success. For this reason, I really think that you need to be careful about using the PC for non-business purposes. You don't, for example, want your 11-year-old to delete a bunch of documents (ostensibly part of a misguided clean-up effort) because he wants to install a new game. You don't want your spouse to inadvertently corrupt a bunch of boilerplates you use for correspondence with customers. And you don't want your dog to foul up your machine by attempting to install some new piece of exotic hardware.

Maybe I shouldn't be bringing all this up. I just want you to be careful, and I want you to have some reasonable, fair ammunition to use in any discussions with family members about how the business PC can and should be used.

On the Road Again

You may have already perused Chapter 11. If you have, you know that Windows includes special tools — including Briefcase and Direct Cable Connection — for mobile computing. (Mobile computing just refers to moving around with a computer and to moving computer information around.) If you haven't read Chapter 11 and this mobile computing stuff sounds like something you want to do, refer back to that chapter.

Multimedia Madness

In some ways, the multimedia craze was largely a flop. Much of the stuff published was less interesting than a bad MTV video. And then very few multimedia titles did as well as they should have (given the money that the publisher's invested).

In spite of all this, you should know that multimedia programs are really, really cool in some applications. I've particularly found this to be the case when it comes to educational software. You can find multimedia programs that teach you about all sorts of stuff including computers, business finance, and taxes. (Much of the good stuff seems to come from Microsoft and Intuit.) What this means is that multimedia learning programs (such as Microsoft's Start Here series) and multimedia versions of popular business programs (such as the multimedia of Intuit's Quicken and QuickBooks programs) can be wonderfully powerful business learning tools.

By the way, if you want to learn more about the tools that Windows provides for multimedia programs, refer to Chapter 11.

I Just Want to Say Something About Quicken

In Chapter 14, I whipped through some quick and dirty descriptions of how you can use popular business software for doing all sorts of stuff. One of things I mentioned was accounting software. Everything I said in Chapter 14 still applies for home-based businesses, but let me say that if you operate a small, home-based business, you may not need to go with a full-blown accounting program like QuickBooks. You may instead get by just fine with a program like Intuit's Quicken or the roughly equivalent program Microsoft Money 98.

Both the Quicken and Money programs amount to computerized check-books, which means they're really easy to use. If you want to use either program but find them confusing, you may want to consider IDG's *Quicken For Dummies* (written by me) or *Microsoft Money 98 For Dummies* (written by my friend, Peter Weverka).

Part VI

Appendixes

In this part . . .

You've probably noticed that companion CD glued into the back cover of this book? This part includes three appendixes that describe how you install and use the new Windows accessories that are available on that CD.

Appendix A
About the CD

● ●

*H*ere's what you can find on the *Small Business Windows 95 For Dummies* CD-ROM:

- ✔ A popular Web browser suite
- ✔ A shareware graphics viewing and editing program
- ✔ A handful of useful utilities for zipping files, making business calculations, and determining break-even points
- ✔ A Web page collection of hyperlinks useful to small business Web sites

System Requirements

Make sure that your computer meets the minimum system requirements listed below. If your computer doesn't match up to most of these requirements, you may have problems in using the contents of the CD.

- ✔ A PC with a 486 or faster processor.
- ✔ Microsoft Windows 95.
- ✔ At least 8MB of total RAM installed on your computer. For best performance, we recommend at least 16MB of RAM installed.
- ✔ At least 40MB of hard drive space available to install all the software from this CD. (You'll need less space if you don't install every program.)
- ✔ A CD-ROM drive — double-speed (2x) or faster.
- ✔ A sound card.
- ✔ A monitor capable of displaying at least 256 colors or grayscale.
- ✔ A modem with a speed of at least 14,400 bps. For best performance, we recommend a modem with a speed of at least 28,800 bps.

If you need more information on the basics, check out *PCs For Dummies,* 4th Edition, by Dan Gookin (published by IDG Books Worldwide, Inc.).

How to Use the CD

To install the items from the CD to your hard drive, follow these steps:

1. **Insert the CD into your computer's CD-ROM drive.**

2. **Click the Start button and click Run.**

3. **In the dialog box that appears, type** D:\SETUP.EXE.

   Most of you probably have your CD-ROM drive listed as drive D under My Computer. Type in the proper drive letter if your CD-ROM drive uses a different letter.

4. **Click OK.**

   A license agreement window appears.

5. **Since I'm sure that you'll want to use the CD, read through the license agreement, nod your head, and then click the Accept button. Once you click Accept, you'll never be bothered by the License Agreement window again.**

   From here, the *CD interface* appears. The CD interface is a little program that shows you what is on the CD and coordinates installing the programs and running the demos. The interface basically lets you click a button or two to make things happen.

6. **The first screen you see is the Welcome screen; click anywhere on this screen to enter the interface.**

   Now you are getting to the action. This next screen lists categories for the software on the CD.

7. **To view the items within a category, just click the category's name.**

   A list of programs in the category appears.

8. **For more information about a program, click the program's name.**

   Be sure to read the information that appears. Sometimes a program may require you to do a few tricks on your computer first, and this screen will tell you where to go for that information, if necessary.

9. **To install the program, click the Install button. If you don't want to install the program, click the Go Back button to return to the previous screen.**

   You can always return to the previous screen by clicking the Go Back button. This feature allows you to browse the different categories and products and decide what you want to install.

After you click an install button, the CD interface drops to the background while the CD begins installation of the program you chose.

10. **To install other items, repeat Steps 7, 8, and 9.**

11. **When you're done installing programs, click the Quit button to close the interface.**

You can eject the CD now. Carefully place it back in the plastic jacket of the book for safekeeping.

What You'll Find

Here's a summary of the software on this CD. If you use Windows, the CD interface helps you install software easily. (If you have no idea what I'm talking about when I say "CD interface," flip back a page or two to find the section, "How to Use the CD.")

Internet Explorer 4, from Microsoft

Category: Internet Software

This is the much-talked-about new version of Microsoft Internet Explorer, a powerful World Wide Web browser. It's also free, making it a true bargain.

To learn more about IE4, visit the Web site: `www.microsoft.com/ie`. To download additional components for Internet Explorer, visit the Internet Explorer Component Download Web site: `www.microsoft.com/ie/ie40/download/rtw/x86/en/download/addon95.htm`.

Note: An Internet connection is required for this software to connect to Web sites on the Internet. Such connections are available through an Internet service provider. To sign up for an account with an Internet service provider, run the Internet Connection wizard in Internet Explorer, as described in Chapter 5.

Internet Utilities 97, from Starfish Software

Category: Internet Software

Starfish calls Internet Utilities an "Internet Survival Kit." It stores your bookmarks, monitors your online connection, and contains a toolkit of online utilities like QuickZip, QuickFTP, and NewsDecoder (which figures out and displays binary files like the ones people send over the newsgroups).

For more information, check out the Starfish Web site at www.starfish.com.

The Small Business Internet Resources Library

Category: Internet Software

This Web page provides dozens of hyperlinks to useful Web sites for small businesses. The Web page is divided into categories so that all you have to do is click a link to move to a category and then click another link to display the Internet resource. The Small Business Internet Resources Library includes hyperlinks to tax form pages, to Web sites that help you predict and solve potential problems converting to the year 2000, to several small business organizations including organizations for minority and women-owned businesses, to payroll and shipping companies, to online business newspapers and magazines, to several government resources including the Small Business Administration and the Department of Commerce, and much more.

Note: This file does not install to your computer. You must have the CD in your CD-ROM drive to view the file. To use the Small Business Internet Resources Library, open the file called SBIRL in the Links folder on the CD by using your Web browser.

Paint Shop Pro, from JASC Inc.

Category: Graphics Software

Paint Shop Pro is a versatile general-purpose bitmap graphics program that also reads *vector formats* (drawings made up of lines and curves and shapes and stuff). These capabilities make Paint Shop Pro extremely useful for file conversion where the originals are drawings.

The program performs a wide range of painting, drawing, and text functions. In addition, it contains a full range of functions for adjusting image quality, color depth, and special effects including GIF transparency.

Check out www.jasc.com/ on the World Wide Web for a full description.

WinZip, by Nico Mak

Category: Utilities

You really need an unzipping program to deal with compressed files that you download, specifically those files with the file extension .zip (these files are called, unsurprisingly, zip files). Zip files are especially useful on the Internet, because compressed files take up less space and take less time to download. You may receive zip files as e-mail attachments, or you may download them from Web pages, particularly shareware sites.

WinZip can both unzip and zip things for you. For more information, check out the Web site at www.winzip.com/.

BizCalculator

Category: Utilities

You can use this business calculator to make loan calculations (balances, terms, interest rates, payment amounts, and balloon payments) as well as investment calculations (present values, terms, rates of return, annuity amounts, and future values). See Appendix B for more details.

PVCAnalyzer

Category: Utilities

This profit-volume-cost analyzer lets you calculate break-even points for new business opportunities. For example, if you're thinking about starting a new business, you can use the PVCAnalyzer to get a rough feel as to how much sales volume you'll need to generate in order to break even or to achieve some minimum level of profits. If you're already in business but occasionally consider new opportunities — a new product or service or a new location — you can use the PVCAnalyzer to estimate the sales volume necessary in order to break even on this new opportunity. You can even use the PVCAnalyzer to consider some investments in business equipment — for example, you can use the PVCAnalyzer to gauge the economics of setting up a Web site. See Appendix C for more details.

If You Have Problems (Of the CD Kind)

I tried my best to compile programs that work on most computers with the minimum system requirements. Alas, your computer may differ, and some programs may not work properly for some reason.

The two likeliest problems are that you don't have enough memory (RAM) for the programs you want to use, or you have other programs running that are affecting installation or running of a program. If you get error messages like `Not enough memory` or `Setup cannot continue`, try one or more of these methods and then try using the software again:

- ✔ **Turn off any anti-virus software that you have on your computer.** Installers sometimes mimic virus activity and may make your computer incorrectly believe that it is being infected by a virus.

- ✔ **Close all running programs.** The more programs you're running, the less memory is available to other programs. Installers also typically update files and programs. So if you keep other programs running, installation may not work properly.

- ✔ **Have your local computer store add more RAM to your computer.** This is, admittedly, a drastic and somewhat expensive step. However, adding more memory can really help the speed of your computer and enable more programs to run at the same time. This may include closing the CD interface and running a product's installation program from Windows Explorer.

If you still have trouble installing the items from the CD, please call the IDG Books Worldwide Customer Service phone number: 800-762-2974 (outside the U.S.: 317-596-5430).

Appendix B:
Using the BizCalculator

*U*nfortunately, Windows doesn't include an accessory that is almost a necessity for many small businesses: a business calculator that lets someone make loan calculations (balances, terms, interest rates, payment amounts, and balloon payments) as well as investment calculations (present values, terms, rates of return, annuity amounts, and future values). For this reason, I created a business calculator program that lets you make these calculations and then stuck the program on the companion CD in the back of this book.

Turn back to Appendix A if you need to install the business calculator and the other programs on the CD. If you've already installed the software, keep reading to find out how to use it.

Starting the BizCalculator

To start the BizCalculator, click Start➪Programs➪BizCalculator. Windows starts the program and displays its simple application window, as shown in Figure B-1.

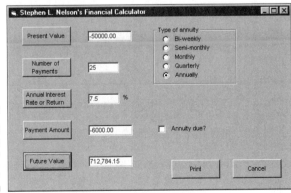

Figure B-1:
The
BizCalculator
window.

Using the BizCalculator Program

You can use the BizCalculator to make both loan and investment calculations. To make either sort of calculation, you supply the loan or investment terms you know and then click the command button that describes the variable you want to calculate. Unfortunately, there is a trick to successfully using the BizCalculator program — or any other financial calculator. You need to enter dollar amounts you pay out as negative values and dollar amounts you collect as positive values. But let me show you how this works by providing step-by-step instructions for making loan calculations and investment calculations.

Making loan calculations

To make loan calculations using the BizCalculator, follow these steps:

1. **Start the BizCalculator program.**

2. **Click the Type of Annuity button that corresponds to your loan payment frequency.**

   For example, if you will make regular loan payments bi-weekly, click the Bi-weekly button. If you will make regular loan payments semi-monthly, click the Semi-monthly button. If you will make payments on a monthly, quarterly, or annual basis, click the Monthly, Quarterly, or Annually button.

3. **If you know the loan balance you want to borrow, enter this amount *as a positive value* into the Present Value text box.**

   Note: If you don't know the loan balance because that's what you want to calculate, you don't have to enter anything into the Present Value text box.

4. **If you know the number of regular loan payments you'll make, enter this value into the Number of payments text box.**

   For example, if you will make monthly payments on a 30-year mortgage, enter 360 because a 30-year mortgage with monthly payments requires 360 payments. If you are borrowing money on a ten-year business loan with annual payments, enter 10 because such a loan requires 10 annual payments. (*Note:* If you don't know the number of payments because that's what you want to calculate, you don't have to enter anything into the Number of Payments text box.)

5. **If you know the annual interest rate a loan charges, enter the interest rate percentage into the Annual Interest Rate or Return text box.**

For example, if you will borrow money by using a loan that charges you a 7.5% annual interest charge, enter **7.5**. Note that you do not enter the decimal equivalent for the interest. In other words, if the annual interest rate is 7.5%, you enter **7.5** into the text box and not **.075**. One other important point to make is that you can't enter fractions into the text boxes so you need to restate interest rates that use fractions. For example, if a loan charges $7^{1}/_{2}$ percent interest, you must enter this interest rate as **7.5**. (*Note:* If you don't know the annual interest rate a loan charges because that's what you want to calculate, you don't have to enter anything into the Annual Interest Rate or Return text box.)

6. **If you know the regular loan payment that a loan requires, enter the amount *as a negative value* into the Payment Amount text box.**

   For example, if you will pay monthly principal and interest charges equal to $500, enter **-500**. (*Note:* If you don't know the regular loan payment because that's what you want to calculate, you don't have to enter anything into the Payment Amount text box.)

7. **If a loan requires a balloon payment, enter the balloon amount *as a negative value* into the Future Value text box.**

   For example, if in addition to the regular monthly payment, you will also pay a final $10,000 balloon payment, enter **-10000**. (*Note:* If you don't know the balloon payment because that's what you want to calculate, you don't have to enter anything into the Future Value text box. If the balloon payment is zero, you can enter **0** into the Future Value text box or leave the text box blank.)

8. **If your loan requires you to make payments at the beginning of payment period, check the Annuity Due box.**

   Typically loans do not require you to make payments at the beginning of the payment period. For example, a mortgage or car loan with monthly payments typically requires you to make payments at the end of the month. Leases, however, often do require you to make payments at the beginning of the payment period. A car lease with monthly payments often requires you to make payments at the beginning of the month (which actually means you often make your first payment at the same time as you sign the lease).

9. **Click the command button that corresponds to the loan variable you want to calculate:**

   - **Loan Balance.** Click the Present Value button to calculate the loan balance given the number of regular loan payments, an annual interest rate, the payment amount, and, optionally, a balloon payment.

   - **Number of Payments.** Click the Number of Payments button to calculate the number of regular loan payments given the loan balance, the annual interest rate, the regular payment amount, and, optionally, a balloon payment amount.

A sample loan calculation

Suppose, for the sake of illustration, that you want to know what the mortgage payment would be on Bill Gates' new, $50,000,000 mansion. Assume that Bill uses a 30-year, $50,000,000 mortgage charging a 7¼ annual interest and that he doesn't have a balloon payment.

To make this calculation, you enter the **50000000** into the Present Value text box, **360** into the Number of Payments text box, and **7.25** into the Annual Interest Rate or Return text box. (You can go ahead and leave the Annuity Due box unchecked and the Future Value empty.) To calculate Bill's monthly mortgage payment, you click the Payment Amount command. If you enter the loan variables correctly, the monthly mortgage payment equals –341,088.14. Notice that the value is a negative number because this is the amount that Bill will have to pay out.

- **Annual Interest Rate.** Click the Annual Interest Rate or Return button to calculate the annual interest rate given the loan balance, the number of regular payments, the regular payment amount, and, optionally, a balloon payment amount.

- **Payment Amount.** Click the Payment Amount button to calculate the regular loan payment given the loan balance, the number of payments, the annual interest rate, and, optionally, a balloon payment amount.

- **Balloon Payment.** Click the Future Value button to calculate the balloon payment amount given the loan balance, the number of payments, the annual interest rate, and the regular payment amount.

Making investment calculations

To make investment calculations by using the BizCalculator, follow these steps:

1. **Start the BizCalculator program.**

2. **Click the Type of Annuity button that corresponds to how frequently you'll add money, or savings, to some investment.**

   For example, if you will regularly add to an investment bi-weekly, click the Bi-weekly button. If you will regularly add to an investment semi-monthly, click the Semi-monthly button. If you will regularly add to an investment on a monthly, quarterly, or annual basis, click the Monthly, Quarterly, or Annually button.

3. **If you know the investment's current balance — its present value, in other words — enter this amount *as a negative value* into the Present Value text box.**

   (*Note:* If you don't know the present value because that's what you want to calculate, you don't have to enter anything into the Present Value text box.)

4. **If you know the number of regular additions to the investment you'll make, enter this value into the Number of payments text box.**

   For example, if you will make annual payments into an Individual Retirement Account over 25 years, enter **25**. If you will make monthly payments into a 401(k) plan over 10 years, enter 120 because such an investment plan results in 120 monthly payments. (*Note:* If you don't know the number of payments because that's what you want to calculate, you don't have to enter anything into the Number of Payments text box.)

5. **If you know the annual interest rate or rate of return an investment will earn, enter the interest rate or return percentage into the Annual Interest Rate or Return text box.**

   For example, if you will invest money in bonds that pay an 8.5% annual interest charge, enter **8.5**. Note that you do not enter the decimal equivalent for the interest. In other words, if the annual interest rate is 8.5%, you enter **8.5** into the text box and not **.085**. One other important point to make is that you can't enter fractions into the text boxes so you need to restate interest rates that use fractions. For example, if you expect an investment to payment $9^{3}/_{8}$ interest, you must enter this interest as 9.375. (*Note:* If you don't know the annual interest rate or return an investment will earn because that's what you want to calculate, you don't have to enter anything into the Annual Interest Rate or Return text box.)

6. **If you know the regular amount you will add to some investment, enter the amount *as a negative value* into the Payment Amount text box.**

   For example, if you will save $500 each month, enter **500**. (*Note:* If you don't know the regular payment because that's what you want to calculate, you don't have to enter anything into the Payment Amount text box.)

7. **If you know the investment's ultimate future value, enter that amount *as a positive value* into the Future Value text box.**

   For example, if you want to create an investment plan that produces a $1,000,000 future value, enter **1000000**. (*Note:* If you don't know the investment's future value because that's what you want to calculate, you don't have to enter anything into the Future Value text box.)

8. **If you anticipate making payments at the beginning of the payment period, check the Annuity Due box.**

For example, if you will put $2,000 a year into an IRA but will save this amount at the beginning of the year, then check the Annuity Due box.

9. **Click the command button that corresponds to the investment variable you want to calculate:**

- **Current Investment Balance.** Click the Present Value button to calculate the current investment balance given the number of payments amount, an annual interest rate or rate of return, the regular payment amount, and the investment's future value.

- **Number of Payments.** Click the Number of Payments button to calculate the number of regular payments made given the current investment balance, the annual interest rate or rate of return, the regular payment amount, and the future value.

- **Return on Investment.** Click the Annual Interest Rate or Return button to calculate the return on investment given the current investment balance, the number of regular payments, the regular payment amount, and the investment's future value.

- **Payment Amount.** Click the Payment Amount button to calculate the regular payment given the current investment balance, the number of payments, the annual interest rate or rate of return, and the investment's future balance.

- **Investment Future Balance.** Click the Future Value button to calculate the investment's future balance given the current investment balance, the number of payments, the annual interest rate or rate of return, and the regular payment amount.

A sample investment calculation

Suppose that you want to estimate how much money you'll accumulate in a new Simple-IRA plan that you've set up for yourself and your employees. Assume that you haven't yet saved any money (because it's a brand-new plan), but that you'll save $200 a month over the next 25 years. Further assume that you'll invest the money in the stock market and expect to earn the historical average stock market return of 9 percent and will make your payments to the Simple-IRA at the beginning of the month. Note, by the way, that in this example, you make 300 monthly payments to the Simple-IRA because 12 payments a year for 25 years equals 300.

To make this calculation, you enter the **0** into the Present Value text box, **300** into the Number of Payments text box, **9** into the Annual Interest Rate or Return text box, and **–200** into the Payment Amount text box. You also need to check the Annuity Due box. To estimate the future value of the Simple-IRA, click the Future Value command button. If you enter the investment variables correctly, the investment future value equals 224,224.39. Notice that the value is a positive number because this is the amount your Simple-IRA will ultimately pay to you.

Some General Tips on Using the BizCalculator

The principal trick to getting the BizCalculator to work correctly (and the same is true of all financial calculators) is that you need to get the signs of your cash flows right. If some dollar amount gets paid by you to a lender or into an investment account, it needs to be entered as a negative value. If some dollar amounts gets paid to you from a lender or out of an investment account, it needs to entered as a positive value. If you remember this, you typically shouldn't have serious problems using the BizCalculator.

Just for safety's sake, however, let me mention a couple of other quick points. First, make sure that you enter the number of payments value correctly (if that's not something you're calculating). Secondly, make sure that you mark the appropriate Type of annuity button. I guess this seems like kinda obvious advice. ("Hey, reader! Do the right thing, not the wrong thing!") But getting mixed up on these calculation variables is an easy thing to do. For example, if you're working with a 30-year mortgage that requires monthly payments, you need to enter **360** into the Number of Payments text box and then mark the Monthly radio button. Even though you think of the mortgage as 30-year mortgage, it requires payments on a monthly basis, and well, that's the way the BizCalculator needs to see it.

One other thing to note is that it's possible to describe a loan calculation or an investment calculation that the BizCalculator can't calculate. If this happens, you'll see a message box that says, basically, "Hey, Dude. I just give up. This one is too tough!" The problem in this case, by the way, is that some of the numbers that the calculator needs to crunch in order to produce the final result get so wild that the BizCalculator can't handle them. For example, if you try to calculate the mortgage payment on a 150-year mortgage with semi-monthly payments, well, my little calculator will freak out. Sorry.

Appendix C

Using the PVCAnalyzer

●●

*T*he companion CD stuck in that plastic envelope in the back of this book also provides a profit-volume-cost analyzer. This handy software program lets you calculate break-even points for new business opportunities.

For example, if you're thinking about starting a new business, you can use the PVCAnalyzer to get a rough feel as to how much sales volume you'll need to generate in order to break even or to achieve some minimum level of profits. If you're already in business but occasionally consider new opportunities — a new product or service or a new location — you can use the PVCAnalyzer to estimate the sales volume necessary in order to break even on this new opportunity. You can even use the PVCAnalyzer to consider some investments in business equipment — for example, you can use the PVCAnalyzer to gauge the economics of setting up a Web site.

Before you can use the PVCAnalyzer, you must install it. See Appendix A if you need to do so.

Starting the PVCAnalyzer

To start the PVCAnalyzer program, click Start⇨Programs⇨PVCAnalyzer. Windows starts the program and displays its simple application window, as shown in Figure C-1.

Using the PVCAnalyzer Program

To use the PVCAnalyzer program, you describe some business opportunity by entering half a dozen inputs and then have the calculator estimate your break-even point. This process requires you to take the following steps:

1. **Use the Sales revenue per unit text box to enter the sales revenue per unit you'll record in the new business opportunity.**

   For example, if you're thinking about selling some new widget for $15.00, you enter **15**. If you're thinking about selling consulting services for $75 per hour, you enter **75**.

2. **Use the Fixed costs text box to enter the fixed costs you'll incur because you pursue some new opportunity.**

   Fixed costs are costs you have to pay regardless of whether you actually generate any sales volume. For example, if some new opportunity requires you to hire an employee and pay the employee even if you don't sell anything, that employee's salary is a fixed cost. If the opportunity also requires you to rent space and you pay the rent whether you have customers or not, the rent expense is a fixed cost.

3. **Use the Vary-with-units costs text box to enter any variable costs that depend on the number of units you sell.**

   For example, if you sell widgets that you purchase for $5, you have a unit variable cost equal to $5.

4. **Use the Vary-with-revenue costs text box to enter any variable costs that depend on the dollars of sales you sell.**

   For example, if you're a retailer and you pay 12 percent of your sales to the landlord, you have a variable cost equal to 12 percent of revenues.

5. **Use the Vary-with-profit costs text to enter any variable costs that depend on the profits you generate.**

   For example, if you will pay a 34 percent income tax, you have a variable cost equal to 34 percent of profits.

6. **Optionally, use the Target profit amount text box to specify that you want some minimum level of profits included in your break-even analyzer.**

   In other words, if you must earn a specific level of profits — say $50,000 — in order to consider a new opportunity as "breaking even," you can enter this amount into the Target profit amount text box.

7. **Click the Calculate button to calculate the break-even point in units, and then the sales revenue, costs, and profits at the break-even point.**

8. **Optionally, click the Print button to print a hard copy of the PVCAnalyzer window so you have a record of your break-even calculations.**

9. **Click the Clear Inputs button to erase your data.**

10. **Click the Close button to stop the PVCAnalyzer program.**

Note: If you have questions about how to fill in the text boxes, click the Show Example button. When you do, the PVCAnalyzer fills in its text boxes with data from an example business opportunity where a small business is selling some item for $15, will incur $150,000 of fixed costs, pays variable unit costs of $5, another variable cost equal to 12% of revenue, an income tax of 34% on its profits, and wants to earn a minimum profit of $50,000.

Some General Tips on Using the PVCAnalyzer

You shouldn't have any trouble using the PVCAnalyzer. All you do is fill in some blanks and then click appropriate command buttons. Nevertheless, I want to provide you with some general tips that may help you perform more meaningful profit-volume-cost analysis.

The first thing to note is that you need to perform profit-volume-cost, or PVC, analysis (which is what you're doing when you make break-even calculations), for a specific time period. In other words, you calculate how much sales volume some new business opportunity needs to generate over a day, a month, a year, or the product's life. That's probably obvious to you, but note that this means your fixed costs need to be expressed as the amount you'll pay over the specific time period. Does that make sense? In other words, if you're calculating the break-even point on a daily basis, the fixed cost amount needs to be expressed as daily amount. If you're calculating the break-even point on an annual basis, the fixed cost amount needs to be expressed as an annual amount.

A second thing to note is that PVC analysis really only works well for simple business opportunities. You can rather easily use it to figure out, for example, whether it makes sense to hire some new, $15/hour employee who will repair people's computers, for example, for a $30/hour repair fee. And you can easily figure out whether it makes sense to sell $15 widgets if you can buy them for $5. But analyzing opportunities where, for example, you're both selling hours of a repair person's time and widgets, is very difficult. Oh sure, you can sort of do this by using averages for the sales revenue per unit and the variable costs and then combined totals for the fixed costs and the target profit amount. But your analysis results often aren't very good because, to butcher a cliché, you lose sight of how an individual tree is doing because all you see is a forest.

Another minor point to just note here is that the PVCAnalyzer rounds numbers to the nearest whole unit or even dollar. This typically shouldn't cause you problems because the extra precision you get from working with fractional units, cents of revenue, and cents of costs doesn't really make sense — it's only an illusion. But this rounding does mean that you may see minor rounding errors of a dollar or two in the PVCAnalyzer's calculations. The calculator may consider you to be breaking even though you're making a 1, for example, or it may say that you've reached your target profit amount even though you're a couple of bucks short.

One other idiosyncrasy related to this number-rounding business is that the calculator also rounds decimal input values to whole numbers. For example, the calculator rounds the value $9.95 to $10. If this causes you trouble, simply enter all your values as pennies rather than as dollars. In other words, rather than enter **$9.95**, enter **995** (for 995 cents). Just remember that doing so means your output values also will be calculated in pennies, so you'll have to add the decimal point to the calculator's answers.

Index

IDG Books Worldwide, Inc., End-User License Agreement

READ THIS. You should carefully read these terms and conditions before opening the software packet(s) included with this book ("Book"). This is a license agreement ("Agreement") between you and IDG Books Worldwide, Inc. ("IDGB"). By opening the accompanying software packet(s), you acknowledge that you have read and accept the following terms and conditions. If you do not agree and do not want to be bound by such terms and conditions, promptly return the Book and the unopened software packet(s) to the place you obtained them for a full refund.

1. **License Grant.** IDGB grants to you (either an individual or entity) a nonexclusive license to use one copy of the enclosed software program(s) (collectively, the "Software") solely for your own personal or business purposes on a single computer (whether a standard computer or a workstation component of a multiuser network). The Software is in use on a computer when it is loaded into temporary memory (RAM) or installed into permanent memory (hard disk, CD-ROM, or other storage device). IDGB reserves all rights not expressly granted herein.

2. **Ownership.** IDGB is the owner of all right, title, and interest, including copyright, in and to the compilation of the Software recorded on the disk(s) or CD-ROM ("Software Media"). Copyright to the individual programs recorded on the Software Media is owned by the author or other authorized copyright owner of each program. Ownership of the Software and all proprietary rights relating thereto remain with IDGB and its licensers.

3. **Restrictions on Use and Transfer.**

   (a) You may only (i) make one copy of the Software for backup or archival purposes, or (ii) transfer the Software to a single hard disk, provided that you keep the original for backup or archival purposes. You may not (i) rent or lease the Software, (ii) copy or reproduce the Software through a LAN or other network system or through any computer subscriber system or bulletin-board system, or (iii) modify, adapt, or create derivative works based on the Software.

   (b) You may not reverse engineer, decompile, or disassemble the Software. You may transfer the Software and user documentation on a permanent basis, provided that the transferee agrees to accept the terms and conditions of this Agreement and you retain no copies. If the Software is an update or has been updated, any transfer must include the most recent update and all prior versions.

4. **Restrictions on Use of Individual Programs.** You must follow the individual requirements and restrictions detailed for each individual program in Appendix A, "About the CD," of this Book. These limitations are also contained in the individual license agreements recorded on the Software Media. These limitations may include a requirement that after using the program for a specified period of time, the user must pay a registration fee or discontinue use. By opening the Software packet(s), you will be agreeing to abide by the licenses and restrictions for these individual programs that are detailed in Appendix A and on the Software Media. None of the material on this Software Media or listed in this Book may ever be redistributed, in original or modified form, for commercial purposes.

5. Limited Warranty.

    (a) IDGB warrants that the Software and Software Media are free from defects in materials and workmanship under normal use for a period of sixty (60) days from the date of purchase of this Book. If IDGB receives notification within the warranty period of defects in materials or workmanship, IDGB will replace the defective Software Media.

    (b) IDGB AND THE AUTHOR OF THE BOOK DISCLAIM ALL OTHER WARRANTIES, EXPRESS OR IMPLIED, INCLUDING WITHOUT LIMITATION IMPLIED WARRANTIES OF MER-CHANTABILITY AND FITNESS FOR A PARTICULAR PURPOSE, WITH RESPECT TO THE SOFTWARE, THE PROGRAMS, THE SOURCE CODE CONTAINED THEREIN, AND/OR THE TECHNIQUES DESCRIBED IN THIS BOOK. IDGB DOES NOT WARRANT THAT THE FUNCTIONS CONTAINED IN THE SOFTWARE WILL MEET YOUR REQUIREMENTS OR THAT THE OPERATION OF THE SOFTWARE WILL BE ERROR FREE.

    (c) This limited warranty gives you specific legal rights, and you may have other rights that vary from jurisdiction to jurisdiction.

6. Remedies.

    (a) IDGB's entire liability and your exclusive remedy for defects in materials and workmanship shall be limited to replacement of the Software Media, which may be returned to IDGB with a copy of your receipt at the following address: Software Media Fulfillment Department, Attn.: *Small Business Windows 95 For Dummies*, IDG Books Worldwide, Inc., 7260 Shadeland Station, Ste. 100, Indianapolis, IN 46256, or call 800-762-2974. Please allow three to four weeks for delivery. This Limited Warranty is void if failure of the Software Media has resulted from accident, abuse, or misapplication. Any replacement Software Media will be warranted for the remainder of the original warranty period or thirty (30) days, whichever is longer.

    (b) In no event shall IDGB or the author be liable for any damages whatsoever (including without limitation damages for loss of business profits, business interruption, loss of business information, or any other pecuniary loss) arising from the use of or inability to use the Book or the Software, even if IDGB has been advised of the possibility of such damages.

    (c) Because some jurisdictions do not allow the exclusion or limitation of liability for consequential or incidental damages, the above limitation or exclusion may not apply to you.

7. U.S. Government Restricted Rights. Use, duplication, or disclosure of the Software by the U.S. Government is subject to restrictions stated in paragraph (c)(1)(ii) of the Rights in Technical Data and Computer Software clause of DFARS 252.227-7013, and in subparagraphs (a) through (d) of the Commercial Computer–Restricted Rights clause at FAR 52.227-19, and in similar clauses in the NASA FAR supplement, when applicable.

8. General. This Agreement constitutes the entire understanding of the parties and revokes and supersedes all prior agreements, oral or written, between them and may not be modified or amended except in a writing signed by both parties hereto that specifically refers to this Agreement. This Agreement shall take precedence over any other documents that may be in conflict herewith. If any one or more provisions contained in this Agreement are held by any court or tribunal to be invalid, illegal, or otherwise unenforceable, each and every other provision shall remain in full force and effect.

Installation Instructions

To install the items from the CD to your hard drive, follow these steps:

1. **Insert the CD into your computer's CD-ROM drive.**

2. **Click the Start button and click Run.**

3. **In the dialog box that appears, type** D:\SETUP.EXE **(or substitute the appropriate drive letter for D if your CD-ROM drive is assigned to another letter).**

4. **Click OK.**

5. **Read through the license agreement, nod your head, and then click the Accept button.**

   From here, the CD interface appears.

6. **The first screen you see is the Welcome screen; click anywhere on this screen to enter the interface.**

   This next screen lists categories for the software on the CD.

7. **To view the items within a category, just click the category's name.**

   A list of programs in the category appears.

8. **For more information about a program, click the program's name.**

9. **To install the program, click the Install button.**

   If you don't want to install the program, click the Go Back button to return to the previous screen. You can always return to the previous screen by clicking the Go Back button.

   After you click an Install button, the CD interface drops to the background while the CD begins installation of the program you chose.

10. **To install other items, repeat Steps 7, 8 and 9.**

11. **When you're done installing programs, click the Quit button to close the interface.**

    You can eject the CD now. Carefully place it back in the plastic jacket of the book for safekeeping.

YOUR ONLINE RESOURCE

WWW.DUMMIES.COM

Discover Dummies Online!

The Dummies Web Site is your fun and friendly online resource for the latest information about ...*For Dummies*® books and your favorite topics. The Web site is the place to communicate with us, exchange ideas with other ...*For Dummies* readers, chat with authors, and have fun!

Ten Fun and Useful Things You Can Do at www.dummies.com

1. Win free ...*For Dummies* books and more!
2. Register your book and be entered in a prize drawing.
3. Meet your favorite authors through the IDG Books Author Chat Series.
4. Exchange helpful information with other ...*For Dummies* readers.
5. Discover other great ...*For Dummies* books you must have!
6. Purchase Dummieswear™ exclusively from our Web site.
7. Buy ...*For Dummies* books online.
8. Talk to us. Make comments, ask questions, get answers!
9. Download free software.
10. Find additional useful resources from authors.

Link directly to these ten fun and useful things at
http://www.dummies.com/10useful

WWW.DUMMIES.COM

SURF THE NET

For other technology titles from IDG Books Worldwide, go to
www.idgbooks.com

Not on the Web yet? It's easy to get started with *Dummies 101*®: *The Internet For Windows*®*95* or *The Internet For Dummies*®, 4th Edition, at local retailers everywhere.

IDG BOOKS WORLDWIDE

Find other ...*For Dummies* books on these topics:

Business • Career • Databases • Food & Beverage • Games • Gardening • Graphics • Hardware
Health & Fitness • Internet and the World Wide Web • Networking • Office Suites
Operating Systems • Personal Finance • Pets • Programming • Recreation • Sports
Spreadsheets • Teacher Resources • Test Prep • Word Processing

IDG BOOKS WORLDWIDE
BOOK REGISTRATION

Register This Book and Win!

We want to hear from you!

Visit **http://my2cents.dummies.com** to register this book and tell us how you liked it!

- ✔ Get entered in our monthly prize giveaway.

- ✔ Give us feedback about this book — tell us what you like best, what you like least, or maybe what you'd like to ask the author and us to change!

- ✔ Let us know any other ...*For Dummies*® topics that interest you.

Your feedback helps us determine what books to publish, tells us what coverage to add as we revise our books, and lets us know whether we're meeting your needs as a ...*For Dummies* reader. You're our most valuable resource, and what you have to say is important to us!

Not on the Web yet? It's easy to get started with *Dummies 101*®*: The Internet For Windows*® *95* or *The Internet For Dummies*®, 4th Edition, at local retailers everywhere.

Or let us know what you think by sending us a letter at the following address:

...*For Dummies* Book Registration
Dummies Press
7260 Shadeland Station, Suite 100
Indianapolis, IN 46256-3945
Fax 317-596-5498

BUSINESS AND GENERAL REFERENCE BOOK SERIES FROM IDG

COMPUTER BOOK SERIES FROM IDG